A House Divided

A House Divided

SEXUALITY, MORALITY, AND CHRISTIAN CULTURES

GEOFFREY W. SUTTON

⌒PICKWICK *Publications* · Eugene, Oregon

A HOUSE DIVIDED
Sexuality, Morality, and Christian Cultures

Copyright © 2016 Geoffrey W. Sutton. All rights reserved. Except for brief quotations in critical publications or reviews, no part of this book may be reproduced in any manner without prior written permission from the publisher. Write: Permissions, Wipf and Stock Publishers, 199 W. 8th Ave., Suite 3, Eugene, OR 97401.

Pickwick Publications
An Imprint of Wipf and Stock Publishers
199 W. 8th Ave., Suite 3
Eugene, OR 97401

www.wipfandstock.com

ISBN 13: 978-1-4982-2488-8

Cataloging-in-Publication data:

Sutton, Geoffrey William.

A house divided : sexuality, morality, and Christian cultures / Geoffrey W. Sutton.

xviii + 260 p. ; 23 cm. Includes bibliographical references.

ISBN 13: 978-1-4982-2488-8

1. Sex—Religious aspects—Christianity. 2. Sex (Psychology). 3. Sex—Biblical teaching. I. Title.

BT111.3 S87 2016

Manufactured in the U.S.A.

All rights reserved worldwide. Unless otherwise indicated, all scripture quotations are from the New Revised Standard Version Bible. New Revised Standard Version Bible, copyright © 1989 the Division of Christian Education of the National Council of the Churches of Christ in the United States of America. Used by permission. All rights reserved

To my students who taught me more than they will know

TABLE OF CONTENTS

Acknowledgements ix
Introduction xi

PART I: *Pathways to Understanding Christianity, Morality, and Sexuality*

Chapter 1: Biblical Texts and Christian Perspectives 3
Chapter 2: The Influence of Spirituality and Thinking on Morality 26
Chapter 3: The Influence of Personality, Physiology, Emotions, and Social Context on Morality 49
Chapter 4: Moral Psychology 57
Chapter 5: Psychology and Sexuality 79
Chapter 6: Sexuality and Healthy Relationships 96

PART II: *Christian Cultures and Contemporary Sexuality: Biblical texts and Christian Perspectives*

Chapter 7: Beginnings: From Pregnancy to Adolescence 123
Chapter 8: Marriage, Divorce, and Sexual Relationships 149
Chapter 9: Sexual Orientation and Same Sex Relationships 172
Chapter 10: Sex and Gender Roles 195
Chapter 11: Sexual Violence and Christianity 209

PART III: *Redemption and Reflections*

Chapter 12: Sexuality, Morality, and Redemption 231
Chapter 13: Reflections: Sexuality, Morality, and Christian Cultures 236

Bibliography 245

ACKNOWLEDGEMENTS

Many people reviewed parts of this manuscript and offered comments that helped me rethink and revise this manuscript. My wife, Sandra Sutton, and son, Nathan Sutton, were always faithful to read and comment. I have also benefitted immensely from the faithful comments of colleagues and friends: Travis Cooper, Brandon Schmidly, Eloise Thomas, Robert Berg, Kamden Strunk, and Monte Harris.

I sincerely appreciate the careful editing of Beth Barker with comments from her husband, Jeremiah Barker.

I am especially grateful to those who agreed to provide comments for readers who might consider this book: Jennifer S. Ripley of Regent University, Kelly Reiner at Virginia Commonwealth University, Rodney Bassett of Roberts Wesleyan College. I also appreciate the comments of my editor, Robin Parry, and the work of the staff at Wipf and Stock Publishers.

INTRODUCTION

Stories about sex grab headlines. When the story offers something unique, interest peaks. In the last decade, advances in medicine have introduced a variety of new contraceptives and improvements in sexual health. Stories also reported on the harm done when people attempted to change sexual orientation. The public became more aware than ever about the way sexual minorities have been discriminated against in education, employment, and housing. And the media informed us of the horrors of sex trafficking.

People in Western cultures have different restrictions on sexual activity than they had a century ago. Public attitudes have changed in recent decades. New laws regulate various aspects of sexuality such as birth control, abortion, age of consent to sex, who can marry, what level of exposure to sex-related art may be shown at what time on TV, discussed on the radio, or made available in libraries. And the diverse voices within Christianity, which is the dominant religion for many in Europe and the Americas, offer different opinions about what is right and wrong. Christians often quote biblical texts to make their points, teach children, or explain why they work to change laws and policies governing the sexual behavior of others in their communities. They carry placards, write letters to government officials, and lobby to change laws they hope will change the way people have sex or what happens when a sex act creates a new life. How can a person make sense of these public battles over sex and morality? How can counselors, clergy, and consultants be helpful when people hold widely divergent moral views from those of their family members or from those in the helping professions? And how can business consultants promote understanding and problem-solving when values seem so far apart? The purpose of this book is to either answer those questions or suggest ways that people can meaningfully discuss divergent views about the topics that divide Christian groups or pit Christian groups against secular and non-Christian religious groups.

How is it possible that Christians can read the same sacred text, the Holy Bible, and come up with different interpretations? Why are some moral issues so important that people warn of sin on social media pages and TV, while other moral issues barely get noticed? Judging by all the news stories about abortion, birth control, same-sex marriage, sex abuse, campus rape, and sex-based discrimination, I'm guessing millions of people are asking the same questions.

My purpose in writing this book is to offer students, educators, psychotherapists, clergy, consultants, business leaders, and educated readers, research and analyses about the intriguing interconnections among beliefs about human sexuality, morality, and Christianity. I hope to expand the public conversation as well as offer practical suggestions for thinking about differences. I do not think anyone can get far in a discussion about morality and sexuality without discovering that someone's interpretation of a religious belief has informed the discussion. The point of this book is that Christians simply do not agree about many of the sexual issues that make headline news. It turns out that many Christian beliefs that seem like ancient traditions are really not very old. And some biblical justifications for and against restrictions of sex-related behavior have only been contentious in recent history. So, I will take a look at how people come to the biblical texts and reach their conclusions. I will examine those conservative perspectives that rely heavily on select portions of the biblical texts, and I will examine alternative voices. Finally, I will provide an overview of new findings in moral psychology research and suggest how these findings might promote a richer understanding and informed communication about the moral issues that divide people who identify with the world's largest religion, Christianity.

I believe that Christian moral judgment about sex-related issues is based on four factors: Scripture, beliefs about human nature, multidimensional moral reasoning, and beliefs about sexuality.

Part One: Pathways to Understanding

Part one consists of six chapters that provide a basis for understanding how Christians form a moral judgment.

In chapter one, "Biblical Texts and Christian Perspectives," I look at the biblical texts and offer a brief overview of how the ancient stories became documents that eventually became part of the Christian Bible. For most Christians, the Bible provides an important basis for moral decisions, including those pertaining to sexuality. Our Bibles include a collection of documents from thousands of years ago in ancient Israel. The stories and laws were passed down from one generation to the next in an oral tradition. Eventually, these documents were written on separate scrolls, which formed the Hebrew Bible. Christianity began with the story of Jesus, which is presented in four documents called Gospels. Leaders in the early Christian movement wrote other documents, mostly letters, which gained wide circulation. Eventually, church leaders selected some documents for inclusion in the Christian Bible and rejected others. Christian groups agree on a core of biblical documents referred to as books, but they continue to disagree on some other books.

I also look at what it means to be a Christian. First, I briefly consider the early statements of beliefs known as creeds. Next, I offer some ideas about how we might differentiate between conservative Christians—often called fundamentalists or evangelicals —and those with alternative beliefs —often called liberals or progressives.

In the second and third chapters, I examine six sources of influence on morality by referring to six dimensions of human functioning commonly referred to by clinicians and researchers. The SCOPES model is a six-factor approach to understanding human nature and is the second consideration in forming moral judgments. These six dimensions can be labeled to form an acronym, *SCOPES*. The letters refer to Spirituality, Cognitive or thought processes, Observable behavior patterns (personality traits), Physiological or biological processes, Emotions, and Social context. In chapter 2 I examine the spiritual dimension by considering such topics as religious orientation and the influence of religion on decision-making and coping. I also look at differences in how much religion is a part of a person's life. Cognitive processes constitute the second dimension covered in chapter two. Here I examine cognitive processes related to morality. These processes include beliefs, memory, knowledge, intelligence, prejudice, bias, valuing, projection, sunk costs, and self-control.

In chapter 3 I review research focused on the remaining four of the six dimensions. First, I look at research on behavior patterns, which includes a discussion of personality factors linked to morality. Second, I consider physiological factors related to moral judgments. Third, I examine the influence of both positive and negative emotional responses on moral decision-making. For example, sexuality evokes pleasurable emotions, but some aspects of sexuality evoke negative emotions of fear and disgust. Finally, I consider the role of our social context on morality. People influence each other when it comes to making a moral decision. And time is a factor as well. Moral responses differ based on the time of day and at different times in a person's life.

Moral psychology is the subject of chapter 4. In the last ten years, psychological scientists have conducted numerous studies to learn how people make moral decisions. I summarize the problem of moral tribes described by Joshua Greene[1] as a way of thinking about the problem of people with different moral and religious beliefs who come to an impasse when trying to resolve a difference. Their morality works well within their tribes, but they can be deeply divided when their beliefs seem so far apart from those in other religious tribes. Then, after briefly considering the traditional approach to moral development, which was heavily dependent on intellectual development, I introduce the new and exciting work of a leading psychological scientist, Jonathan Haidt,[2] who, along with many colleagues, has found a basis for moral foundations on which people seem to rely when giving reasons for their moral beliefs. These foundations have a murky past and appear to develop from powerful emotional responses like disgust. I will use these six foundations as part of the process of analyzing how Christians end up with such different ideas about morality. Reasoning based on one or more of the six dimensions of morality represents a third factor in moral judgment.

I end Part 1 with two chapters on sexuality. Beliefs about sexuality represent the fourth of four factors Christians consider when forming a moral judgment about sex-related issues. In chapter 5, "Psychology and Sexuality," I review some basic findings about love, which dominates contemporary views about the context for a happy relationship. I then look at a number of other topics including sexual arousal and desire, sexual attraction, and self-control. I close the chapter by looking at biopsychological aspects of contraception, pregnancy, and abortion.

Chapter 6 discusses "Sexuality, Health, and Healthy Relationships." I follow a developmental progression from childhood through adolescence and into adulthood. Among the topics are sections on sex education, premarital sex, and teen pregnancy. I review psychosocial issues in marriage, divorce, and remarriage. In the next section, I look at research findings related to sexual orientation and same-sex relationships, including same-sex marriage. Then I look briefly at sex and gender differences, sex linked fear and disgust, and sexual disorders.

Part Two: Christian Cultures and Contemporary Sexuality: Biblical Texts and Christian Perspectives

In chapter 7, *Beginnings: From Pregnancy to Adolescence*, I examine Christian teaching about the controversial topics of sexuality during development. I present conservative and progressive views about contraception,

1. Greene, *Moral Tribes*, 19–144.
2. Haidt, *Righteous Mind*, 295–309.

pregnancy, abortion, circumcision, sex education, masturbation, pornography, and teen pregnancy. After considering how different Christians view these topics, I show how they may be analyzed using the six moral dimensions referred to in chapter 4.

"Marriage, Divorce, and Sexual Relationships" is the subject of chapter 8. I review conservative and progressive views on the biblical texts covering these important life events. Throughout history, Christians have struggled with biblically-based rules about divorce. Not only was divorce considered sinful in most cases, but remarriage was rarely considered acceptable. Despite a greater acceptance of divorced and remarried persons within Christian congregations, conservative groups continue to place a high value on marriage, consider all or most reasons for divorce unacceptable, and limit acceptable reasons for remarriage. Although most non-Catholic clergy are permitted to marry, conservative groups sometimes insist that their clergy never divorce or remarry As before, I will review these issues from diverse perspectives on Scripture and the six moral dimensions.

In chapter 9, "Sexual Orientation and Same Sex Relationships," I look at the way Christians express their disapproval or approval of same-sex relationships and marriage based on various interpretations of the biblical texts. The analysis is somewhat detailed because people have written books and argued at length to justify one position or another about same-sex activity, lifestyles, relationships, and marriage. Following a summary of the various perspectives, I show how the six moral dimensions can promote an understanding of the positions held by people with strong opinions.

Chapter 10 is about "Sex and Gender Roles." It is no surprise that women have had a minor role in the history of the Christian religion just as they have had in the social, economic, and political arenas of society until recent decades. To be sure, there were exceptions, but in Christianity, a woman is not permitted to become a Catholic priest or bishop. And women are restricted from select clergy or organizational roles in many Protestant denominations and other Christian groups. I consider the texts Christians use as a basis for discrimination and analyze the moral dimensions of sex-linked discrimination.

Chapter 11 concerns an incredibly sad part of sexual morality. I consider the problem of "Sexual Violence and Christianity." I will look at the biblical accounts of incest and rape and the attitudes toward women who are the usual victims of sexual violence. I also look at the problem of sex abuse within the church. Although there is no disagreement that sexual violence is morally wrong, I look at possible reasons behind the cover-up of abuse and the devastating consequences when such activity is not stopped.

Part III: Redemption and Reflections

Part III consists of two brief chapters that bring the book to a close. First, I consider a Christian's moral obligation to forgive others, which promotes the repair of damaged relationships. And second, I offer a summary and some final thoughts.

In chapter 12, I look at "Sexuality, Morality, and Redemption." The purpose of the chapter is to focus on redemption. Christian leaders have made public apologies for their harmful acts throughout history. And Christian leaders continue to battle each other in the public arena over matters of sex-linked moral values. In the process, people are hurt. Redemption is called for and involves forgiveness, reconciliation, and restoration.

I close the book with a brief chapter on "Reflections." I focus on some of the major concerns that continue to drive acrimonious debate in Western cultures. I suggest ways that promoting an understanding of human nature and moral psychology might help lessen the intensity of the rhetoric at least among those tribal leaders willing to re-examine old beliefs and moral facts. By the time you reach the conclusion, I hope you find some value in thinking about the four factors influencing Christian moral judgment about sex-related issues: Scripture, beliefs about human nature, multidimensional moral reasoning, and beliefs about sexuality.

Disclosure

I have attempted to come to the subject of sexuality and morality from an objective point of view, but my education and life experiences likely influence me in ways I may not fully recognize. Perhaps the best I can do is present potential sources of bias so that you can better determine where my personal experiences have unduly influenced my perspective on one issue or another.

I am a psychologist. For years I have evaluated and consulted with many people to explore solutions to life problems. Many of the people I saw discussed distressed relationships and some aspect of sexuality. Like many psychotherapists, I have evaluated and treated people victimized by sexual violence and have explored concerns about sexual orientation and the distress brought on by verbal violence. Because I am a Christian, many Christians were referred to me by other Christians. In various ways, Christian beliefs influenced the process of psychotherapy.

In recent years I have taught research methods, a university course titled *The Psychology of Religion*, and published on topics of psychology and religion. In preparing for courses and advising students, I have learned a lot about spirituality and psychology. Finally, my upbringing likely continues to affect my thinking. Although I come from a large city (London, England), my parents attended a small Evangelical church. When I was still a boy, we came to the United States, where we continued to be involved in small Evangelical congregations. Although I no longer identify with those aspects of Christianity described by literal or fundamentalist beliefs, I am a Christian.

Geoffrey W. Sutton
Springfield, Missouri, USA

PART I

Pathways to Understanding Christianity, Morality, and Sexuality

1

BIBLICAL TEXTS AND CHRISTIAN PERSPECTIVES

Christianity had a rough start. Jesus of Nazareth, born a Jew in the ancient lands of Roman-occupied Israel, taught a new way of faith in a loving and forgiving God who, like a loving father, was intent on having a large family of children who loved one another. When he taught, he quoted the Hebrew Scriptures. He also associated with people considered unclean and unwelcome in Jewish society. He challenged the interpretations of contemporary religious leaders on points of law and tradition. He was beaten and crucified. His followers hid in fear that they too might suffer the same fate, but he appeared to them and encouraged them to share the good news of this new way of living before he left the earth. Then his followers spread the good news of freedom from spiritual bondage and a new way of faith based on a loving relationship with God. He offered forgiveness and hope to people weighed down by onerous laws and traditions.

In this chapter I plan to answer two main questions important to anyone striving to understand diverse Christian views on morality. First, a two-part question: what are the sacred texts of Christianity, and how did they become the book widely known as the Holy Bible, which governs how Christians frame morality? And second, how can we identify a Christian perspective on morality?

How Was the Bible Formed?

The sacred text of Christianity known as the Bible, or Holy Bible, is a collection of ancient writings called books that were written over a period of centuries by many persons. The collections vary from the sixty-six books in the Protestant Bible to several more in Catholic and Orthodox Church

Bibles. Early on, Christians accepted the Hebrew Scriptures as part of their canon. Religious scholars use the term *canon* to mean a religious group's official collection of sacred texts.[1] Because Christians accept Jesus' teaching as a new covenant between God and people, the term *old covenant* referred to the agreement between God and the descendants of Abraham while *new covenant* referred to the new message presented by Jesus and written about by his followers. The different sets of texts became known among Christians as Old and New Testaments, indicating that the documents bear witness to the two different covenants.

The Hebrew Bible

The Hebrew Bible includes twenty-four sets of documents referred to as books in three sections: The Torah (five books of the law, or teaching, traditionally attributed to Moses), Nevi'im (prophets), and Ketuvim (writings). The variety of documents is broadly identified as law, poetry, and prose.[2] In contemporary Western Christian versions of the Bible, the Hebrew Bible is presented as thirty-nine Old Testament books. Traditionally, the Jewish canon was considered firm since about 100 CE (Common Era), but Toorn suggests that what came to be the official collection of scrolls had more to do with the end of the canonical era sometime after the Hebrew prophet Ezra.[3]

There are different theories as to how the ancient writings were eventually organized into a collection. References in 2 Kings 22 and 1 Samuel 10:25 indicate the presence of scrolls in the Hebrew temple. Also 2 Maccabees 1:20—2:18 refers to a temple library. Outside of Scripture, there are references by Flavius Josephus to a collection of twenty-two books that, depending on how books are counted, could refer to the collection in use by Jews. The Hebrew language collection of books is the official version of the Hebrew Bible in contrast to a Greek translation, *The Septuagint*, which had wide use sometime before the Christian era among Greek-speaking Jews and later, among Christians.[4]

Other Jewish writings appear in the Bibles of the Catholic Church and the Eastern Christian churches, but not in the Protestant Bible. These additional books are referred to as the Apocrypha, which means hidden. The Apocrypha are not part of the Bibles of either Judaism or Protestant

---

1. From Greek meaning measuring stick, rule, or measure. Sanders, "Canon: Hebrew Bible," 837.
2. Friedman and Dolansky, *The Bible Now*, 1.
3. Toorn, "Constructing the Canon," 233–64.
4. Gabel and Wheeler, *The Bible as Literature*, 168–69.

Christianity. There are other collections of ancient writings such as the Pseudepigrapha and the New Testament Apocrypha, but these are not commonly found in official canons.[5]

The Christian Bible

Because the early Christians were Jews who followed Jesus, they, like Jesus, accepted the Hebrew Bible as their sacred text. Early followers of Jesus and his teachings created a number of documents, which were circulated among the newly formed congregations. Two major collections were used in the early years of the church. One collection consists of writings by Jews close to the time of Jesus and, as previously mentioned, this collection is known as the Apocrypha. Another collection, which eventually became the New Testament, consisted of the four Gospels, the Acts of the Apostles (history), twenty-one Epistles (letters), and the book of Revelation. This latter collection of New Testament books was a work in progress for many years because different groups maintained different lists of sacred texts.

The four Gospels explain the importance of Jesus' life and teaching to different audiences. There is some overlap of content among the four Gospels as well as some differences in what the writers include. One writer, Luke, produced a two-volume work known as Luke-Acts. The book titled *Luke* is one of the four Gospels. In the Acts of the Apostles, Luke explains that the name *Christian* was used to refer to a follower of Jesus. The term *Christian* refers to a particular role that is key in separating traditional Jews from the Jews in the new group that followed Jesus. In the Hebrew Bible, Jews looked forward to a man sent from God as a savior of their status as a people under foreign rule. This savior is also known as the Messiah, meaning the anointed one. The followers of Jesus accepted Jesus as God's Messiah. In the Greek language, the Hebrew word for messiah is *christos*, which is the origin of the name translated into English as Christ and the term *Christian*. What looks like a two-part contemporary name—Jesus Christ—is actually a name (Jesus) and a title (Christ, the anointed one). However, many Christians use the phrase, Jesus Christ, as if his name were similar to the two names common in contemporary Western cultures. Eventually the Jews who followed Jesus' way became known as Christians. In addition to their acceptance of Jesus as the Christ, they created new documents and welcomed non-Jewish converts into their congregations. As this group of Jews expanded, another event happened to change the course of Judaism. The Romans put down a Jewish rebellion and destroyed the Jewish temple at Jerusalem in the year

---

5. Ibid., 165–81.

70. The destruction put an end to a focal point of Jewish faith and the important rite of sacrifice.[6]

One early Jewish convert, Saul of Tarsus, persecuted the first-century Jewish followers of Jesus for their heretical teachings, but following a dramatic conversion, he—now using the name Paul—embarked on a series of missionary journeys throughout the Roman Empire. He communicated with towns where early Christians formed groups by sending letters known as Epistles. These letters of Paul form a large part of the New Testament. But scholars like Victor Furnish disagree over who actually wrote some of the letters attributed to Paul based on analyses of dates and the characteristics of the writings themselves.[7] Other letters are traditionally attributed to the apostle Peter and Jesus' brothers, Jude and John.

As the Gospels and letters began to circulate among the early congregations, a collection began to form. There were disputes over some books, such as Hebrews and Revelation, that ultimately made it into the official canon. Other writings were rejected despite strong support from some leaders. Examples of rejected documents include *The Gospel of Thomas* and *The Letter of Barnabas*.[8]

As noted above, the official canon varies with the Christian traditions. The Hebrew Torah and Prophets were in use by Jews before Jesus, but the addition of the other Jewish writings appears to have taken place within a few decades after Jesus. Roman Catholics fixed their canon at the Council of Trent (1545–63). They included forty-six books from the Old Testament and twenty-seven for the New Testament. The books in the Apocrypha were reviewed and included as part of the official Catholic Bible. These books have since been known as Deuterocanonical (of the second canon). In current versions of the Catholic list, these apocryphal books are part of the Old Testament booklist. As already noted, most Protestants do not accept these additional Old Testament texts, so Protestant Bibles have only thirty-nine Old Testament books. Variations in what books were included appear in Greek, Russian, Georgian, and Eastern Orthodox Bibles. The Anglican Church uses some apocryphal books in their liturgies.

No original Bible texts have been found. The twenty-seven books of the New Testament were officially recognized by Bishop Athanasius on Easter 367.[9] The Vulgate, a Latin translation by Jerome, was available about 400 CE and helped solidify the biblical canon. Stephen Langton, Archbishop

---

6. Borg, *Reading the Bible*, location 2404.
7. Furnish, *The Moral Teaching of Paul*, 11–12.
8. Ibid., 179.
9. Brakke, "Canon Formation," 395–419.

of Canterbury, has been credited with the division of the Bible books into chapters during the thirteenth century.[10] More refined divisions into numbered verses have been traced to Robert Stephanus for the Greek New Testament and William Whittingham for the English New Testament.[11]

Contemporary translators select texts from various parts of the ancient world and try to determine which text is likely closer to the original document when preparing a translation. Unfortunately, there are no original documents. Translators attempt to be faithful to the likely original text by footnoting which ancient manuscripts they used and by including alternative translations for obscure words and phrases. However, some groups of Western Protestant Christians still consider a version of the Bible authorized by King James I of England in 1611 as The Holy Bible. This version, known as the KJV, dominated English-speaking societies until other versions gained wide acceptance in the last few decades.

Perhaps several factors contributed to the decline of the KJV. Archeologists discovered older versions of biblical texts, which varied from the documents used to translate the KJV. In general, Bible scholars believe the words and phrases in older texts are probably closer to the original. Differences among the old manuscripts can be due to copying errors or a preference for a particular word or phrase. Bible scholars learned more about ancient languages, which allowed for more accurate translations. Translators became more sophisticated not only in their understanding of ancient languages but also in the science of linguistics.[12] And the public became less and less aware of the meaning of the English words in use some four hundred years ago. Today there is a plethora of translations available to users of English and other contemporary languages.

Many have asked who wrote the Bible. For conservative Christians, the ultimate author is God. On a simple level this idea works for many who believe that God inspired different people to write the documents that compose the Bible. Some believers have little knowledge about the history of the Bible and simply accept what they are told by their religious leaders (e.g., pastors, priests, or teachers). But even knowledgeable Christians may view God as the author if they have a strong view of what it means for God to inspire people to write one lengthy text over many centuries. Other Christian scholars emphasize the different views in the Bible and consider the texts as

---

10. Gilmore, "Langton," 111.
11. Ibid., "Stephanus," 186.
12. Black, *New Testament*, 11–26.

documents produced by a community of believers who saw God in different ways at different times in history.[13]

The question of authorship is important to understanding Christian morality because people who believe God wrote the entire Bible are going to be very careful about how to interpret God's word. If God is the author, then Christians need to be careful about questioning what the Bible teaches about morality. Anyone who begins to ask questions that seem to challenge Bible-based beliefs about sexual morality will soon encounter an oft-quoted verse from 2 Timothy 3:16. Kern Trembath is an Evangelical scholar who explains the problem with the way conservatives use this quotation to prove that the Bible is God's Word.[14] Following the text, I will review Trembath's points: "All scripture is inspired by God and is useful for teaching, for reproof, for correction, and for training in righteousness" (2 Tim 3:16).

Trembath explains the difficulty this verse poses. First, we do not know to what Scripture the author of Timothy was referring: the author could have meant the Old Testament. He could have referred to a Hebrew text or Greek translation of the Old Testament, which are not the same. He may have included other writings known as the Apocrypha. And he may have referred to some of the early church letters that were in circulation. The second problem: what does the word *inspiration* mean? The Greek word translated as inspiration is only found in the biblical text I quoted and is not found much outside the Bible. As we will see, even when people view the Bible as God's word, they often come to different conclusions as to whether a particular act is moral or immoral.

Certainly, the Bible is important to Christians. Christians turn to the Bible for guidance in their faith. And most Christians will also consult the Bible for guidance on matters of morality. Whether conservative or liberal, Fundamentalist, Evangelical, or progressive, the Bible provides the context for an understanding of Christian morality. Of particular importance to this book is the way Christians interpret what the Bible says or does not say about contemporary sexual issues.

Other Texts

The Dead Sea Scrolls were found between 1946 and 1956 and may have included about one thousand texts found near the northwest shore of the Dead Sea. They have been dated between 408 BCE and 318 CE. The Dead Sea Scrolls include texts from the Hebrew Bible, religious texts found in

---

13. Borg, *Reading the Bible*, locations 309–16.
14. Trembath, *Evangelical Theories*, 5–6.

various Christian canons, and texts that related to various aspects of social life.[15] The Dead Sea Scrolls and other discoveries of texts are important—as noted previously—because newer translations of the Bible often use the oldest available texts in an effort to be true to the original writings.

The rapid spread of Mormonism began in the 1820s when Joseph Smith introduced a new sacred text to the world. *The Book of Mormon* was originally intended as a companion to the Bible,[16] but it soon became the basis for the new movement known as Mormonism.[17] The point of mentioning the Mormons is to recognize that some consider members of the Latter Day Saints (LDS) church as Christians and some do not; but they have an additional text, which is only recognized as a sacred text by the LDS church.

Who Are the Christians?

Christians are a diverse group of more than two billion adherents worldwide. Most people in the Americas continue to identify themselves as Christian. Most Europeans who identify as religious also identify as Christian. Among Christians, most identify as either Catholic or Evangelical, although many Christians, primarily in Eastern Europe, identify as Orthodox. An exception can be found in England. The Church of England was reformed when King Henry VIII broke away from the Roman Catholic Church over a divorce decision. Those affiliated with the Church of England are known as Anglicans. In the U.S., Episcopalians have their roots in the Church of England, the official church of the English during the Colonial Era. To scholars, most Christians who are not Anglican, Orthodox, or Catholic are classified as Protestants because their beliefs originated with leaders such as Martin Luther and John Calvin, who protested against some of the beliefs and practices of the Roman Catholic Church and formed new religious groups. The various subgroups of Protestants are often called denominations. It is important to keep in mind that although news stories often refer to Catholics and Protestants, there are other Christian groups.

---

15. Wise, et al., *The Dead Sea Scrolls*, 3–13.

16. Hansen, "Mormonism," 142–59.

17. The official name for the Mormon Church is *The Church of Jesus Christ of Latter-day Saints*, often abbreviated as LDS.

Christian Beginnings

Early Christians were people who followed the teachings of Jesus of Nazareth. Like Jesus, they were Jews. In those days, people who followed religious leaders were known as disciples or followers. Jesus selected a dozen of his male followers to be leaders. After listening to Jesus, seeing his work amongst the people, and witnessing his death, resurrection, and ascension into heaven, they were convinced he was God's Messiah or Christ. To follow Jesus' teachings was to follow God's new way.

Judas—one of the original twelve disciples—had betrayed Jesus and was replaced. This group of twelve became known as the apostles. In the decades following Jesus' ministry, the apostles spread the good news of Jesus' way throughout the known world. This good news is known as the gospel. Four manuscripts containing the sayings and acts of Jesus—the good news—became known as the Gospels, which are the first four books in the New Testament. The early Jewish followers who changed their beliefs to accept Jesus as the Messiah continued to meet in synagogues. Other people who were not Jews were also convinced of the truth of Jesus' way and gave up their old belief systems. This changing of an entire set of beliefs and a way of living is known as conversion. From the biblical book of Acts, we learn that the early converts assembled in homes. Later they constructed places of worship, which have become known as churches rather than synagogues.

The early letters from Paul, Peter, and others writers were circulated, read, and copied. After the apostles died, new church leaders interpreted the gospels and letters in different ways. Major beliefs considered in error by those in power were labeled as heresies.

In the context of various beliefs, early Christians met to formulate a statement of Christian beliefs, which came to be known as the Apostles' Creed. It appears to have been an early statement of faith spoken by a person about to be baptized into the Christian faith.[18] Here's a formulation of that creed:

> I believe in God the Father almighty,
> creator of heaven and earth.
>
> And in Jesus Christ, his only Son, our Lord;
> Who was conceived by the Holy Spirit
> Born of the virgin Mary.
> He suffered under Pontius Pilate,

---

18. Phipps, *The Apostle's' Creed*, i.

> was crucified, died, and was buried;
> he descended into hell;
> The third day he rose again from the dead.
> He ascended into heaven
> And is seated at the right hand of God the Father almighty.
> From there he will come to judge the living and the dead.
>
> I believe in the Holy Spirit,
> the holy catholic church,
> the communion of saints,
> the forgiveness of sins,
> the resurrection of the body,
> and the life everlasting.
> AMEN.[19]

Christian leaders—bishops—met at Nicaea—modern Iznik, Turkey—in 325 CE to resolve differences in beliefs about the nature of Jesus Christ. Essentially, people held different opinions about what it meant to be a Son of God: was Jesus a human being, a divine being, or was his nature something else? Eventually, a revised document was created and it became known as the Nicene Creed. Here is that creed.

> We believe in one God the Father, the Almighty, maker of heaven and earth, of all that is, seen and unseen.
>
> We believe in one Lord, Jesus Christ, the only Son of God, eternally begotten of the Father, God from God, Light from Light, true God from true God, begotten, not made, of one being with the Father.
>
> Through him all things were made.
>
> For us and for our salvation he came down from heaven: by the power of the Holy Spirit he became incarnate from the Virgin Mary, and was made man.
>
> For our sake he was crucified under Pontius Pilate; he suffered, died, and was buried.
>
> On the third day he rose again in accordance with the Scriptures; he ascended into heaven and is seated at the right hand of the Father.

---

19. Van Harn, *Exploring and Proclaiming*, xviii.

He will come again in glory to judge the living and the dead, and his kingdom will have no end.

We believe in the Holy Spirit, the Lord, the giver of life, who proceeds from the Father and the Son.

With the Father and the Son he is worshiped and glorified.

He has spoken through the prophets.

We believe in one holy, catholic and apostolic Church.

We acknowledge one baptism for the forgiveness of sins.

We look for the resurrection of the dead and the life of the world to come.

Amen.[20]

Christian Diversity

Christian diversity has been evident for nearly two thousand years. The Bible itself reveals different opinions on how one should live, as can be seen in the disagreement between the apostles Peter and Paul (Gal 2:11–21). Since those early days, a variety of Christian groups continued to interpret particular texts in different ways that led to the formation of doctrinally distinct groups. Two major movements made significant contributions to the range of diversity we see today. Many contemporary Christian groups may be traced to the Protestant Reformation beginning about 500 years ago. In Western Europe, men like Martin Luther and John Calvin led movements that eventually created new religious groups with distinct interpretations of Scripture and leaders no longer obligated to follow the teachings of the dominant Roman Catholic Church.

The second major movement, associated with the seventeenth and eighteenth centuries, is known as the Enlightenment. This movement was marked by an emphasis on critical thinking informed by reason and scientific inquiry to advance knowledge. Since the Enlightenment, scientists challenged many assumptions about nature, which led to an explosion of scientific knowledge. In this context, religious scholars also challenged assumptions derived from simplistic interpretations of biblical texts, which appeared at variance with such scientific discoveries as the age and vastness of the universe.

20. Walsh, *Roman Catholicism*, 2.

Perhaps the most controversial challenge has been the scientific research on evolution in general and human evolution in particular. And in more recent decades, the behavioral sciences (e.g., anthropology, psychology, and sociology) have explained aspects of human nature that some Christians consider to be at odds with Christian teaching. Psychology in particular was offensive because findings about mental illness seemed to contradict biblical beliefs about sin and the spiritual path to transformation from the effects of sin rather than the secular process of change—psychotherapy. Also, many psychologists explained biblical stories of demon possession as ancient ways of describing mental illness rather than reports of spiritual beings invading or controlling human beings.

In response to various challenges to faith, conservative groups hammered out a set of fundamental beliefs, hence the term *Fundamentalists*. Christian Fundamentalists and theological conservatives view the Bible as the Word of God. God is the author of the text, and the Bible is the ultimate guide for life. Fundamentalists do not reject all extrabiblical knowledge. What they reject is knowledge of things like evolution and mental disorders that appear to contradict the biblical texts. These perceived contradictions often include contemporary ideas about morality and sexuality.

Many Christians do not identify as Fundamentalists because the term has become associated with negative stereotypes of poorly educated and simple-minded people who are rightwing authoritarians, closed minded, and highly judgmental.[21] Instead of viewing themselves as Fundamentalists, many conservative Christians identify as Evangelicals. Evangelicals rely on the Protestant Bible to form their view of the world; thus, the Bible is of primary importance in matters of the Christian life.

But the term *Evangelical* can also be elusive because it can be used to represent a classification of Christians based on surveys of beliefs, or it can refer to people who attend churches that either belong to the National Association of Evangelicals (NAE) or who share all—or most—of the doctrinal beliefs of the NAE.[22] Some researchers ask a series of questions to form the basis for identifying a respondent as an Evangelical or nonEvangelical. When reading news and research about Evangelicals or any other group, it is important to note how the authors define the group.

Many Pentecostals also identify as Evangelicals, and some Pentecostal groups are members of the National Association of Evangelicals (e.g., the Assemblies of God). The Latter Day Saints (LDS) share many Fundamentalist

---

21. Hood et al., *The Psychology of Religious Fundamentalism*, 12–13.

22. You can find the current statement of beliefs and membership on the NAE website: www.nae.net.

values although a number of Christians—including Fundamentalists—do not consider adherents to the LDS to be Christians.

Pentecostal and charismatic Christians share many of the core beliefs of Fundamentalists and Evangelicals but add two key components to their theology. First, they believe divine healing and other miracles are available to contemporary believers as was true in the Gospel stories. Second, based primarily on the biblical books of Acts and 1 Corinthians, they believe in an active role of God's Spirit to gift people for various ministries. These gifts follow a second baptism often accompanied by glossolalia—i.e., speaking in tongues—and include discernment of spirits and prophecy. Pentecostal scholars have identified a diversity of theological beliefs among Pentecostal and charismatic Christians.[23]

Similar to other Evangelicals, Pentecostals view the Bible as authoritative. Pentecostals examine the Scriptures expecting to see God's Spirit at work in the lives of the ancient Israelites and expecting those same experiences to be part of their contemporary Christian life, which is sometimes referred to as the abundant life. God is present now. Believers can speak to God and expect him to respond. A helpful study of this personal sense of God's presence is T. M. Luhrmann's research as summarized in her highly readable book, *When God Talks Back*.[24] The negative side of God at work is the devil at work. For Pentecostals and charismatics, Satan is an active person-like being with hordes of demons seeking to entrap unwary believers.[25] When caught in sexual sin, some Pentecostals and charismatics attribute the sin to the work of the devil and pray for deliverance. Sexual sins and other moral failures and can be viewed as evidence of spiritual warfare.

I should point out that some variations of beliefs among Pentecostal believers do not always carry official recognition. For example, the U.S. Pentecostal fellowship known as the Assemblies of God responds to problematic beliefs with position papers.[26] Another example of a unique group of Pentecostals is the snake-handling believers from Appalachia, which is located in the Southeastern United States. They became popular in a show titled *Snake Salvation*, which aired in the U.S. on the National Geographic channel.[27] The death of pastor Jaime Coots in February 2014 drew attention to their handling of poisonous snakes during worship. Pastor Coots

---

23. Macchia, "Baptized in the Spirit," 13–28.
24. The entire book contains the results of her study.
25. In Christianity, Satan is a leading fallen angel and synonymous with the devil.
26. The AG position papers can be found online http://ag.org/top/Beliefs/position_papers/index.cfm
27. www.nationalgeographic.com

was bitten by a snake and refused treatment because of his interpretation of a biblical text suggesting that believers will not be harmed if they handle poisonous snakes.[28]

Protestant denominations that accept a broader interpretation of the biblical texts and a more flexible understanding of faith became known as mainline denominations and were said to have a liberal theology. In the U.S., *liberal* has become a negative political label hurled against politicians who appear to fight against the traditional moral values espoused by religious and political conservatives. Scholars associated with the seminaries and universities founded by these mainline denominations drew upon a growing body of research to challenge the traditional interpretations of the biblical texts. Perhaps as a stereotype, they were disparagingly known for their social gospel rather than for their enthusiastic personal relationship with Jesus and a desire to evangelize—that is, preach the gospel message of salvation from personal sin. The list of liberal denominations may vary, but most lists include Episcopalians, some groups of Lutherans, Presbyterians, and Methodists. Another way this class of denominations differs from the Evangelicals is on social values such as divorce, remarriage, same-sex relations, and abortion. Of course, not every person who serves as clergy or attends a mainline or liberal church holds the same religious beliefs.

Catholics rely on the Bible, conscience, and prayer, as well as guidance from the official teachings of the church to address moral issues.[29] It so happens when it comes to contemporary social issues like marriage, divorce, same-sex relationships, and abortion that Catholics, Evangelicals, and Latter Day Saints have much in common. Again, it would be a mistake to conclude that all Catholic clergy, church leaders, and church members share the same beliefs.

Christian Beliefs and Research

A great deal can be learned about changing trends in Christian beliefs and values from polling data. Harris Interactive polled 2,250 adults between November 13 and 18, 2013.[30] A summary of their findings is available online. A few findings are highly relevant to this chapter. First, most in the U.S. continue to believe in God (74 percent), and about two-thirds believe Jesus is God or the Son of God (68 percent). Age makes a significant difference.

---

28. Fantz, "Reality Show," para. 1–3.

29. See the section on "Morality" at http://www.usccb.org/beliefs-and-teachings/what-we-believe/morality/index.cfm

30. Harris Interactive, "Americans' Belief."

Those working with seniors will find a much higher rate of believers in God (83 percent) and Jesus as God or God's Son (75 percent) than those working with younger persons aged eighteen through thirty-six (64 and 58 percent). Women (59 percent) reported a higher level of certainty that God exists than did men (48 percent).

I have mentioned the importance of the Bible to an understanding of Christian morality. Polling data reveal that about half of U.S. adults view the Bible as God's Word. The percentages holding the belief were similar for the Old (49 percent) and New Testaments (48 percent) as God's Word. When the researchers at Gallup asked similar questions in 2014, the importance of the Bible to U.S. Christians was even more evident.[31] In a representative sample of U.S. adults (May 8–11, 2014) about 75 percent considered the Bible to be the Word of God. When the question was more specific, about one quarter agreed: "The Bible is the actual word of God and is to be taken literally." The researchers observed that when they analyzed the sample, about 90 percent of those who identified as Christian, link the Bible to God. Regardless of personal belief, readers need to understand the biblical texts in order to understand diverse Christian moral perspectives.

Morality: From Text to Life

I am sure you are aware that whatever term I use to refer to a group of people and their beliefs, it will be inadequate and subject to criticism. Rightly or wrongly, I have selected two terms to group two broad cultures of moral perspectives on the social issues in this book: *Conservative* and *Progressive*.

Conservative Perspectives

I use the term *conservative perspectives* for the views of Christians who express social values based on a close-to-literal interpretation of the Bible. I also use the term for views derived from an interpretation of the Bible that represents a desire to maintain a recent status quo or return to a social policy that was changed in recent decades. When I consider the way Christians cite biblical texts to support marriage or oppose such social issues as abortion and same-sex relationships, I find some writers describe the conservative opinions as Fundamentalist or literalist. Fundamentalist interpretations of the Bible often rely on translations of ancient words or phrases. The interpretations are often presented without explanations regarding the meaning

---

31. Saad, "Three in Four."

of the words in the original language, considerations of biblical or historical contexts that can influence the meaning of words, or guidance about how Christians can apply an ancient proverb or law to contemporary issues. I think the terms *Fundamentalist* and *literalist* are unsatisfactory because Christian groups that are not clearly Fundamentalist in their approach to biblical texts have reached similar conclusions about the morality of certain social behavior patterns.

Although Evangelicals, Pentecostals, Catholics, and Mormons often hold similar social values, their approaches to the biblical texts reflect an appeal to church teaching and a consideration of biblical studies. In contrast, Fundamentalists eschew extrabiblical documents, research, and traditions when arriving at the interpretation of key texts. That is, they claim to rely solely on the biblical texts to interpret other biblical texts. In their view, the biblical text is primary. The Bible has one voice. The Bible is the Word of God. However, it should be pointed out that although Fundamentalists stress their reliance on the biblical text, they can disagree with other Fundamentalists over such matters as the role of women in the church and worship styles; thus, Fundamentalists also vary in their interpretation of the Word of God and the implication of select texts for morality. In contrast with Fundamentalists, Roman Catholics and some Evangelicals consider scholarly research and church tradition when reaching a conclusion about how God would have people live in response to any social trends that may appear. For these reasons, I will use the term *conservative perspectives* for moral values shared by these Christian groups despite some quite distinctive differences on matters of theology.

Mark Driscoll is a U.S. Evangelical preacher who addressed many aspects of sexual conduct in a bestselling book he wrote with his wife Grace: *Real marriage: The Truth about Sex, Friendship & Life Together*. I refer to the Driscolls' book as one example of how conservative Evangelicals use the Bible as a basis for generating recommendations to Christians who want to live a moral life. Another reason to mention the book is to show that, unlike a Fundamentalist who might be expected to rely solely on the Bible, the Driscolls quote scholarly resources, such as the work of sociologist W. Bradford Wilcox.[32] Again, my purpose here is only to show how a conservative Evangelical can consider both findings from behavioral science and reason to reach a nuanced conclusion about how contemporary Christians ought to act.

Clifford and Joyce Penner also offer a conservative view of Christian sexuality in their book, *A Gift for all Ages*. Like many authors, the Penners

---

32. Driscoll and Driscoll, *Real Marriage*, 57.

begin their work with a reference to being created in the image of God and affirm, "Sex is part of God's design for us."[33]

A third example of a conservative approach to Christian morality comes from John S. and Paul D. Feinberg—both of Trinity Evangelical Divinity School. In their scholarly book, *Ethics for a Brave New World*, they examine relevant biblical texts and use reason to derive principles of morality, which they apply to such contemporary issues as abortion, birth control, and sexual orientation.

Traditional Perspectives

Are conservative views the same as traditional views? The answer to the question depends on how long a view needs to be held to count as a tradition. Conservative perspectives give great weight to the way common biblical texts have been interpreted by many Christians for decades. Why decades? I wanted to write traditional views have been present for centuries or millennia, but that would not be true. Aside from the long-standing limitations of the restricted role of women in Christian churches, many of the social issues that have divided Christians are recent. Some specific changes that occurred in the twentieth century are linked to recent changes in sexual activity. Protestant Fundamentalists, Evangelicals, Pentecostals, Roman Catholics, Orthodox churches, and Mormons continue to find common ground in affirming the long-standing European-American tradition of marriage as that between one man and one woman, which they link to Old and New Testament Scriptures. They also condemn the increase in sexual activity outside of marriage, which was associated with the widespread availability of medically safe and effective contraceptive techniques—never before available in the history of humankind. Prohibitions against sex outside of marriage can be traced to the writings of the apostle Paul, but the changes in contraception are new and nuanced.

Medically safe abortion procedures became possible with advances in medical technologies. The medical abortion is a relatively new social issue. Another recent social factor is the major change in abortion laws, linked to the influence of the 1973 U.S. Supreme Court ruling in *Roe v. Wade*. The new technology and the changes in law prompted Christians to consult the Bible and form policy statements about abortion. One example of their ability to cooperate on matters of social value may be their success in changing laws in various U.S. states to impose restrictions on abortion, which has led to the closure of clinics that offer abortions.

33. Penner and Penner, *A Gift*, ix.

Many twentieth-century social changes and technological advances changed the way women and men earn a living and divide their responsibilities for childcare and other household duties. These and other factors—including two world wars—involved large numbers of women in the workplace. Eventually and unevenly, people came to recognize the important contribution of women in a diversity of fields beyond their traditional expertise within the home. Women continued to make progress toward equality with men. They attended universities in large numbers and in some cases outnumbered their male counterparts. In 2013, the U.S. military announced a plan to increase the integration of women by opening combat positions in 2016.[34] The social changes, which opened well-paying careers to women, afforded women the opportunity to support themselves without relying on a man's income. In fact, some men find themselves depending on a woman's income for all or most of a couple's income.

Before the twentieth century, divorces were difficult to obtain, especially for women. Not surprisingly, when women had the same recourse to divorce as men did, they were able to seek divorce from those who mistreated them. Easing of divorce restrictions naturally resulted in increased divorce rates, which in turn led to more single men and women interested in remarriage. Of course, without employment opportunities for women, the possibility of divorce from a painful marriage could hardly be enticing.

The traditional teaching of the church presented the ideal of a lifelong monogamous marriage with the only official basis for divorce being adultery. And depending on a group's interpretation, there was either no biblical basis for remarriage or a highly restricted biblical option for remarriage, which was at odds with the behavior of people attending church. Denominations were prompted to address this social trend. In fact, many Christian denominations changed policies to be more accepting toward divorced and remarried persons. Also, many initiated premarital counseling and marriage enrichment programs to support marriage.

Marriage between one man and one woman is not a long-standing tradition. As we will see in other chapters, plural marriage has a long history, not only in the Bible but also in other cultures. Polygamy continues to be practiced in many countries. It can be said that most marriages in the United States and Europe were between one man and one woman until recently. It can also be said that polygamy is illegal in the United States.

Another example of problems with the concept of traditional marriage is the widespread existence of laws forbidding marriages between people of different racial groups. Biblical laws limited the Israelites to marrying those

---

34. Brook, "Pentagon Opening," para. 1.

who were members of the Israelite tribes (Deut 7:3–4). Marrying outside the Jewish community was forbidden. These ideas became the basis for modern laws prohibiting marriages between Blacks and Whites. In the Southern U.S. states, black and white marriages were specifically forbidden. In 1967, the U.S. Supreme Court decided in *Loving v. Virginia* that the law preventing marriage between a black woman and a white man violated the Fourteenth Amendment to the U.S. Constitution. Eventually the laws changed, but for centuries, traditional marriage meant marrying within your racial group where race was based on skin color. You will still find Christians who maintain a long-standing view that it is a violation of God's Word for black and white Christians to date and marry.

Related to the concept of marriage and tradition was the 1996 U.S. Defense of Marriage Act. This act included an official definition of marriage as being between one man and one woman. The change in laws permitting same-sex marriage is my final example of a recent break from traditional marriage. Only in the past decade have several nations changed their laws to grant gay and lesbian persons the right to a legally recognized marriage. The U.S. Supreme Court decision in *The United States v. Windsor* handed down on June 26, 2013 found critical portions of the Defense of Marriage Act violated equal protection guaranteed in the Due Process clause of the Fifth Amendment to the U.S. Constitution. On June 26, 2015, the U.S. Supreme Court ruled that same-sex couples had the right to marry.

In view of the changes in marriage relationships, what should we consider when referring to a marriage belief as traditional? The Fifth Amendment was added to the U.S. Constitution December 15, 1791. The Defense of Marriage Act only became law in 1996. Of course, by referring to the dates of laws, I am referring to a nonreligious codification of beliefs or traditions. However, although the Bible contains verses related to same-sex activity, the concepts of same-sex marriage are recent phenomena in Western cultures, which prompted Christians to search the Bible before producing policy statements about same-sex marriage.

Progressive Perspectives

I use the term *progressive perspectives* to identify the views of those Christians who have favored social changes that went beyond the restrictions desired by Christians favoring a conservative view. Although many U.S. Christians support conservative interpretations as the only correct biblical view, other Christians interpret the same sacred texts in different ways. Progressive Christians rely more on general principles of Scripture, such as love and justice, rather than laws or teachings that may be viewed as specific to a cultural context. Progressives embrace changes that promote equality for all and do not wish to restrict the blessings of life to a majority, or even a minority. The term *progress* refers to change that advances the wellbeing of those who heretofore had some aspect of their life restricted because of an interpretation of the Bible, which required that a restriction based in a biblical law or other biblical text remain as a part of contemporary social policy in order for people to live according to God's law. Progressive perspectives represent a different Christian culture when it comes to social values.

Progressives point to such biblical examples as Jesus' summary of the entire Law encapsulated in the expression, "Love God and love your neighbor." Progressives also point to other favorite texts, such as Matthew 9:16–17, in which Jesus explained changes by way of illustrating that people do not patch old garments with new cloth or put new wine into old wineskins. And the apostle Peter learned a lesson of change or progress in thinking about acceptable people when God showed him a vision of religiously unclean animals and asked him to eat them (Acts 10). Progressives also point to Paul's understanding that the new converts did not need to follow the God-ordained Jewish tradition of circumcision. Instead, according to Paul, circumcision could be seen as an inner attitude toward God (Rom 2:25–3:2). These and other examples represent progress—going beyond ancient Israelite laws and traditions. The progress in attitudes toward old rules comes from Jesus and two leading apostles—Peter and Paul—who wrote much of the New Testament. Progressive Christians continue to apply this way of thinking when new issues like abortion, birth control, stem cell research, and other ethical issues invite a Christian response.

At this point it might be reasonable to ask how progressive Christian approaches differ from Evangelical approaches. Unfortunately, there is no easy answer. The boundary between an Evangelical and a progressive approach can be fuzzy in the midrange between Fundamentalists on one extreme and liberal progressives on the other. Perhaps one guideline will help make the difference clear. An Evangelical approach continually refers back to biblical teachings and laws. In addition, many Evangelicals believe some Old Testament laws about moral issues continue to provide a basis for the contemporary Christian life. Evangelicals will often refer to three kinds of biblical laws: ceremonial, civil, and moral. In this view, ceremonial laws are those that governed the way ancient Israelites worshipped God. Because Christians accept Jesus as their priest and view his life and death as a one-time sacrifice, Christians no longer need to follow ceremonial laws about Jewish worship. The civil laws are also not binding on Christians because they regulated how Israel governed their nation. And contemporary

Christians are to obey existing governments as taught by the apostle Paul in Romans 13:1–7. Finally, moral laws are considered binding on Christians. These moral laws deal with such things as murder and theft but also include the sexual issues addressed in this book.

In contrast to the more moderate Evangelical approaches to Scripture, progressive views toward the biblical texts vary considerably. Progressives are generally more willing to give greater weight to more universal moral rules as exemplified by the golden rule: "Do unto others as you would have them do unto you" (Matt 7:12). Progressives are generally more open to consider various interpretations of biblical texts. Progressives are open to considering the historical context that might explain why a biblical rule existed in the first place. And they are more willing to evaluate the impact on the lives of contemporary people if an ancient rule is applied without consideration of actual or potential harmful consequences.

Progressive Christians are concerned about social justice. They hear the call of Isaiah to serve God by serving others (Isa 58), the message of Jesus to serve him by serving the needy (Matt 25), and the importance of living a loving and humble life (John 13:34–35).

Two Christians often linked to the progressive movement are Brian D. McLaren and Tony Campolo. Their 2003 book, *Adventures in Missing the Point*, offers chapters on several challenges to Christian traditions, including women in ministry and homosexuality. Another progressive author and popular speaker is Rob Bell. Bell is a graduate of the conservative Wheaton College. In 2011 he was listed as one of *Time Magazine's* top one hundred most influential people in the world. He garnered widespread attention that year when he challenged traditional beliefs about hell in his popular book, *Love Wins*. Another of his controversial works relevant to this book is *Sex God*, which challenges interpretations of what constitutes traditional marriage. An example of a more scholarly perspective on moral issues can be found in *The Moral Teaching of Paul* by Victor Furnish.

As a final note, sometimes I will use the phrase *alternative perspectives* to refer to those views of Christians who hold nontraditional perspectives on a moral issue. In this case, *alternative* simply means another view or a different view that is clearly not conservative but not easily identified with a progressive perspective.

Summary

In this chapter, I laid the foundation for understanding Christian moral perspectives by looking at how the Bible came into existence and what makes for a Christian identity. I began by answering the question about how the Bible was formed. The Christian Bible begins with a collection of writings known to Jews as the Bible. This Hebrew Bible was the collection of manuscripts available to the first followers of the Jewish teacher, Jesus of Nazareth. When his followers accepted him as God's Messiah or Christ, they became known as Christians. A new collection of teachings and stories about Jesus became known as the Gospels. Those close to Jesus, known as apostles, wrote letters to the new Christian groups throughout the Roman Empire. The Gospels and letters formed a collection known as the New Testament and among Christians, the Hebrew Scriptures became known as the Old Testament.

The second compound question was about the identity of Christians. Who are they and what do they believe? Because there were disagreements about Christian beliefs, church leaders created a set of belief statements, which were agreed to by many representatives of the growing Christian movement. I included copies of two of these documents known as the Apostles' Creed and the Nicene Creed. The Roman Catholic and Orthodox Churches trace their roots to the early days of Christianity. In the last few centuries, new Christian groups have formed. The Church of England in its Protestant form began when the King of England broke ties with the Catholic Church. Several leaders broke away from the Catholic Church and formed new groups. Those Christians who became members of non-Catholic churches came to be known as Protestants.

I referred to a 2013 Harris Poll that provided recent data on selected religious beliefs of U.S. adults. Most in the U.S. affirm a belief in God and in Jesus as either God or God's Son. Older adults and women tend to have beliefs closer to the official teaching of the church. And of high importance to this book is the 2014 Gallup Poll indicating that most U.S. Christians view the Bible as God's Word. This belief about the Bible as God's Word establishes the text as an authority for morality.

Today there is a diversity of perspectives on what it means to be a Christian. But when it comes to moral values, groups with different views about Christian doctrine often share common social values about abortion, contraception, marriage, and same-sex relationships. I identified two metagroups who seem to hold similar perspectives on how to apply scriptural principles to contemporary moral issues.

I refer to one metagroup as conservative Christians. Although some conservatives are Fundamentalists who focus exclusively on the biblical texts, others—like Evangelicals and Catholics—use extrabiblical knowledge to understand Christian morality. When forming their perspectives on morality, these nonFundamentalist Christians employ reason, knowledge of the customs and culture that existed when the biblical documents were written, and—to varying extents—church traditions. Although all Fundamentalist Christians hold conservative (perhaps ultraconservative is more accurate) perspectives on moral matters, not all conservatives are Fundamentalists in their approach to understanding biblical morality.

There are a variety of alternative perspectives on Christian morality. The name of a recent movement, progressive Christianity, is the term I have selected for those Christians who seek to identify general principles of Christian morality. They are more likely to focus on how a principle like loving one's neighbor ought to apply to a contemporary social issue rather than rely on a law for ancient Israel or a letter written by Paul to a group of people in Corinth nearly two thousand years ago. Progressive Christians view Jesus' teaching as progressing beyond rigid adherence to old rules in favor of moral principles. They view his focus on humanity as more important than following an ancient law without regard for the impact of the law on a person.

An understanding of Scripture is the first of four factors that contributes to understanding how Christians form moral judgments.

Additional Resources

1. The Bible as the Word of God. Gallup routinely conducts a variety of polls. One poll relevant to this chapter was reported on June 4, 2014. They found that 28 percent of Americans believe the Bible is the actual word of God and that it should be taken literally. See the post by Lydia Saad for more details. http://www.gallup.com/poll/170834/three-four-Bible-word-god.aspx

2. Catholic beliefs. The largest Christian group is the Catholic Church. This website offers you access to their beliefs: http://www.vatican.va/archive/ENG0015/_INDEX.HTM

3. Evangelicals. What is an Evangelical? The National Association of Evangelicals provides their answer to the question: http://www.nae.net/church-and-faith-partners/what-is-an-Evangelical

4. Progressives. Progressive perspectives are sometimes hard to pin down. Author James F. McGrath, a regular blogger on the Patheos Progressive Christian Channel offers a statement of faith in his June 4, 2014 post, "Progressive Religion." http://www.patheos.com/blogs/exploringourmatrix/2014/06/progressive-religion.html

Discussion Questions

1. How popular is the Bible? For some statistics on Bible sales, see Guinness World Records. Why do you think the Bible is so popular? http://www.guinnessworldrecords.com/records-1/best-selling-book-of-non-fiction/

2. Why might it be important for atheists and people of other religions to know some of the major teachings in the Bible?

3. Estimate how many people you interact with at work or school during a week or month. Use recent polling data to estimate answers to the following questions. How many of the people you see are likely to affirm a belief in God? How many would you expect to value the Bible as God's Word? And how many might be inclined to view the biblical texts in a literal fashion?

2

THE INFLUENCE OF SPIRITUALITY AND THINKING ON MORALITY

Imagine a couple and their two daughters with wide, unbelieving eyes as they hear the intense warning—"You must leave now! Your house and entire village is about to be destroyed." Running for their lives, they head off toward a nearby mountain. Behind them, fire consumes their house. Smoke billows into the air. The mother stops and takes a fatal look back at her smoldering hometown. Shaking with fear, the father and his two daughters continue until they find a cave. Isolated, motherless, bereft of all they had, the two girls hatch a plan to have children. Each daughter takes a turn. And both become pregnant by their father. The incestual story of Lot and his two daughters (Gen 19) has puzzled Christians for centuries. Why don't the biblical writers condemn Lot for his actions? Why is Lot considered a righteous man (2 Pet 2:7)?

Religion is such an important aspect of life that it is not surprising to find it a topic of interest to behavioral scientists. The modern study of the psychology of religion arguably started with William James, an American philosopher and psychologist who wrote *The Varieties of Religious Experience* in 1902. In the past century, scientists have studied many aspects of religion and spirituality with a focus on beliefs and behavior. As a science, psychology is limited to that which is observable and testable. So, psychological scientists can identify factors in the environment as well as personal factors, such as beliefs and emotions, that influence religious experiences, but they cannot study the supernatural. Psychological scientists are interested in how religious beliefs and practices affect other dimensions of life, such as general health and mental health as well as relationships.

My purpose in this chapter is to review scientific findings about human nature. Beliefs about human nature constitute the second of four factors influencing how Christians form moral judgments.

I am going to present a six-dimensional model of human functioning to illustrate how various factors influence the way people make decisions—especially moral decisions. A second purpose is to understand basic components of human nature in order to consider how moral judgments affect people. Those six factors are spirituality or religion, cognition, behavior patterns, physiology, emotions, and social influences. Said another way, people act morally because of their spirituality, thinking, habits, biological status, feelings, and their social context. A related question is: how does acting on a moral judgment affect a person spiritually, cognitively, behaviorally, physically, emotionally, and socially?

One reason it is difficult to understand why people do what they do is that the answer is complex. We will need to examine many factors to explain moral behavior. If you are wondering about Christian perspectives on the incest story mentioned above, I will address the subject of incest in a later chapter.

Six Dimensions of Human Functioning: The SCOPES model

Those involved in the study of psychology are used to organizing information about the various dimensions of human functioning; however, those new to the vast expanse of theory and research on the psychology of religion can find the task of organizing overwhelming. A recent *Handbook of the Psychology of Religion and Spirituality* includes thirty-three chapters and spans nearly seven hundred pages.[1] I will try to make the task easier by using a six-dimensional model that is largely an expansion of the widely used Cognition-Affect-Behavior triad referred to by cognitive-behavioral psychotherapists.[2] The SCOPES model bares some similarity to the multimodal model developed by Arnold Lazarus.[3] I use the term *SCOPES* as an acronym for six dimensions: Spiritual, Cognitive, Observable (behavior patterns), Physiological, Emotional, and Social (context). The six dimensions are somewhat artificial in that people cannot be literally divided into discrete units of functioning. Nevertheless, you will find these six dimensions are commonly used by psychotherapists and psychological scientists even when they do not refer to these aspects of functioning as a group of six dimensions as I do in the SCOPES model. In this chapter I will present

---

1. Paloutzian and Park, *Handbook*.

2. Sutton and Mittelstadt, "Loving God," 157–66; Sutton and Thomas, "Restoring Christian," 28–29.

3. Lazarus, *The Practice of Multimodal*, 13–17.

the first two dimensions: Spirituality and Cognition (i.e., thinking). I will discuss the other four dimensions in the next chapter.

Spirituality and Religiosity

I use the term *spirituality* in a broad sense to include traditional religiosity associated with the beliefs and ceremonies of an established religious tradition like Christianity, Judaism, and Islam familiar to people in Western cultures. *Spirituality* can also be used for the beliefs and rituals of those who follow the practices of Buddhism, Hinduism, and Shintoism commonly associated with Eastern cultures. In addition, I use *spirituality* to refer to that sense of the sacred that many people report even if they are not affiliated with a specific religion. Many psychology of religion writers have noted the difficulty in defining religion and spirituality.[4] In this book, my task is somewhat easier because my focus is on how people—identified as members of the Christian religion—live that aspect of their Christian spirituality identified as morality.

I view the spiritual dimension of human functioning as an important core-orienting system that helps people make sense of their life experiences. I share the view of Raymond Paloutzian and Crystal Park, who view religion and spirituality as a part of human meaning systems.[5] People connect the events of life in ways commonly held by those around them as well as in unique ways. Whether people closely affiliate themselves with an identifiable religious group or not, ordinary people connect life events as they tell others about their day or some interesting experience. Gifted persons create extensive narratives, music, sculpture, paintings, and other artistic works that organize the experiences of a culture in meaningful ways. For some psychological scientists, religion and spirituality are additional ways people organize and make sense of life experiences. Because all humans organize life in meaningful ways, a meaning system appears to be a durable component of the human brain.

The concept of a worldview is part of a spiritual orientation. A worldview is close to a cognitive framework, which is one influential aspect of a spiritual core. The idea of a worldview functioning as a framework can be illustrated by thinking of a window frame. Your view of the world can be wide or narrow depending on the size of your window frame and how much of the world you wish to see. You may have one large window frame

---

4. For example, Hood et al., *The Psychology of Religion*, 6–12; Oman, "Defining Religion," 23–47.

5. Paloutzian and Park, "Recent progress," 3–22.

or a window with many smaller panes—each in its own smaller frame. Your windowpanes may be clear or colored. You may opt for glass that distorts an image so people cannot look in but you get some light. You may have a clear window but prefer to cover the window for most of a day, thereby only catching glimpses of what goes on in the world outside. I do not want to push the framework idea too far. The point is that Christian educators often speak about a Christian worldview in contrast to a secular worldview. In a Christian worldview, Christians see God at work in the world bringing organization and purpose to life. And they appraise human activities as moral or immoral based upon their belief system. Assuming a broad Christian window frame, you can easily see how people can add variety so they are seeing events from different angles, perspectives, and filters. Those on the outside of the window frame have a different perspective on morality. There is an exception, though. All people have some cognitive constraints common to the ability of the human brain to perceive and interpret information about the world.

I view the spiritual dimension as encompassing a worldview along with an interwoven network of influence from the other components of the SCOPES model—thoughts, emotions, behavior patterns, physiology, and social interactions. Many Christians report feeling the presence of God and they behave in certain ways when worshipping. Their spirituality affects their health and their state of health influences their spirituality. Finally, their spirituality both influences their social interactions and is influenced by the social setting and the people in that setting. For example, a person's spirituality may be positively influenced by listening to sacred music and be negatively influenced by viewing a faith-insulting artistic project.

In this book, we will consider Christian spirituality by referring to the Bible, interpretations of the Bible, and beliefs reported by Christians in surveys and other research studies.

Religious Orientations

Psychologists have studied religious orientations since the seminal work of Gordon Allport, who developed a scale to measure two components identified as intrinsic and extrinsic religiosity.[6] Numerous studies have explored the concept of religious orientation and its relationship to other aspects of functioning, e.g., behavior patterns and social prejudice. More recent formulations of religious orientation retain the intrinsic factor, which reflects a person's valuation of the importance of their faith. The extrinsic factor has

6. Hill, "Measurement," 49.

been subdivided into two components: extrinsic-personal and extrinsic-social.[7] People who view religion from an extrinsic personal perspective value the way religion contributes to their personal wellbeing. They may value the protection, comfort, and self-control afforded by their faith. Those who value the extrinsic-social aspect of religion are focused on the social interactions and relationships that are part of their faith. In recent research, the religious orientation set of questions is sometimes reduced to three items that capture each of the three religiosity factors.[8] I have included the three items, which can be rated on a nine-point scale from Strongly Disagree (1) to Strongly Agree (9).

> Intrinsic: "My whole approach to life is based upon religion"

> Extrinsic-personal: "What religion offers me most is comfort in times of trouble and sorrow"

> Extrinsic-social: "I go to church mainly because I enjoy seeing people I know there."

The concepts of intrinsic and extrinsic religion can be helpful. And the three-item scale offers clinicians and consultants a quick way to estimate this aspect of a religious orientation. But religion as an orientation includes more than an intrinsic or extrinsic focus. Psychology of religion researcher Ken Pargament offers a broader perspective. Here is his definition of religious orientation:

> In the face of crisis, we are guided and grounded by an orienting system. The orienting system is a general way of viewing and dealing with the world. It consists of habits, values, relationships, generalized beliefs, and personality. The orienting system is a frame of reference, a blueprint of oneself and the world that is used to anticipate and come to terms with life's events. The orienting system directs us to some life events and away from others.[9]

If we were to consider the components of religious orientation identified by Pargament in his definition, we would cover most of the elements in the SCOPES model. In fact, the only item he does not mention is the contribution from our physiology. So, in a sense, you can see the acronym *SCOPE* or *SCOPES* works not just to organize different dimensions of functioning, but *scope* is a metaphor for the different ways people view the world.

7. Gorsuch and McPherson, "Intrinsic," 348–54.
8. Williamson et al., "The Intratextual," 721–47.
9. Pargament, *The Psychology of Religion*, 99–100.

Scientists use scopes to study the world in detail, but the type and power of the scopes vary and offer different perspectives.

Religion and Decision-Making

If you know the religious beliefs of a judge, you can predict how the judge will decide some cases. Brian Bornstein and Monica Miller reviewed several studies of U.S. judges and their decisions that spanned many decades.[10] In general, most judges are considered supportive of religion, but the strongest support comes from Catholic and Baptist judges. A 2004 review of 729 cases indicated that religion had the greatest influence on how judges made their decisions. Not surprisingly, in matters of gender discrimination and obscenity, Evangelical Christian judges were more conservative when compared to judges who identified as Jewish or Protestant. In matters concerning LGBT issues between the years 1981 and 2000, Jewish judges offered more liberal opinions than did Protestant or Catholic judges. In short, we may say judges take their faith to work.

The research on judges illustrates the role religion plays in the way people make judgments. A religious worldview has an influence on how people approach life problems. Christians make moral judgments in part based on their worldview. The research about judges offers an example of influence on decision-making by people who are among the professions best prepared to think carefully about rule violations, including the moral issues covered in this book.

Religion and Coping

When faced with a threat, many people turn to God or their religious faith for support. For many Christians, the liberalization of laws and policies that govern sexual behavior is a threat to their way of life. A classic treatment of religion and coping can be found in Kenneth Pargament's *The Psychology of Religion and Coping*. The subject of coping is quite broad and cannot be adequately addressed in this chapter. However, several points are relevant to improve our understanding of the intersection of Christianity, sexuality, and morality. Both religion and coping style may be brought into play when people are faced with a threat. I use the term *threat* broadly to mean an event that people view as stressful.

---

10. Bornstein and Miller, "Does a Judge's," 112–15.

It is not surprising that many people draw upon their religious beliefs to cope with stressful life events. The issues of sexuality discussed in this book clearly qualify as stressful for many people. Consider the following few examples.

1. Coping with the social pressure to have sex in High School or College in contrast to years of religious teaching against sex outside marriage.

2. Coping with an unplanned pregnancy as a single woman, especially in a subculture like a Christian school that strongly condemns sex outside of marriage.

3. Coping with feelings of same-sex attraction in a subculture that condemns any attraction that is not heterosexual, e.g., a gay employee working in a Christian ministry.

4. Coping with divorce and a sense of failure in a culture that stresses forgiveness—interpreted to mean reconciling with one's spouse and maintaining a lifelong marriage even when a spouse is abusive.

5. Coping with rape and other forms of sexual abuse by clergy—a situation made even more complex for a woman who has become pregnant as a result of an assault in a religious community that opposes abortion and desires to protect the clergy and the church from unfavorable exposure.

Cognition or Thinking

The cognitive dimension of human functioning deals primarily with thoughts and images that people process and store in memory. We learn about sex via verbal communication as well as pictures, illustrations, and video productions. We find some presentations disgusting, some humorous, and others erotic. During our waking hours, we are constantly thinking about life events in habitual ways. It is only when we encounter some difficulty that we seem to slow down and engage in effortful thinking to solve a problem. Decades of research on these two primary modes of thinking (i.e., automatic and effortful) have been masterfully summarized in the book, *Thinking, Fast and Slow* by Nobel Prize-winning psychological scientist, Daniel Kahneman.[11] I will refer to the fast and slow thinking processes again in the next chapter when I review the fast, emotion-linked thinking

---

11. Kahneman, *Thinking, Fast and Slow*, 20–24.

that seems to drive sexual behavior and the often quick moral responses to "hot-button" social issues.

In the following sections I will review several aspects of cognition that influence how people decide what is right and wrong. The cognitive elements include perceptions, thoughts, beliefs, and memories.

Perceptions and Beliefs about the Bible Can Influence Morality

You probably have seen a Bible. If you have one, take a look. It is one book and likely has the words "Holy Bible" on the cover. For a few centuries, Christians have been able to view one sacred book. Since the era of the printing press and widespread literacy, people have been able to start at the beginning (i.e., Genesis) and read the entire collection. This appearance of a compact single volume makes it easy to accept the view of Christian Fundamentalists that the book is God's word—one official communication from God containing everything that God wanted people to know. Most people are unaware of the span of years involved in the creation and copying of the documents they read in translation. Most do not know of the translator's tasks of deciding which set of documents constitutes the text to translate or which variation to accept as authentic from the hundreds of variations available. Nor do people understand the difficulties of finding contemporary words and phrases to capture the meaning of ancient words and phrases written in old languages, which were spoken in a sociohistorical context we often know little about. The physical appearance of the book affects the way many Christians interpret the words and phrases they read or hear. Because the different Christian traditions long ago settled the question of which writings belong in their version of the Holy Bible, many contemporary Christians usually do not reconsider those decisions. Beliefs about what God said may be influenced not only by traditional interpretations of the text but by the physical appearance of one book attributed by conservative Christian groups to one author—God. Perceptions about the Bible influence beliefs about the Bible.

If people pick up a book written by God and read a few words that tell them something they should not do, how likely is it they will argue with God? They may not follow a rule because some rules are hard to follow but they will argue that people ought to obey the rule because God says so. Sound simplistic? Maybe. But I suspect that many people do not ask questions of the biblical texts because they fail to realize how they came into existence. They do not see the richly diverse opinions of Jewish male authors from different historical contexts who wrote the documents Fundamentalists label—*God's Word*. Those who have not studied the ancient biblical texts do not have a systematic way of analyzing things written by different human authors who wrote about things said by God and different human beings in the Scriptures to different people in different places at different points in time. For some Christians, the Bible is treated as if it were just one set of instructions by God given to all people for all time.

Now consider a view of the Bible that includes the interaction of human authors with God. Ancient people told many stories about how God spoke to them or performed great acts. After a while, some people wrote down these inspirational stories along with the rules about how to live—rules about what was right and wrong. And they included important traditions and customs that identified their culture. Later, scribes copied the writings and passed them on to others. Even later, people argued about who wrote what document. They wondered which copy of a scroll was more authentic. When they were able to organize all those scrolls into books, they argued about which ones to include in the Bible. More recently, they argued about the best way to translate those old words and phrases into hundreds of local languages. Christians who believe the Bible is one book with God as the sole author will approach the Bible from a different perspective than do those who believe the Bible is a diverse collection of inspired writings by different human authors with unique perspectives on how God interacted with people at different times in history.

As noted previously, many Christian beliefs about right and wrong are derived from the way people interpret the Bible. Psychological scientists have long known the obvious: beliefs are difficult to change, and beliefs can lead to behavior. What Christians believe about the Bible can make a difference in how they think, feel, and behave. Anyone working with Christian Fundamentalists or those similar to the approximately one-quarter of Americans who view the Bible as literally God's Word will likely find that this belief about biblical inspiration and its contents will drive their understanding of the moral life. In traditional Christian theology, God knows everything (i.e., he is omniscient) and is a perfectly moral being. In this view, humans have a minimal role in the process of deciding what is moral.

There are several alternatives to this Fundamentalist view. The alternatives allow for more flexibility when it comes to making a moral decision. The general alternative is to consider that human beings had a greater role in writing the contents of the Bible. Their experiences with God inspired different people in different ways. The Bible contains many voices, which can still inspire people today. But inspiration does not require a rigid adherence to moral rules that governed ancient cultures. And inspiration does not mean people ought to treat each other in the same way that people treated each other thousands of years ago. Understanding what Christians believe about the Bible is part of understanding how Christians come to different beliefs about morality and understanding how much flexibility a person has in discussing moral facts and reasoning based on sources of knowledge not contained in the Bible.

Human Memory Can Influence Morality

Psychological scientists have long documented the difficulties people have with memory. It is a commonplace for people to complain about problems of concentration and memory when they feel stressed, experience pain, struggle with a variety of health problems, or realize they forget a thing or two as their age increases. The problem with memory is a matter of life and death. In a summary statement, researcher A. Daniel Yarmey wrote, "mistaken eyewitness identification is responsible for more wrongful convictions than all other causes combined."[12] The understanding of the fallibility of eyewitness testimony is a recent phenomenon in human history. When Hugo Munsterberg suggested problems in his 1908 book, *On the Witness Stand*, he met with significant resistance. Only recently has sufficient scientific evidence accumulated to convince scientists and societal leaders that too many people were wrongly convicted because of the unreliable evidence from eyewitnesses.[13]

Memory is a diversified storage network mostly within the brain. Various biological processes are involved in determining how well we recall something we heard years ago. Here are a few things that make a difference when hearing a message that we want to remember:

1. The clarity of the original message
2. How well we paid attention to and concentrated on the message
3. How well we understood the words and phrases in the message
4. What emotions we felt when the message was received (e.g., feeling happy, sad, or angry)
5. What substances were in our bodies when the message was presented (e.g., the presence of alcohol or too much or too little food)
6. What life experiences and beliefs influence our understanding of the words and phrases in the message

---

12. Yarmey, "Expert Testimony," 92.
13. Pedzek, "Fallible Eyewitness," 105–24.

There is another set of processes at work when we are asked to remember something we were told a few years or decades ago. What did teachers and parents say when we were ten years old? What was that teaching we learned from a minister or priest last year? The process of remembering, or recalling, varies in people. Some are more accurate than others. Most people remember the gist of a message and forget the details. Our life histories and feelings affect what we remember. Given what we know about human memory, a supernatural intervention would be needed for a perfectly accurate oral transmission of ancient stories and rules until the time they were written.

Common experiences and research results demonstrate that eyewitnesses do not recall the same details when asked about an accident or other shared experience. At any family gathering, suspicions arise as to the accuracy of old stories often missing significant details or embellished beyond recognition. Juries struggle to discover the truth when witnesses present different versions of events. Sometimes those decisions are matters of life and death. You do not have to be a neuroscientist to know people make mistakes when recalling the past. When it comes to reading translations of ancient texts, conservative Christians seem to believe that ancient people possessed a supernatural ability to relay the exact words they heard from an original speaker. Alternatively, they might believe God performed a miracle to ensure his words were accurately remembered.

Is there evidence that Bible scholars recognize that difficulties with human memory may be reflected in the biblical texts? In a book-length review of the evidence, New Testament scholar Robert McIver summarizes human memory and how such cognitive factors as transience (i.e., fleeting memory of details), suggestibility, and bias may have influenced the parables and sayings of Jesus in the Gospels.[14]

Several factors are at work in determining how Christians view the inspiration of the biblical texts that offer moral guidance about sex and other life matters. Christians who believe humans had a significant role in writing the Bible believe problems of human memory about conversations and events long ago require a humble stance when a moral decision is based on a few words and phrases or on one or two biblical events.

Human Errors Can Influence Morality

It does not take much life experience to know people make mistakes when carrying out even simple tasks. Now we turn to the problem of accurate

14. McIver, *Memory, Jesus*, 183–88.

copying of biblical texts. It is a problem because many Christians seek a biblical basis for their morality although Bible scholars do not have the original biblical documents. Instead, scholars have thousands of copies of biblical texts, which contain different words and phrases. And in some cases, large sections of the texts are different. Scholars agree that various people were responsible for the eventual writing of the texts following many years of oral traditions. That is, the ancient laws, poems, and stories were passed along by word of mouth before they were written.[15] Once written, scribes made copies of the texts, which were kept in the libraries of different communities scattered throughout the ancient world. Because some copies of biblical texts contain different words, human judgment must be employed to decide which parts of the text are likely original and which parts were added by those responsible for making copies. Recently, translators included footnotes that document variations in the texts they relied upon to decide on the best manuscripts to translate. The translators' notes offer readers examples of variations in human accuracy.

How do conservative Christians respond to copying errors in the Bible? First, the variations in the copies are minimal and have little impact on doctrine. Second, the original documents were without error. Because conservatives view the Bible as God's Word, they have no doubt that the text accurately reflects God's instructions about morality. Because progressive Christians focus on an appreciation of the different ways biblical writers were inspired and focus more on themes and principles than the literal interpretation of words and phrases, the problem of human errors in the biblical documents is to be expected and is not a key to making a moral decision based on principles. But progressive Christians may point out the variations in the texts when discussing moral matters with Fundamentalists or other conservatives who minimize the error problem inherent in textual variations.[16]

Understanding Can Influence Morality

Since the days of the Bible, our understanding of the natural world has grown tremendously, and this expansion of knowledge includes an increased understanding of human nature. Ancient people had no evident appreciation of the age of the universe or the earth. They had a limited understanding of

---

15. Van Seters, "The Origins," 89

16. Conservative Greek scholar Daniel Wallace of Dallas Theological Seminary calls for honesty when it comes to the thousands of text variations in the New Testament alone.

genetics, disease processes, and ways to cure diseases. They did not appear to have much knowledge of debilitating mental illnesses or how to cure such conditions. They were at the mercy of mysterious forces when it came to birthing and raising healthy children or recovering from serious injury or illness. There was no effective natural treatment for stroke, cancer, depression, or head injury. There was no cesarean section delivery of babies. There was no effective means of birth control and perhaps no reason to control the number of children a family could have. Few people could read or write. And because of the culture, those who did learn to read and write were men. Knowledge has increased. The limited scientific knowledge about human nature and particularly human sexuality allows progressive Christians to draw heavily on contemporary knowledge when making moral decisions. Conservatives who view God as all-knowing may argue that God overcame the limited understanding of the ancient men who wrote the biblical texts. How Christians weigh scientific evidence will make a difference in how they arrive at moral decisions.

Problem-Solving Ability Can Influence Morality

Many people are particularly talented with their portrayal of beauty and truth in stories, poems, songs, and plays. When it comes to literature, art, science or other endeavors, we can easily recognize people who stand out as gifted or talented. We also recognize people who have a difficult time grasping basic concepts. Many struggle with statistics, physics, and creative writing. Others struggle to keep up with changes in technology. Many feel woefully inadequate when it comes to carpentry, quilting, sculpture, or other creative works. Unfortunately, some people struggle to such an extent that they require a guardian. Problem-solving ability varies from an inability to solve simple problems needed for basic survival to superior abilities needed to solve complex problems. And most people have abilities within a broad average range.

In addition to our inherited capacity for understanding, we vary in our educational experiences. Given the range of variation in the capacity to understand and analyze anything that is written, it is not surprising that education will influence how people interpret biblical texts and think logically about moral problems.

When it comes to understanding how people form their ideas about sexuality and morality, their capacity to solve problems by analyzing, synthesizing, and evaluating written language and scientific evidence are factors that deserve additional consideration. We might say that a capacity to understand how moral principles may be derived from biblical texts is a necessary but not sufficient condition to create a foundation for Christian morality.

Prejudice and Bias Can Influence Moral Decisions

Prejudice and bias can influence contemporary opinions about biblical texts. Prejudice is an unjustifiable negative attitude toward a group of people and the individuals within that group. Groups can be people of a different nation, culture, or gender. The negative attitude is a complex association of beliefs about the group, uncomfortable emotions (e.g., anger, fear), and actions or predispositions to act against a group. These negative actions result in discrimination. Discrimination is showing a favorable response to one group and an unfavorable response to another group. For example, if an employer hired more men than women, then the employer would appear to discriminate on the basis of gender.

Although conditions have improved in recent decades, prejudice against people based on skin color, national or group identity, gender, and age has been common throughout history and continues to influence decisions about employment, education, housing, and other aspects of social functioning. In the Bible, Jesus acted contrary to the prejudices of his times by interacting with people who were shunned by society, such as lepers (Matt 8:1–4) and Samaritans (John 4:1–26).

Bias is a tendency to think in a certain way. The research support for some common biases suggests these are ways that most minds work most of the time. In general, people are more favorable toward members of their own group (*ingroup bias*) than toward members of other groups (*outgroup bias*). We would expect that the people in the Bible stories acted more favorably toward those in their own tribes and were less supportive of their neighbors.

Human beings quickly categorize people, which allows for a way to simplify their lives, but in doing so, they can mistakenly assume things about others. For example, if we observed a few people from another tribe (i.e., ethnic or religious group) committing an act of violence, we may falsely assume all other people from that tribe are equally aggressive. We may never know the extent to which ancient people mischaracterized people from other tribes.

A *general belief bias* exists when people fail to recognize how the beliefs they hold about certain issues influence their reasoning. For example, conservative Christians traditionally believe that sex is only acceptable within marriage. When they read the Genesis 38 story of Onan, who ejaculated on the ground instead of having intercourse with a woman as expected, and learn that God killed him, they believed Onan was punished for masturbation, which was named in his so-called honor as "onanism". Although few contemporary Christians believe that masturbation is a sin—at least not a sin punishable by death—the persistence of the old interpretation of the story illustrates the operation of belief bias.

The *just world phenomenon* is a common belief that people get what they deserve. People who seem to have many good things are rewarded for a life well lived. And people who suffer might just deserve their punishment. Sometimes this belief is subtle to the point that people do not realize how they blame victims as if they deserved what they got. Some people thought that AIDS victims were punished by God for their sinful sexual behavior. Some believe women who are raped deserved to be raped or were "asking for it."

Beliefs persist in the face of contradictory evidence. This *belief perseverance bias* has been studied by offering supportive and nonsupportive research findings to people who hold various beliefs. Participants in the experiment found the supportive studies to be more persuasive.[17] Human beings approach evidence with a *confirmation bias*. They seek to confirm what they believe and ignore or downplay contradictory evidence. It is very difficult to change a person's beliefs.

Who might have prejudices or biases related to biblical views on morality? Here's a list to consider:

1. The ancient people described in the Bible had opinions about their own tribes, appropriate roles for men and women, and the people in other tribes.

2. The scribes who recorded the Bible stories had their own prejudices and biases that could affect what they included and how they interpreted blessings and punishments.

3. The scholars who translated the biblical texts from ancient languages into contemporary languages brought their current perspectives on people and the social and moral issues that challenge Christians. Biases can influence which ancient manuscripts are selected for translation and which words and phrases are chosen as the best translation of an ancient word or phrase. All this might not matter much to the average Bible reader, but it can matter when readers make moral decisions

---

17. Myers, *Psychology*, 408.

and fight for social policies based on the perceived meaning of a few words.

4. People who interpret the translated biblical texts have their own set of prejudices and biases that can influence the comments they express.

5. People who lead congregations or denominations also have prejudices and biases that influence what Bible translations they use, what Bible commentaries they select, and how they present moral teaching to their constituents.

The topic of sexuality evokes a unique bias. The variety of words for sex organs and sexual behavior poses a challenge to understanding the thoughts of people from any culture. And it matters when contemporary Christians attribute modern understandings to translated words and phrases. People of any culture use euphemisms for sexual organs and sexual behavior as if they are afraid to speak openly about sex. Any tube-like object substitutes for a penis, and people hearing the substitute word in the context of romance on TV get the idea and laugh. A counselor told me about a person "sleeping" with someone. I feigned puzzlement and responded, "I don't care who she sleeps with. It's who she had sex with that matters." As Michael Coogan and Teresa Hornsby point out, the Bible uses many euphemisms for sex.[18] Sometimes the words and phrases in Hebrew are quite graphic, and translators do not always convey the starkness found in the original languages.

Valuing the Bible Differently Can Influence Morality

One way to distinguish between different Christian groups is to analyze the view they have of the role of Scripture in determining right belief (orthodoxy) and right behavior (orthopraxy). The anchor words *high* and *low* are used to denote the end points on many scales of values. In this valuation process, Fundamentalists have a high view of Scripture as captured in the words they use to refer to the biblical collection as God's Word or when they support a position in an argument by quoting a Bible verse prefaced by "God says." Notice the use of the present tense, which emphasizes that God is still speaking to people today with the same words recorded thousands of years ago.

Those who take a high view of Scripture will search the Bible for laws and teachings that guide them in making today's moral and other life decisions. They want to do what is right and believe that God's words will direct them. In addition, they want the *plain truth* from God—not a truth coming

---

18. Coogan, *God and Sex*, 15; Hornsby, *Sex Texts*, 3–10.

from a consideration of extrabiblical sources. This way of searching the text for truth was labeled the "principle of intratextuality" by Ralph Hood, Peter Hill, and Paul Williamson.[19] Since then, Williamson and his colleagues developed a scale to measure the principle and found that five items representing five attitudes toward sacred texts yielded adequate psychometric properties in three samples.[20] Two samples were U.S. Christians and one was a sample of Muslims living in Pakistan. The five attitudes Fundamentalists tend to take toward their texts represent strong beliefs. I think this is an important contribution to understanding how some Christians derive their values from the Bible, so let's consider those five attitudes.

1. Inerrant: The Bible does not contain errors. There are no mistakes, inconsistencies, or contradictions.

2. Authoritative: The contents of the Bible are an authoritative guide for life. If there is a conflict between what the Bible says and some other source, the Bible wins.

3. Divine origin: God is the author. Even though other people were involved in writing the Bible, God inspired all of them. What is written is what God wanted them to communicate.

4. Unchanging: The truths of the Bible are true for all people and for all time. The truths are absolute.

5. Privileged: The Bible has a special place of high importance above all other sources of knowledge or law. God's law is above every law. Fundamentalists can respect other religious traditions and documents, including the laws of society. But the Bible is above all other teachings and ideas.

A corollary to the belief that the Bible is God's word is the belief that the entire text may be searched to understand what God means when a particular phrase or passage seems obscure.

Finally, consistent with their stance toward Scripture is a strong sense of conviction that what God says is true and disobedience toward God will result in eternal punishment. Taking God at his word is a matter of life and death now and forever. Arguments about what texts mean can be heated. Failure to accept how a group understands the Bible, evidenced in verbal assent and observant behavior, obliges a Fundamentalist to leave a particular congregation. People who do not follow the prescribed beliefs and behavior

---

19. Hood et al., *The Psychology of Religious*, 22–28.
20. Williamson et al., "The Intratextual," 721–47.

patterns of the church are deemed less spiritual or may even be judged to be an unbeliever.

Evangelicals can still take a high view of Scripture and search the Scriptures for guidance, but they are often more willing to consider the role of reason and other sources of truth to gain a better understanding of biblical truth than are Fundamentalists. Evangelicals attempt to find principles of interpretation that allow them to view the Scriptures the way Jesus did when he quoted the Hebrew texts. A classic work among Evangelicals is a book by Gordon D. Fee and Douglas Stuart: *How to Read the Bible for All Its Worth*. The authors explained the different literary genres found within the Bible and provided educated readers with an introduction to interpreting the different texts. A quote from the back cover illustrates their aim: "How does a psalm addressed to God over 2500 years ago function as a word from God for today?" While holding a high view of Scripture, some Evangelicals prefer to take a humble or low stance on interpretation, confessing they are willing to be wrong when it comes to a particular interpretation that has been held as absolute truth by one Christian group or another.

There is a phrase that may help consultants guide Christians toward a weighing of extrabiblical evidence when attempting to resolve moral dilemmas. In my years of living amongst U.S. Evangelicals, I have often heard the phrase, "All truth is God's truth." This phrase is frequently used in Christian schools to offer a guiding principle: whatever turns out to be true in any academic discipline need not be discarded simply because the information is not a part of the Bible. Often unsaid is the implication that God is the ultimate source of truth. Because God is the creator of the universe, any discovered truth is ultimately derived from God. "All truth is God's truth" is a way of attributing importance or value to academic studies other than the Bible. Its use suggests the difficulty in convincing students from Fundamentalist homes that academic studies other than Bible study have value. Usually, this "all truth is God's truth" attribution is taken at face value with no discussion about what might constitute truth in the sciences, which use probabilistic models to assess evidence confirming or disconfirming a guiding theory. Scientific theories explain a finite set of evidence. And theories change when new data are not easily explained by previous theories. This scientific approach used by psychologists, biologists, and other scientists is quite different from that of an Evangelical theologian who seeks to find absolute truth by understanding the statements in a biblical text. "All truth is God's truth" appears to help Evangelicals broaden their perspective of the meaning of Scripture but will not affect a Fundamentalist's approach to Scripture. Perhaps the best recent example is the ongoing struggle between U.S. Christian Fundamentalists who seek ways to demand that the biblical creation narratives be included in public schools (unlike European public schools, public schools in the U.S. are government-funded schools open to all persons).

Pentecostal and charismatic Christians offer a variation on a typical conservative theme when interpreting the biblical text. The Pentecostal or charismatic view is quite similar to the views of Fundamentalists and Evangelicals for much of Scripture. There is, however, a notable exception. Pentecostals and charismatics emphasize the experienced power of God in their lives by virtue of the presence of God's Spirit. This sense of God speaking and acting in the present allows for a highly personalized application of the text to daily life. Some view Jesus as a friend walking beside them or an elder brother who can offer advice. The well-known acronym *WWJD*—What Would Jesus Do—captures the sense that a believer can ask Jesus for advice on matters of sex, marriage, career, and other aspects of daily life. Believers can turn to the Bible and trust the Holy Spirit to speak to them. When it comes to morality, Pentecostals and charismatics generally find common ground with Evangelicals. But sometimes there is a difference based on their experience. For example, in the early 1900s women experienced the baptism in the Holy Spirit. They spoke in tongues and gave prophecies. Although many groups succumbed to the general male-dominated culture, some Pentecostal women continued to be licensed or ordained as clergy. To be sure, women did not experience equality in Pentecostal or charismatic traditions. But as Western cultures became more supportive of women in leadership positions, the Pentecostal tradition of women in ministry appeared to trump the biblical teaching about male leadership still widely accepted in many Christian traditions. I suggest that the flexibility Pentecostals and charismatics have shown toward women offers possibilities for less rigid approaches to such topics as sex education and birth control, which the Bible does not explicitly address.

When progressives discuss problems with biblical texts, their interpretations may be dismissed by Fundamentalists and Evangelicals as representing a low view of Scripture. Progressive Christians value the texts as historical documents that offer insights into the ways ancient peoples came to an understanding of God and morality. They value Jesus' summary of the law (Luke 10:25–37) and elevate the principle of love of God and others. They also point to Jesus' reformulation of old ways of viewing the laws as Jesus attempted to lead the people toward an inner spirituality not bound by tradition or custom. Scholars in other traditions have investigated the origins of biblical texts and rely on a variety of discoveries and disciplines to better understand the likely meaning of the texts for the ancient people who would have first heard the message. Clergy in these traditions learn varied ways to interpret the ancient texts and evaluate different ways to apply principles to contemporary life. Progressives recognize that sometimes there are no ideal words or phrases to translate an ancient word or phrase. And in other cases, more than one word or phrase may be reasonable.

All people assign values to things in their world. Valuing is one way people create meaning. Religious people value objects differently, imbuing some and not others with sacred meaning. Christians value their texts differently, and this difference in assigning values matters when it comes to interpreting texts about morality and sexuality.

Projection Can Influence Moral Decisions

People view the world based on their personal history. Part of our history is shared with those of our culture, such as family, friends, and coworkers. When we encounter new or vague situations, it is natural to approach these new events by drawing upon our experiences. We tend to view the new in terms of the old. Like a movie projected onto a large screen, we project the images of our experience onto the words of Scripture. Sometimes people share what a verse or passage meant to them, and others are encouraged by this new insight. Most of the time, projections do not matter. Projections help people connect their lives to texts about people who lived thousands of years ago. However, there were times when people came to the texts with their own prejudices against people of other races, skin color, or gender and created laws that favored one group over another resulting in real harm. Looking back, it is hard to believe that people used the Bible to justify murderous crusades, genocidal wars, severe beatings, excruciating torture, and slavery. In part, we are products of our time as well as our personal experiences. It is difficult to avoid interpreting any literary work without projecting part of who we are onto the text. Some may endorse projection as a beautiful way to find meaning. The downside of projection occurs when our patterns of biases and prejudices hurt others. Perhaps realizing this aspect of human nature can help some take another view of what texts mean about morality and sexuality.

Sunk Costs Can Influence Moral Decisions

The social psychology principle of sunk costs helps explain why some Christians remain fixed in traditional views about morality or sexuality in contrast to the views of those who seem able to throw off old ways of thinking or behaving with relative ease. In finance, people who have invested heavily in a business, home purchase, or company stock tend to hold on when the value of the investment declines. Some will purchase more of a falling stock or add new money to a failing business venture. Unfortunately, many new businesses fail. Governments can go bankrupt. And the value of company stock can go to zero. People who add more money to failing investments provide evidence supporting the proverb, "Don't throw good money after bad."

The principle of sunk costs may be used to explain the way some people invest emotional energy into preserving religious traditions even when they become aware of beliefs or traditions that no longer make sense to them. Some invest time in religious causes or programs; others consume new Christian books with vigor as if the search for new insights will reassure them that their faith investment makes sense. Some have found themselves trapped as pastors or leaders in religious organizations.[21] One professor at an Evangelical university quipped that students in seminary are there because they need Jesus. Many clergy who no longer accept the tenets of their faith feel they have no alternative career. Christians find that the social costs of expressing a liberal view are too great. Recently, a woman told me of a pastor who was stripped of his clerical credentials because of his views supporting same-sex marriage. To leave a church or religious position can result in both condemnation and the painful loss of family and friends. A religious way of life is an investment. Perhaps this is reflected in Jesus' call to commitment (Matt 10:37–38). In any church there may be those who personally favor a more moderate view toward a particular moral or social issue but fear speaking out because of the personal cost.

Sometimes the odds favor leaving a group, such as when a Christian gives up an old belief in order to maintain an important life relationship with a spouse or child. Pravinkumar Israel tells the story of how members of his family left the local Hindu faith to become Christians. When a male Hindu dies, his wife is expected to die on the funeral pyre of her husband. Christian missionaries offered an alternative belief. The costs of shame and dishonor were strong, but the family chose the life of their female kin over the cultural costs and converted to Christianity, which offered an alternative set of rules.[22] We will often find it helpful to consider the personal costs involved for a particular Christian to make a specific moral decision.

---

21. Dennett and LaScola, *Caught*, 198.
22. Pravinkumar Israel, in discussion, June 2, 2013.

Self-control and Self-regulation Influence Morality

Self-control and the self-regulation of behavior begin in the brain. People often feel like attacking someone who insulted them, but they usually hold back. They experience the thought but control their behavior in conformity to the rules of their culture. They may lash out with verbal behavior but refrain from doing physical damage. Similarly, people often experience sexual thoughts, but most people control their sexual behavior. In general, people who are highly religious have more self-control than others. Christian organizations actively encourage both moral thinking as well as moral behavior in sermons, books, and audio/video presentations.

Self-regulation is a mental process that actively monitors and adjusts internal responses in response to external events. At times we may be aware of self-regulating activity, such as when we are asked to think about what we have done wrong. Other examples of awareness include the practice of Catholics prepare for confession, and the custom of many Christians who regulate their activities during Lent. When Christian students in the U.S. state of Alabama were asked to consider their wrongdoing, they were more likely than others to report an interest in religious goals.[23]

Summary

My purpose in this chapter was to review scientific findings about human nature and consider how they might help explain how different Christian groups sometimes reach widely different conclusions about morality. I began by describing a six-dimensional model that includes the multiple ways people respond to any situation, including moral matters—the six dimensions form the acronym SCOPES. The letters refer to Spiritual core, Cognitive processes, Observable behavior patterns, Physiological responses, Emotional responses, and Social considerations of one's spatial location and time of day or period in one's life.

Most of the second half of chapter 2 describes how spiritual and cognitive factors influence moral decisions. The spiritual components include religious orientation and the role of religion in decision making and coping. The second dimension is cognition or thinking. Cognition includes perceptions, thoughts and beliefs, understanding, memory, biases, and prejudices. Cognitive processes include the sunk cost phenomenon, projection, self-control, and self-regulation. I will discuss the remaining four components of the SCOPES model in the next chapter.

23. Wenger, "The Implicit," 47–60.

Additional Resources

1. Can you trust your memory? A short video summarizes some of the problems with human memory. https://www.youtube.com/watch?v=lkvOMt34hAo

2. Challenges of Bible Translation. In a two-part presentation hosted by Dallas Theological Seminary, scholars explain the difficulties of translating Bible words and ideas from one language to another. Part 1: http://www.dts.edu/media/play/the-challenges-of-Bible-translation-1-of-2-darrell-l-bock-robert-b-chisholm-jr-and-w-hall-harris-iii/?audio=true#transcript Part 2: http://www.dts.edu/media/play/the-challenges-of-Bible-translation-2-of-2-darrell-l-bock-robert-b-chisholm-jr-and-w-hall-harris-iii/?audio=true

Discussion Questions and Topics

1. How much of a difference do you think it would make if people were to hear preachers say "Moses wrote" or "Matthew wrote" instead of hearing "God's Word says?"

2. Can you think of examples of a matter of right and wrong that changed based on how people interpreted the meaning of a few words in a statement, rule, or law?

3. Think of an example of sunk costs. Explore how people clung to an idea or belief even as evidence mounted that the idea or belief was unhelpful or actually wrong.

4. How might the phrase "all truth is God's truth" help an Evangelical Christian consider a range of birth control options or scientific evidence about same-sex orientation?

3

THE INFLUENCE OF PERSONALITY, PHYSIOLOGY, EMOTIONS, AND SOCIAL CONTEXT ON MORALITY

My purpose in this chapter is to continue an overview of scientific findings about human nature by referring to the remaining four dimensions of the SCOPES model, which I introduced in chapter 2. The six dimensions are Spiritual core, Cognitive processes, Observable behavior patterns, Physiological responses, Emotional responses, and Social considerations of one's spatial location and time of day or period in one's life. Said another way, people act morally because of their spirituality, thinking, habits, biological status, feelings, and environment. As I mentioned at the beginning of chapter 2, one reason it is difficult to understand why people do what they do is because the answer requires an evaluation of multiple sources of influence.

Observable Behavior Patterns or Habits

I use the letter *O* here because if fits nicely with the acronym, SCOPES. The patterns of behavior that can be viewed by others and oneself are what I am referring to by *observable behavior*. We describe people in many ways, e.g., conscientious, agreeable, and closed-minded. When a person consistently behaves in a similar fashion, we form opinions about their personality. At this point in the history of psychology, there is reasonable research support for five major behavior patterns or traits known simply as the Big Five. These five traits represent a continuum with most people falling somewhere in the middle. The five traits also have a commonly used acronym—*OCEAN*: openness, conscientiousness, extraversion, agreeableness, and neuroticism. Here's a little more detail.

- **O-Openness:** an interest in new experiences and a willingness to consider various points of view in contrast to being closed or rigid. We would expect people high on openness to respect diverse perspectives on sexual morality.
- **C-Conscientiousness:** a concern about doing what is right and doing things well. In their review of research, Michael McCullough and Brian Willoughby found that highly religious people, including Christians, were also highly conscientious.[1] In research, Christians see conscientiousness as a desirable trait. And conscientiousness is highly correlated with self-control.
- **E-Extraversion:** a preferred pattern of activity with others rather than alone. Extroversion is contrasted with introversion.
- **A-Agreeableness:** a friendly, positive outlook that makes a person easy to get along with in contrast to the opposite extreme of disagreeable and oppositional patterns. Highly religious people tend to be highly agreeable. And like conscientiousness, agreeableness is highly valued among Christians. Using a measure of Fundamentalism, Paul Williamson and his colleagues found Fundamentalists were also high in agreeableness.[2]
- **N-Neuroticism:** a pattern of worry, distress, and uneasiness in contrast to a stable and calm demeanor. *Neuroticism* is the traditional term, but some prefer to focus on the positive pole of the trait using the label, *Emotional Stability*. Several studies have found that highly religious people tend to have better mental health. The relationship is weak, but consistent.[3]

Physiology

The physiological dimension is that aspect of functioning we often refer to as physical or biological. Of course, our biology is affected by things we ingest, such as food, medicines, and drugs as well as our degree of general health and exercise. Danziger and his colleagues found a surprising link between snacks and judgments made by experienced judges.[4] They ana-

---

1. McCullough and Willouughby, "Religion," 69–93.

2. Williamson et al., "The Intratextual," 721–47.

3. McCullough and Willoughby, "Religion," 69–93; Smith et al., "Religiousness," 614–36.

4. Danziger et al., "Extraneous Factors," 6889–92.

lyzed 1,112 rulings made by eight Israeli judges over a ten-month period. The judges reviewed parole requests and were advised by a criminologist and a social worker. The crimes ranged from misdemeanors to felonies. The judges had an average of 22.5 years of experience. The researchers were able to consider factors that were part of the judicial record. The time of the decisions was part of the record. People make better decisions after a break. A rest restores the brain. Small things make a difference—looking at a nature scene and having a snack that increases brain glucose levels is important. So what did they find? If you want a favorable decision, see the judge early in the morning or just after a break. As breaktime approaches, the probability of a favorable outcome declines to near zero. The status quo prevails—i.e., denying the request—when mental resources are depleted.

We will look more at the biopsychology of sex in another chapter, but for now we would certainly include within the physiological dimension all of the anatomical components and processes of reproduction along with the nervous system that controls sexual functioning and the various neurochemical processes involved.

Emotion

Our feeling state is obviously an important part of being human. Religious experiences are often reported in terms of feeling the presence of God or feeling at a distance from God. People feel joyful, angry, sad, and guilty during religious experiences and in religious settings. Feelings occur in association with thoughts, behavior patterns, and physiological events. People often experience strong feelings associated with sexual experiences. Emotions appear to be associated with a common pattern of facial expressions recognized across multiple cultures. The studies of common basic emotions by Paul Ekman and his colleagues are cited in psychology texts.[5] Researchers disagree about what might constitute a common set of basic emotions. However, the literature suggests something close to an agreement for three basic expressions: anger or rage, fear or anxiety, and sadness.[6] Other strong candidates for basic emotions include disgust, surprise, and happiness.

As I will discuss later, a particularly dramatic emotional response is disgust, which includes a strong negative feeling and a verbal response of "yuck" (or worse). Physiological reactions are common in the behavioral contortions of faces of people in many cultures. Disgust also causes a physiological sensation of nausea, avoidance behavior, and moral condemnation.

5. For example, Schirmer, *Emotion*, 45–47.
6. Schirmer, *Emotion*, 49.

And disgust is related to aspects of spirituality concerned with purity, holiness, and keeping the sacred separate from that which is dirty, vulgar, and immoral.

How do emotions work? Emotions are feeling states that are linked to the dimensions of functioning in the SCOPES model. We think (Cognition) about our feelings (Emotion), and when asked, we label them (e.g., happy, angry, disgusted). This thinking about an emotion and identifying it is termed *appraisal* by psychologists. We have a biological response (Physiological). For example, fear produces reactions in the amygdala. And we act (Observable Behavior). For example, a loud noise motivates us to duck for cover.[7] In addition to these factors, we may interpret our emotions in part based on our spirituality (Spiritual). For example, Christians can feel guilty about adultery because they broke a commandment and because they experience the destructive effects on their relationship. Finally, people and settings influence emotions (Social context). A survivor of sexual abuse may experience strong fear, anger, and disgust in response to the presence of his or her abuser and the situation in which the abuse occurred.

There are several theories about how emotions work. The exploration of these theories would require a substantial study of neuropsychology, which is beyond the scope of this chapter. After reviewing various ideas, I find myself in agreement with the view of Shiota and Kalat, who support a modification of the James-Lange Theory.[8] In this theory, many emotional appraisals occur quickly (cognitions) before physiological responses and observable behavior occur. But feedback from our physiological state and behavior can influence our feelings. For example, we may quickly appraise an oncoming car as a threat slightly before our heart races and we swerve to safety. We are aware of our racing heart and swerving, which intensifies the feeling of fear.

Emotions have a significant influence on what people consider morally right and wrong. In fact, six foundations of moral reasoning appear to be linked to some very basic emotions. This six-factor grid will be a primary focus in the next chapter.

Social Context

The final dimension of human functioning is different from the others because it involves our social context. Our social context includes people and objects and where they are located geographically as well as in time. Social

---

7. For a summary of four aspects of emotion see Shiota and Kalat, *Emotion*, 30.
8. Shiota and Kalat, *Emotion*, 25.

context influences our spirituality, thoughts, feelings, behavioral responses, and even our health. People are often moved deeply during worship. Romantic encounters provoke strong positive and negative responses—responses that can include feelings, behavioral acts, and physiological activity, which can vary with the person, the setting (e.g., work, school, home) and the time of day (e.g., people think of romantic evenings rather than mornings). The social settings, including the people present, make a difference in appraising a sexual experience. Being with a loved one is vastly different from struggling with a rapist. Listening to a talk about sexual attraction is different from feeling warm toward or repulsed by a sexual touch. A comment suggesting sexuality can be funny in a restaurant but labeled sexual harassment or inappropriate in the work place.

People are often unaware of the influence of situational elements on moral behavior. In most religions, human behavior is observed by gods or spirits. The supernatural beings know what people think, judge their behavior, and control rewards and punishments.[9] In the Bible, God is often depicted as administering rewards or punishments to nations and individuals who obey or disobey commandments. Psychological scientists find that the presence of eyes influences moral behavior. American university students were more generous when eyes appeared on a computer screen. And British faculty contributed substantially more to a break room donation box when the box was decorated with eyes compared to when it was decorated with flowers.[10] These studies suggest that Christians who view God as observing their behavior and controlling the consequences of their behavior may demonstrate more self-control when it comes to sexual behavior.

Time is a social context factor too. People respond differently to similar events not only based on time of day but the time frame of their lives. As a society, we try to protect all people from sexual abuse, but we especially focus on protecting children and adolescents. Obviously, the younger the victims, the less life experience they have that may help them better deal with trauma. In addition, since children have many more post-trauma years to live than older persons, there exists a possibility they will experience more traumatic experiences. The experience of multiple traumas leads to severe, complex, and lifelong struggles to survive.[11]

---

9. Bering and Johnson, "O Lord," 118–42.
10. Bateson et al., "Cues," 412–14.
11. van Deusen and Courtois, *Spirituality*, 29–54.

Summary

In this introduction to moral psychology, I introduced you to six dimensions of human functioning; the six letters form the acronym SCOPES. I have explained the six dimensions by using examples of research to highlight key facets of each dimension. Now I will present a series of questions that will demonstrate how we can systematically collect information to help us better understand how Christians might evaluate an act as moral or immoral. The questions will serve as a summary of key facets of each dimension related to morality. The questions are examples of multidimensional thinking about people and the many sources of influence on the way they judge behavior as moral or immoral.

Spirituality

1. How do their spiritual beliefs and practices make their lives meaningful?
2. To what extent do their spiritual beliefs provide a framework for viewing life experiences—especially issues involving morality and sexuality?
3. How well does a religious orientation style (intrinsic/extrinsic) influence the role of their faith in moral decisions?
4. What examples of previous behavior indicate how their faith influences important moral decisions (e.g., relationships, integrity).
5. How does their faith help them cope with life's moral challenges (e.g., relationships, marriage, divorce, abuse)?

Cognition (i.e., perceptions, memory, ability to solve problems, thoughts, beliefs, prejudices, biases)

1. How do they understand the contributions of people to the books in the Bible? And how does this influence their perspectives on sexuality and morality? For example, is the Bible all God's direct communication, or are the writings produced by people with different views of God at work?

PERSONALITY, PHYSIOLOGY, EMOTIONS, & SOCIAL CONTEXT 55

2. How do they view the accuracy of the Bible? Do they view the translations as perfectly accurate words and phrases to guide judgments about sexuality and morality?

3. How much do they allow scientific findings (e.g., medical, biopsychological) to be considered in addition to Scripture when deciding the morally correct thing to do?

4. How does their ability to understand the Bible and life problems influence their capacity for moral judgments? How well can they analyze facts, concepts, and principles related to deciding on the morally right thing to do?

5. What prejudices and biases might influence their view of morality and sexuality?

6. To what extent do they seem to project their own life experiences onto Scripture rather than focus on understanding the personal and cultural experiences of the people who wrote the biblical texts?

7. To what extent are they invested in a Christian tradition (e.g., Catholic, Orthodox, Protestant) such that they have little freedom to openly consider a moral judgment that is different from the official position of their faith tradition? How much will they lose if they speak or act in a way that is not approved by the religious authorities in their tradition?

Observable Behavior Patterns (personality patterns and traits)

1. Are there habitual ways of acting that predispose them to a way of acting considered moral or immoral? For example, are they generally agreeable, conscientious, open to new information, outgoing, or impulsive (any many other traits)?

Physiology

1. How does their health and biological status influence their decisions?

2. Do they have a condition or take medication that affects their capacity to exercise moral judgment, regulate impulsivity, or regulate their sexual desire?

Emotion

1. What emotions do they experience when dealing with common moral problems, including sexual issues? For example, do they experience anxiety, anger, sadness, or disgust related to abortion, sexual orientation, or various sex acts?
2. Do they have a history of abuse or trauma that influences their emotional response to any of the topics in this book?

Social Context

1. Does a particular *place* influence their moral behavior (e.g., party, gym, work, church)?
2. Do certain *people* influence their moral behavior (friends, relatives, others)?
3. Is *time* a factor? For example, did they "sow wild oats" in their youth? Were they subject to sexual trauma in a religious home as a young child and subject to other traumas during childhood and adolescence?

At this point in the book we have considered two of four factors influencing how Christians form moral judgments about sex-related issues. The two factors are beliefs about Scripture and an understanding of human nature. The third factor, moral reasoning, is next.

Discussion Topics

1. Explore your personality by taking a version of the Big Five online at the Berkeley Personality Lab. http://www.ocf.berkeley.edu/~johnlab/bfi.htm
2. If you took the Big Five test or another personality test, discuss how the results are or are not related to your ideas about spirituality or religion.

4

MORAL PSYCHOLOGY

On 24 March 2014, Richard Stearns, President of the U.S. branch of the humanitarian organization, World Vision, announced that World Vision would change their policies and begin to hire employees who were in same-sex marriages. Many Evangelical Christians were outraged and called to cancel their donations.[1] How did conservative Christians justify their moral outrage? Albert Mohler, President of the Southern Baptist Theological Seminary expressed his differences with several of the points made by Richard Stearns. After several points, Mohler expressed his ultimate concern:

> The worst aspect of the World Vision U.S. policy shift is the fact that it will mislead the world about the reality of sin and the urgent need of salvation. Willingly recognizing same-sex marriage and validating openly homosexual employees in their homosexuality is a grave and tragic act that confirms sinners in their sin—and that is an act that violates the gospel of Christ.[2]

The story about World Vision's announcement and the response of some Christians illustrate the point of this chapter and the entire book: Christians come to different conclusions about what is morally right and morally wrong. Christian leaders are affiliated with different religious groups that all identify with Christianity. The leaders of these different groups make public proclamations when they perceive that a moral issue is critically important. And those public statements influence human behavior. For society, positive and negative outcomes are often linked to the moral decisions of Christian leaders. World Vision lost a lot of donors. On March 26, 2014, World Vision announced their decision to undo their

---

1. Gracey and Weber, "World Vision."
2. Mohler, "Pointing to Disaster."

policy change.³ How do Christians reach such different conclusions about morality? We have seen that many turn to the Bible. In this chapter, we will consider what we can learn from psychological research.

In the previous chapter, I provided an overview of various psychological factors that influence actions people identify as moral or immoral. For Christians, moral acts are righteous and immoral acts are sinful. An understanding of right and wrong comes from the way Christians interpret the Bible. And many psychological factors can be linked to biblical interpretations. In this chapter, I focus on psychological research specifically dealing with morality. There has been a substantial shift away from an emphasis on the role of reason or thinking as a viable explanation for moral decision making to a new emphasis on the powerful role of sentiment, which can drive the explanations people offer to explain why some things are right and some things are wrong. Morality and immorality and righteous conduct and sinfulness may be deeply rooted in the feelings people experience and the six ways groups of people assess right and wrong.

For decades, the work of Jean Piaget and Lawrence Kohlberg dominated moral psychology. Both viewed morality from the perspective of cognitive development. Their ideas were routinely included in textbooks about child and adolescent development. In this chapter, I will briefly review the traditional approach to moral psychology then focus on three principles and six dimensions of a social intuitionist model developed by Jonathan Haidt and his colleagues, which I think offers a useful way of viewing how different Christians come to different conclusions when faced with contemporary moral challenges.⁴ But before I review the new research on moral sentiments, I will present a broader perspective offered by Joshua Greene, who has studied the problem of differences in moral views held by different groups of people.

Moral Tribes

Greene's thinking about the problem of moral tribes is nicely summarized in his book, *Moral Tribes: Emotion, Reason, and the Gap Between Us and Them*.⁵ Moral tribes are groups of people holding similar moral views. Tribes may be nations or religious groups like Catholics, Evangelical Christians, and Orthodox Jews. Greene makes the point that in contemporary societies tribes have moral rules for their people but often do not expect people from

---

3. Gracey and Weber, "World Vision," para. 1.
4. Haidt, *The Righteous Mind*, 295–309.
5. Greene, *Moral Tribes*, 19–144.

other groups to follow their rules. Catholics do not expect Orthodox Jews to eat pork and Orthodox Jews do not expect Christians to circumcise their baby boys. But Greene observes there are social issues that are disruptive and interfere with respectful discourse. And in recent years these major moral issues happen to deal with problems of sex and death.

> The tribal differences that erupt into public controversy typically concern sex (e.g., gay marriage, gays in the military, the sex lives of public officials) and death at the margins of life (e.g., abortion, physician-assisted suicide, the use of embryonic stem cells in research). That such issues are moral issues is surely not arbitrary. Sex and death are the gas pedals and brakes of tribal growth (Gay sex and abortion, for example, are both alternatives to reproduction.) What's less clear is why different tribes hold different views about sex, life, and death, and why some tribes are more willing than others to impose their views on outsiders.[6]

In addition to his expertise in philosophy, Greene is knowledgeable about cognitive psychology and moral thinking. He observes that although humans are naturally selfish, they band together in small groups to enhance their survival. There is an important affiliation with members of one's own tribe because as a group, they competed with other tribes for scant resources. Both cooperation and competition are a part of human nature. Greene defines morality as "a set of psychological adaptations that allow otherwise selfish individuals to reap the benefits of cooperation."[7] Overcoming excessive individual concerns or selfish behavior is important to survival. As Greene explains, "The essence of morality is altruism, unselfishness, a willingness to pay a personal cost to benefit others."[8]

Psychological scientists seek to identify natural causes for the origins of human behavior. But discovering the causes of moral behavior can be difficult and involves some speculation. There is a certain amount of circular reasoning involved in concluding that the behavior we observe in people must be adaptive. After all, if people are alive, they obviously survived whatever challenges the nonsurvivors failed to overcome. The problem of the natural origins of morality is beyond the scope of this book. The importance of considering origins is to understand the perspective of moral psychologists. The actions of human beings have their origins in biological mechanisms of survival and reproduction. People are naturally competitive. They compete for the resources they need to survive. And they compete

6. Ibid., 11.
7. Ibid., 22.
8. Ibid.

for mates. People are social creatures who form strong attachments to family members. The concept of family expands to some loose sense of My People or Us, to use Greene's terms. In many easily observable ways, such as clothing and language, we discriminate between Us and Them. Although some people compete with close kin, many cooperate with group members to compete against other groups for that which we consider necessary for survival. Nowadays, we speak less of basic biological survival and more of maintaining our way of life. It doesn't take much imagination to see that people need rules to prevent competitive acts from getting out of hand. There is a right way to treat family members and those of one's tribe or nation. And those who fail to follow the rules are the losers.

Morality is about right living. Moral teachings prescribe right conduct. People continually make laws, which often turn beliefs and informal rules about what is right and wrong into enforceable statements. Laws reveal what a community or nation considers to be right, and the harshness of penalties for disobeying the laws reveals how important those laws are to the community or at least to those social leaders who have the power to destroy a person's life for noncompliance.

The Christian traditions officially consider the rules about right and wrong as coming from God, which is obviously quite different from the view of behavioral scientists like psychologists who see rules as a natural outcome of people finding the best way to live and work together in the pursuit of common goals. At a surface level, if a rule comes from God, and if God has unlimited power to enforce that rule, then it is utter foolishness to disobey the rule. Disobedience, called sin in Christian language, can be punishable by the loss of eternal life. But over the centuries, since the first rules or commandments were recorded, numerous Christian groups have interpreted and re-interpreted those rules. There are common rules that large groups of Christians accept as binding upon them. And many of those rules have to do with sexuality and how to govern sexual behavior. Some rules have eternal consequences. Other rules are more like tribal customs and rituals that don't carry the weight of eternal life or death. We will see that some forms of sexual behavior are considered worthy of the death penalty. In recent research, psychological scientists do not focus so much on the origins of morality but rather seek to identify those factors that influence how people identify some behaviors as right and others as wrong.

Like Jonathan Haidt, whose work I will discuss later, Greene finds that, for the most part, we make moral decisions automatically, which works well for most moral issues within our tribes. But when it comes to solving nuanced moral problems, the common approaches often fail, and new thinking is needed. This capacity for moral reasoning can be drawn upon, but there needs to be some universal basis for making moral decisions that will transcend the competing values of different moral tribes. For example, at the time of this writing, conservative and progressive Christians are split when it comes to supporting same-sex marriages. To reach a transcendent moral decision, Greene thinks people should adopt a metamorality based on the reasoning processes inherent in utilitarianism, which he explains as a deep pragmatism. It is his belief in a more powerful role for reason that distinguishes Greene's view of morality from that of Haidt. Haidt does not ignore reason but minimizes its role in the way humans make their moral decisions. Greene finds some value in religion. "The religions of the world have much in common. They tell us to be kind to our neighbors, not to lie, not to steal, not to make moral exceptions of ourselves."[9] But Greene believes most religions do not help people reach agreement on a grander scale: "They exacerbate, rather than ease, conflicts between the values of Us and the values of Them."[10]

What might be a key to the problem of peacefully resolving such moral issues? One consideration might be to look at who is part of a tribe. Conservative groups tend to think of smaller groups of Us in contrast to Them. For example, when natural disasters occur, Americans often respond. But some Americans are resistant or even hostile to working collectively through the United Nations. In contrast, other Americans are more willing to consider all humans as worthy of dignity and respect when it comes to thinking about moral matters of harm and fairness. Some think of people in terms of nations and states. And some think of people as all the same species or, in the language of Christianity, "all God's children." These different groups define the concept of *Us* in different ways. One key to improving relationships is to find ways to become more inclusive and discover how *they* are like *us*. Greene has other ideas as well. But these are essentially implications of how to apply utilitarianism to solving moral dilemmas rather than psychological modes of analyses, to which we now turn.

Moral Development in Stages

Jean Piaget studied the rules children used when playing games. He summarized his findings in a classic book—*The Moral Judgment of the Child*. He learned about moral development by asking boys to explain the rules they used in a game of marbles. He also asked girls to explain the rules for a type

9. Ibid., 183–92.
10. Ibid., 183.

of hide-and-seek activity.[11] The rules were not just about cognition because they governed the right way to interact with others. In this respect, Piaget's idea was a forerunner of game theory, which has made many contributions to moral psychology and behavioral economics.

Piaget also used moral stories to understand how children reached conclusions about fair and just responses when a child or adult misbehaved. Two responses emerged. Some answers required violators to pay for their wrongdoing. *Expiation* would occur as a result of punishments like spanking or confinement. Other answers focused on making things right. The children should see the consequences of their behavior. He identified this focus on cooperation as *reciprocity*.[12]

The Piagetian model of moral development was clearly developmental and followed his four stages of cognitive development. In the sensorimotor stage—from birth to age four—children play individually according to their motor abilities. They accept the rules they are given from adults as sacred. In stage two—ages four through seven—children play games with others from an egocentric perspective. They have some understanding of rules but may make up others as they go along. From age seven to ten, rules emerge. In this stage, labeled incipient cooperation, children learn the basis of cooperative and competitive play. Finally, in the fourth stage, beginning about age eleven or twelve, genuine cooperation emerges. Children are keenly aware of rules. They settle disputes and invent new rules. The children are able to develop mutual respect.

Lawrence Kohlberg and his colleagues built on Piaget's work using a set of moral dilemmas to learn how children arrived at their conclusions about the right thing to do.[13] Based on his analysis, Kohlberg developed a six-stage theory organized into three levels, each having two stages. The first level, preconventional or premoral, begins with an obedience and punishment orientation stage and moves to a naively egoistic orientation stage where that which satisfies one's needs is right. At level two, people attain a conventional level of morality based on social conformity. At stage three they orient toward pleasing others. And at stage four they orient toward duty and respect for authority. Finally, postconventional and self-accepted moral principles define level three. Stage five is known for a contractual or legalistic orientation where norms of right and wrong appear derived from reason. The highest attainment is stage six. Individual principles of conscience are relied upon. People orient toward universal principles.

11. Piaget, *The Moral*, 1–103.
12. Ibid., 203–4.
13. Kohlberg and Hersh, "Moral Development," 53–59.

Kohlberg's theory dominated ideas about moral development for years and was routinely included in textbooks about child and adolescent development. Despite their dominance, Kohlberg's ideas have been criticized for being heavily influenced by Western culture and philosophical bias on what constitutes a high level of morality. His ideas were also critiqued by women because he relied on studies that did not include girls.[14] Carol Gilligan argued that female morality is based more on relationships than rules. And women focus more on compassion and care.[15] Researchers also criticize his theory because the data do not support a fixed progress through the hypothesized stages. Of course, just because people can reason well does not imply they will act morally, so, at best, the theory is limited to describing the development of moral thinking rather than a comprehensive moral psychology.

Morality Grounded in Relationships

It is commonly said that the first four of the Bible's Ten Commandments deal with a person's relationship with God and that the other six deal with a person's relationships with others. Or, to paraphrase Jesus' view of the greatest commandments, people should wholly love God and love their neighbors as themselves (Matt 22:36–40; Mark 12:28–31; Deut 6:5; Lev 19:18). Christians come to morality with some sense of biblical morality, which they learn from parents and teachers at churches or Christian schools. For many, the Ten Commandments are set in stone. They are absolutes—rules that never change. But the devil is in the details as Christians disagree over what the Ten Commandments mean when the text forbids making images, killing (or committing murder), or honoring the Sabbath. For those who focus on Jesus' statement of the greatest commandments, there is still the need to identify what it means to express love for neighbor in a contemporary situation. People of good faith disagree on what constitutes a loving response; surely love does not mean tolerating all kinds of conduct.

Recent research on morality by Jonathan Haidt and many colleagues has identified three principles of morality based on a Social Intuitionist Model. He has aptly summarized this body of research in *The Righteous Mind*. In this section, I am drawing upon the Social Intuitionist Model and the supporting research, which places morality squarely within the context of social relationships. First I will discuss Haidt's three moral principles; then I will review his six foundations of morality.

14. Gilligan, *In a Different*, 18.
15. Ibid., 73.

Moral Thinking

Haidt's first principle of morality is the recognition that moral thinking, like other forms of thinking, is largely governed by quick automatic responses. In Haidt's words, *"Intuitions come first, strategic reasoning second."*[16] These responses are motivated by emotions and shaped by our culture. In a previous chapter, I mentioned Kahneman's summary of thinking, which he calls fast and slow thinking. For years psychologists have recognized that much of what we do is a quick and automatic response to events in our environment. Our brains have developed modules to quickly process the input from our senses and link that input to our memories in order to respond to the ordinary challenges of daily life. Memories and the brain's processing system include a network responsible for emotion. We respond quickly with negative feelings of fear, anger, and disgust as well as positive feelings of joy and happiness. Almost simultaneously, we recognize our mental state and behavioral response. This state of awareness can produce words that explain what we are doing and why we are doing it. The quick and automatic processes are part of human nature. And most of those responses enable us to adequately interact with others in a way that promotes cooperation and good relationships. The specific responses—the rituals and the contents of what we say—we learn within our culture. Obviously, some learn culturally approved ways of behaving better than others. And like other aspects of functioning, some people are more agile at social functioning than are others.

But when it comes to difficult decisions—the challenge to behave in a way different than our traditional way—we must stop and think. Reasoning is not absent from this model of morality, but reasoning does take a backseat because it is a slow and inefficient process. To see a member of a minority group and respond with common cultural insults seems *natural* when that response is common among members of a social group. But it requires effort to act differently. First we need to see the effects of an insult on a victim. Next, we might consider how we would feel if we were the victim. And finally, we apply some moral reasoning, which may not happen unless the matter is called to our attention.

Moral thinking, like most thinking, is a quick and automatic process. A moral response is often motivated by a strong feeling. According to the Bible, Lot has sex with his two daughters. This just seems wrong to us. And we are surprised about the lack of condemnation. Why doesn't the Bible tell us that God punished Lot for the incest? Sometimes we know something is

---

16. Haidt, *The Righteous Mind*, 186 (italics in original).

wrong based on our visceral response to an act. But when called to explain why something is wrong, we often have to search for reasons. We know that in difficult cases we need a moral rule that works to explain why an act is wrong. Why shouldn't something be done? Haidt calls this search for reasons "moral dumbfounding."[17] We know it's wrong but have difficulty offering a list of reasons why.

Haidt uses a metaphor of a rider on an elephant to illustrate the difficulty of a small human rider trying to control the elephant.[18] The elephant takes the rider throughout the day and leans one way or another on life's moral matters. A rider must exert considerable effort to change the direction of the elephant. Another metaphor is also worthy of consideration. Greene prefers to think of the brain's moral modules as functioning like a sophisticated camera on an automatic setting.[19] For the most part, the camera works well and takes acceptable pictures, but there are special times when the automatic settings do not work. Thinking is required to select the best settings demanded by the scenario in front of our lens.

When it comes to powerful urges like the human sexual response, I think I prefer a race horse and rider metaphor. Moral thinking is like a sleepy rider on a feisty horse that has not completed training. The horse follows some orders and is familiar with common routes and some noises. But in different settings, or when startled by new sounds, the horse responds, and the human rider wakes up and gives orders. But the horse is already moving on its own impulse. Most of the time, our reasoning capacity is in sleep mode until a dilemma activates this important feature. Reason offers the promise of stopping an action sequence and changing direction. But at some point in the sequence, sexual activity is hard to interrupt. And reason is hard to access.

Haidt cites many examples of moral judgments that demonstrate how unaware people are about external influences on their behavior.[20] In one study, Alex Todorov of Princeton flashed pictures of political winners and runners-up on a screen for one tenth of one second. Research participants were asked to rate the more competent persons in a pair. Those fast competency judgments turned out to be good predictors of actual winners. A study by Alex Jordan at Stanford University found that students exposed to a foul odor were much harsher in their moral judgments than were students who did not breathe the foul air. A similar finding occurred when people drank

17. Haidt and Bjorkland et al., "Moral Dumbfounding," 1.
18. Haidt, *The Righteous Mind*, 67–70.
19. Greene, *Moral Tribes*, 132.
20. Haidt, *The Righteous Mind*, 58–61.

bitter rather than sweet drinks before making a moral judgment. Chenbo Zhong of the University of Toronto found that people who were asked to wash their hands with soap and water before completing a survey about moral purity issues gave highly moral responses. Zhong also examined the opposite effect in participants who reported their moral transgressions or copied an account of another person's moral wrongdoing. Those exposed to the moral wrongdoing thought more about cleanliness and selected cleaning products like hand wipes to take home after the study. Here's one more example to show how simple factors influence thinking. Eric Helzer and David Pizarro at Cornell University asked students to answer questions about their political attitudes. Just being near to a hand sanitizer increased conservative opinions.

Most humans have a long period of time during which their desire for sex is at a high level. When in close proximity to another person, it is difficult to reign in the natural process of screening for a mate. Regardless of relationship status, preliminary mating activities known as flirting or simply showing off happen almost automatically. The sexual urge drives thinking. And moral teachings often take a back seat—to use a different riding metaphor.

Moral Dimensions

Haidt's research led him to conclude that morality is multidimensional: "There's more to morality than harm and fairness."[21] Haidt finds appeals to care vs. harm and fairness vs. cheating are common when people argue about right and wrong. But his research has led to the conclusion that six dimensions form a foundation for morality. Because I will use these six dimensions of morality in analyzing contemporary Christian concerns, I will explain these six dimensions in more detail following the third principle.

Moral Commitment

Haidt labels his third moral principle "morality binds and blinds."[22] This binding and blinding feature is based on the premise that, like other creatures, we are social. In fact, Haidt argues we are ultrasocial creatures because we live in very large groups. Our social impulse can be seen in our defense of our group's territories, the incredible amount of long term care required

21. Ibid., 186.
22. Ibid.

by our offspring, and the need to work together to care for our families while simultaneously defending our group against threats from other groups. We are in this "life thing" together. We have a strong sense of Us and Them. We are bound to our group members by strong sentiments of honor, respect, and love as well as by fear and aversion to shame. Our groups include our families, our friendship networks, our workgroups, our countries and, of course, our spiritual or religious communities. Even as our sentiments bind us together, we are simultaneously blind to the traditions of others, which seem so strange. Whoever *they* are, *they* are not like *us*. And we tend to find our way of doing things the right way, the moral way, the righteous path.

Multidimensional Morality

I am still drawing upon the work of Haidt, who has identified six dimensions of morality, which he identifies as moral foundations.[23] What I find particularly useful here is the research that helps us see how social conservatives and social liberals can approach moral matters by drawing upon different dimensions of morality. And my hope is that this understanding can help us better appreciate how Christians from different traditions arrive at different conclusions about moral conduct. Conservative and progressive Christians often hold strong beliefs about what is right and wrong and how to treat people with love and respect. Even though the moral arguments of Christians contain references to Scripture, the language of the arguments emphasizes one or more of the moral dimensions. Put another way, a Christian's moral judgment includes Scripture and an analysis of concerns that emphasize one or more of six moral dimensions. As you examine the six moral foundations, consider how acting on moral judgment affects multiple dimensions of human functioning presented in the SCOPES model. The general question about the effects of acting on a moral judgment can be framed this way: how does acting on a moral judgment affect a person spiritually, cognitively, behaviorally, physically, emotionally, and socially?

1. Care versus Harm

The focus of this dimension is caring about the welfare of others, which includes the virtues of caring and compassion and ensuring that no harm is done. The primary emotional basis for this dimension is the natural response to care for our own offspring and family members. Our children

---

23. Ibid., 131–54; 170–76.

are born vulnerable and highly dependent on parental care. The cuteness factor helps a lot because we are naturally drawn toward the faces of babies whether human or animal. We naturally form psychological attachments to our young. Stories abound of the heroic efforts of animals and humans to protect and rescue their young even at the risk of death.

Christians see many examples of Jesus' care for vulnerable persons. He welcomed the children and reached out to the sick, the poor, and those unacceptable in his society, such as those with leprosy. The message of love is in the second greatest commandment (Matt 22:39). This dimension is well represented in Catholic Social Teaching as well as the care ministries of many Protestant denominations. Christian charities are everywhere. The care/harm and fairness dimensions are more highly valued among progressive Christians than are the other moral dimensions.

Caring and kindness are primary virtues. Look for these and similar words in written and spoken communication: protect, care, love, kind, nurture vs. harm, hurt, destroy.

2. Fairness/Reciprocity versus Cheating

Be fair, do not cheat, and treat others the way you wish to be treated. Fairness is a virtue important to very young children as soon as they begin to receive gifts and learn to play games by following rules. Fairness and reciprocity norms represent a basic sense of social justice. People who are stingy with their gifts at a potluck supper are the talk of the meal. Generous givers are praised when funds are needed for building projects or helping needy families. People who fake illness or disability to collect sympathy or funds are condemned; "If you do not work you do not eat."

Young children are taught to repay acts of kindness and small gifts with a "thank you." Parents and teachers constantly remind children to share toys and take turns on playground equipment. Adults become outraged when seemingly arbitrary standards are used by supervisors in offering promotions or special deals at work. In recent years, women have made progress at narrowing the pay gap with men. The phrase "equal pay for equal work" represents this idea of fairness. And the reciprocity principle is enforced by social condemnation of free riders. In Western cultures, if you are invited for a meal, you are expected to return the favor. If you help someone move, you expect him or her to help you. When people are unable to return a favor, we expect expressions of gratitude.

There are clear benefits to members of a society when most people are connected by multiple two-way partnerships. We count on others to help us when we are down because we have helped them. Cheating and deception are roundly condemned openly and by means of gossip. Feelings of anger energize condemnation. Feelings of guilt prompt actions to make things right and express gratitude. When there is a high level of fairness and reciprocity, there is a high level of trust.

Fairness is a virtue linked to other virtues of justice and trustworthiness. Look for these and similar words in written and spoken communication: Fairness, proportion, equality, just, trustworthy, faithful vs. unfair, inequality, unjust, cheat, discrimination.

3. Ingroup Loyalty versus Betrayal

Be loyal and do not betray. If you are a member of a church, you are expected to be loyal to your group. Moral people make sacrifices to promote the group ahead of themselves. Sometimes loyalty means the ultimate sacrifice of dying for their country during military service. Fellow citizens and church members are watchful for signs of betrayal. Citizenship or membership is never free. In some religious groups, you owe your life. Martyrs for the faith are respected in many religions.

Patriotism is highly valued among U.S. Christian conservatives who often display the U.S. flag near the Christian flag on public holidays and during programs for children and youth. Christian colleges and universities sing Christian songs and have prayers and bible reading at commencements as well as extended ceremonies for the students who complete military programs as new officers.

The primary emotions motivating loyalty are pride and rage. Group pride is evident through identity symbols such as tee shirts, caps, uniforms, and attendance at group events. Members are expected to attend church and company events. You are expected to serve your country or, at a minimum, to show respect to and support for those who serve. Those who betray their nation are traitors. Throughout history, traitors have been publicly executed as a lesson to all potential violators.

Those who betray their faith are apostates. In the Bible, those who worshipped other gods were likened to adulterers. In some religions, those who leave the faith deserve death. In some religious cultures, those who leave the faith are no longer welcomed into community. In many contemporary Christian cultures, those who leave their faith are turned over to God with the hope that they will return to faith before they die. The faithful know that turning away from God leads to eternal damnation.

The stakes are high for betraying one's group. I suspect that the loyalty dimension is a powerful reason why it is risky for voices of dissent to be heard. Disagreements with leadership are viewed as evidence of disloyalty. Those who disagree are made to feel unwelcome. Those who complain about government will be publicly challenged to leave the country. Those who complain about church will be encouraged to leave the church. Perhaps an excessive expectation of loyalty to one's church is one factor behind the cover-up of religious leaders who sexually abused children.

Loyalty is a powerful moral attribute. Associated virtues are patriotism, self-sacrifice, and respect for heroes. Look for these and similar words in written and spoken communication: Loyal, patriotic, sacrifice, hero vs. disloyal, unpatriotic, traitor.

4. Authority/Respect versus Disrespect

An old Christian song is titled "Trust and Obey." Conservatives in many cultures value the social order. For Christians, the social order reflects God's plan. Christians are taught to respect authorities except when governments violate God's rules (Rom 13). The same expectation of respect is true within church organizations. The Catholic Church and the Eastern Orthodox churches have popes at the highest level. The Church of England has an Archbishop. All groups have leaders. And the faithful are expected to show respect for their leadership and obey church rules. Speaking against those in high positions is disrespectful and even considered an affront to God. For example, conservative Protestants used to quote from Psalm 105:15 using the King James Version: "Touch not mine anointed." The verse was interpreted to mean you should not say anything bad about pastors and missionaries.

It is interesting to note that Jesus appeared to violate the respect expected by the established leaders of his day. The Gospel writers included examples of Jesus' challenges to leaders about their burdensome rules and obsession with outward religion to the exclusion of the needs of the poor and those on the margins of society (Matt 23). Obviously, they became enraged at his disrespectful teachings, which were contrary to those of the official leaders. Their powerful connections with the Romans led to his arrest. The fear instilled in his disciples is amply documented. It is worth noting that for millennia, God was viewed not only as one who loves but also as one who deserves ultimate respect. The "fear of the Lord" (Ps 111:10; Prov 9:10) is not just a saying when punishment by death or eternal life is at stake.

Within each Christian group, there are leaders responsible for official positions on matters of morality. Christians expect their leaders to offer a biblical foundation for their moral pronouncements. In turn, leaders expect to be treated with respect, which often means accepting the policies of the faith tradition. The biblical moral tradition includes respect for one's rightful place in the theocratic hierarchy. In the New Testament, Jesus obeyed his father—even to the point of death (Phil 2:8). Jesus is head of the church, which consists of all believers. And all Christians are to show respect by submissive obedience to him (Eph 5:22–23). In the Christian household, men are the traditional leaders deserving of respectful submission from their wives (Eph 5:24–33). Children are to respect fathers and mothers (Eph 6:1–3). And slaves are also to respect and honor their masters (Eph 6:5–9). Conservative Christians give much more weight to respect for authority as evidenced in a submissive attitude than do progressive Christians, who are more inclined toward egalitarian relationships within society, the church, and marriage.

Obedience and deference are virtues linked to respect for authority. Look for these and similar words in written and spoken communication: obey, respect, humble, deference, toe the line vs. disobey, disrespect, rebellious, defiant, oppositional, arrogant.

5. Purity or Sanctity versus Degradation

Be holy and pure. Concerns about purity and holy living are a common part of many cultures. Religious groups are known for their rituals of purification. Sometimes it is literal, as in hand washing before religious ceremonies, and at other times purity is symbolic, as in once-in-a-lifetime baptism ceremonies. The virtues of chastity, wholesomeness, and control over fleshly desires fit here.

Evidence from the Bible and other sources documents a long history of taboos associated with touching human blood and bodily fluids, discharges, and waste products (e.g., Lev 15:2–3, 19–24). The primary emotion is a sense of disgust, which motivates cleanliness and propels avoidance. People with diseases are labeled unclean. They are expected to stay away from others so as not to spread contamination. In biblical times, people with conditions that appeared contagious were quarantined. Specified time periods were in place to help community members know when the time of uncleanness was over. Priests viewed a person who had recovered, and they collected an offering. Today we expect people to see a physician before returning to work or school in cases presumed to pose a high risk of infection.

People who have been to certain countries or who have certain diseases are not permitted to contribute their blood to the emergency blood supply.

The strong disgust emotion and the avoidance response are the psychological basis for rules governing sanctity and holy living. People are to be separate from that which contaminates and degrades a person. It is but a short psychological step from getting infected by contact with a person who has a disease or handling bodily waste to treating groups of people as if they were contagious. It is not surprising that people label some forms of sex as dirty and identify pornography as filthy or dirty pictures. Conservative Christians advocate clean living. The phrase oft-quoted by conservative Christians, "Cleanliness is next to godliness," captures a guiding principle: that God expects a clean life. Sexual purity includes no sex outside of marriage for conservatives.

The virtues of temperance, chastity, piety, and cleanliness are linked to the sanctity-degradation dimension. Look for these and similar words in written and spoken communication: pure, purity, clean, chastity, piety, holy, sacred, sacred place vs. depraved, dirty, unclean, pervert.

6. Liberty versus Oppression

Set the captives free. The liberty—or freedom—dimension is not part of the original five dimensions in earlier moral psychology work but was later added by Haidt as an important dimension of morality. Throughout history, people have yearned for freedom from oppression. Liberators are revered and seen as agents of God (e.g., Moses and Joshua). Perhaps the quintessential biblical liberation story is the exodus from Egypt still celebrated each year during Jewish Passover.

Americans justified rebellion against their British King as a righteous rebellion against a tyrant. The writers of the U.S. Declaration of Independence state the opinions that justified the rebellion in the first sentence. Their justification appealed to "the Laws of Nature and Nature's God" as if to justify a change in loyalty. In the next paragraph, they wrote that liberty is one of the rights that come from God. And toward the end of the paragraph, the King of Great Britain is judged guilty of absolute tyranny. Following the declaration, loyalty was an issue for people living in the colonies. And those who remained loyal to their King sought ways to escape the colonial rebellion.

American slaves were inspired by the exodus story and occasionally rose up against their masters or endured significant hardships as they attempted to escape to Canada, where they could find the same freedoms enjoyed by European Americans.[24] Years later, Dr. Martin Luther King Jr. led protests for civil rights. His speeches included themes of freedom.[25] Christians value freedom of religion, and many—like the Amish and Huguenots—left tyrannical regimes in search of this important moral virtue.

The primary emotion that propels people to unify with others against threats to liberty is righteous anger. Such focused anger can motivate the formation of relationships among those who are the targets of bullying and aggression whether on a national or local level. The virtues of unity, liberty, and freedom represent a moral response to tyrannical and oppressive regimes. When Christians sense their freedom of religion is threatened by laws or policies from a governmental body, they fight back through the courts and with the usual ways of social protest.

The freedom to live according to the moral rules of one's group is a highly valued virtue. Look for these and similar words in written and spoken communication: liberty, freedom vs. oppression, tyranny.

Consent and Choice

Having a choice is important in matters of morality. Most people do not blame animals for their conduct because we consider their acts natural, and we assume that animals do not have the capacity for morality. We do hold people responsible for their conduct because we believe they have a choice to act or not act in certain ways. People have biologically based urges to eat, sleep, drink, breathe, urinate, defecate, and have sex. We are biologically driven to satisfy these urges. Put another way, we are *motivated* to eat, sleep, drink, breathe, urinate, defecate, and have sex. We do not have to think about these desires. But to control these urges requires effort. People can learn to restrict eating, get by on less sleep for a while, restrict drinking for a short period of time, hold one's breath when diving, delay urinating and defecating to use toilets, and avoid sexual activity for a while. The capacity to control our biological drives by delaying satisfaction and selecting an appropriate time and place forms the basis for the possibility for consent. When one person's satisfaction depends on the action of another person, we have the possibility of mutual consent. Consent only works when both parties involved have the necessary brain functions to control their biological drives. I have included consent here because it is relevant to contemporary thinking about several moral issues in this book. Because of the problems

---

24. Historica Canada, "Departure of Black Loyalists," para 1.
25. King, "I Have a Dream," 1–6.

with sexual harassment on college campuses, students are advised to make sure they have consent before participating in sexual activity.

Consent implies choice, but psychologists and other human service professionals do not consider all persons capable of giving consent to sexual activity. For example, law and ethical principles do not consider minors to have the right to consent to a variety of societal activities, including marriage and sex. People judged to have diminished capacity because of brain damage or neurological diseases are considered unable to give consent to treatment. In the context of psychotherapy, clinicians are in a power position compared to a client, and thus sexual activity between a clinician and a client is never acceptable. In the case of sexual morality and Christianity, consent takes a back seat to the teachings of the Bible as interpreted by conservative leaders. Obviously, in secular contexts, consent is not enough to justify some acts. Additional protections based on laws and the assignment of legal guardians for vulnerable persons are established by governing bodies and connected in law to severe punishments when violated. In the case of conservative Christian beliefs, choice matters but only in so far as people can choose to go God's way or suffer the consequences.

Finally, consent implies that no party to an agreement is more powerful than the other. When one party has more power in a relationship, consent does not truly exist. Any agreement involves coercion and is never truly voluntary. Clergy can never claim consent to sexual activity from a congregant. Supervisors can never claim consent to sexual activity from supervisees. Educators can never claim consent to sexual activity from their students.

Moral Psychology and Christian Theologies

I think the moral dimension of care and harm is one basis for a unified moral response to certain types of sexual expression. An oft-quoted text shows God's concern for the weak, poor, and oppressed (Ps 82:3). Jesus expressed concern for children (Luke 17:2) and often expressed concern for the poor (e.g., Matt 19:21; Luke 20:46–47). Most would agree that exploitation or harming children and other vulnerable persons is morally wrong; hence, sex acts involving children and other vulnerable persons is a common basis for condemning pornography, human trafficking, and sex abuse as sinful within any Christian worldview.

The commandment to love others as oneself incorporates a notion of reciprocity found in the second moral dimension. Regardless of Christian tradition, each faith group values the freedom to worship in their own way. A sense of fairness prevails among reasonable leaders who promote the freedom for others that they want for themselves. But this fairness is held in tandem with the care/harm dimension because there must be limits to freedom when one group harms another.

Loyalty to country occurs when all are under threat. We "rally 'round the flag." Americans expressed mutual support following the attacks of 9/11. North Americans and Europeans joined with other nations when bound by treaty or common interests during World War II. All Christians can be bound together in serving the victims of a natural disaster such as Hurricane Katrina, Super-Storm Sandy, or Typhoon Haiyan. A nation's flag is one of the first symbols to rise following a natural disaster. The presence of the flag means we are all in this together. Seeing a flag is a deeply emotional experience when under threat. Men and women cry when they see their flag and feel a strong sense of community. And Christians from many traditions are also present at disasters as they share a common purpose often under the unifying symbol of the cross.

The biblical injunctions to respect authority are pervasive. It is clearly in the best interest of nations to promote respect for authority to maintain some sense of order within society. Although Christians reasonably expect respect for authority from those who are members of their group or organization, they compete with the presumed authority of other Christian leaders when making pronouncements about public morality. This can only lead to confusion as nonclergy attempt to make sense of disparate voices. Of course, it makes matters worse when a particular group gets tagged as immoral and as lacking moral authority when a leader is caught in a moral failure—sometimes a sexual sin he or she has preached against. Appeals to biblical authority continue to be made, but the lack of consensus on the correct interpretation of key texts leaves some believers in a moral quandary about how to respect the authority of Scripture.

The moral dimension of sanctity and degradation linked to disgust may be difficult for progressive Christians to accept if they are used to relying on reason to rebut the teachings of conservative voices. The disgust response is powerful and emotional and often eludes reason. Progressive Christians are more easily upset when harm or injustice is at stake. But progressive Christians may be blind to disgust-based motives that move conservatives to keep a safe distance from that which seems dirty, evil, or unclean. Furthermore, overcoming disgust-based prejudices is notoriously difficult. Present some disgusting image or odor, and you can see the reaction on a person's face before they formulate words to explain why they hate whatever obnoxious thing you presented. The disgust response is quick, powerful, and hard to control.

People hide from their prejudices perhaps in part because they are dimly aware that they hold them. The responses that result in separation are so embedded in cultural beliefs and practices that powerful forces are needed if individuals are to make significant changes. Witness, for example, the tremendous loss of life during the U.S. Civil War and the incredible struggle still required a century later for African Americans to obtain basic human rights and access to the same benefits afforded European Americans. Long-term, culture-based learning resulted in white-black segregation at drinking fountains, restrooms, and eating establishments. Even when helping allies during World War II, U.S. forces in England insisted on black-white segregation at eating establishments and social events.[26] This example from the U.S. post-slavery era illustrates how hard it is to change views linked to perceptions of purity by separation. Racial separation was also evident in cultural prohibitions against black-white dating. Mixed race marriages were forbidden by law until 1967.[27]

Finally, we see that under perceived threat, conservative Christians have joined together to seek freedom from the perceived tyranny of governments that infringe on their freedom to live in a moral society. Conservative U.S. Christians were able to pass laws prohibiting the sale of alcohol in the early 1900s. More recently, they passed the Defense of Marriage Act (1996) and worked together to fight laws permitting same-sex marriage. The forcefulness of their arguments illustrates the righteous anger present when liberty is perceived to be under threat. Obviously, other Christians held different opinions and considered the conservatives to be the tyrants who wished to limit the freedoms of minorities.

Summary

I began this chapter on moral psychology by looking at the moral philosophy of Joshua Greene, which has been informed by research in moral psychology. Greene describes the problem of moral tribes by showing how naturally selfish humans join together in small cooperative groups for survival.

Next, I discussed the stage theories of Jean Piaget and Lawrence Kohlberg. These cognitive theories have been replaced by theories based on more recent studies.

In the following section, I examined the new emphasis on moral intuition or moral sentiment. Research by Jonathan Haidt and his colleagues suggests three principles to explain moral responses. First, many—if not

---

26. Murray, "Blacks in Britain."
27. Sheppard, "The Loving."

most—moral responses are automatic and likely based on primitive, emotive responses to moral situations. Haidt's third principle is known as "morality binds and blinds." By this phrase, Haidt means people are committed to the morality of their group and find it difficult to view moral matters from the perspective of another group.

I added a section on the topic of consent, which is not a part of Haidt's moral psychology. But consent is important when considering moral matters.

The general question about the psychology of moral judgments can be framed in two ways. The first question asks about the positive dimension of the moral foundations and the second question asks about the negative dimension of the foundations.

1. How does their language reveal concerns about care, equality, loyalty, authority, purity, or liberty?
2. How does their language reveal concerns about harm, inequality, betrayal, disrespect, degradation, or oppression?

We can consider the impact of a moral judgment on a person by thinking of people in terms of the six aspects of human functioning represented in the SCOPES model. The general question about the effects on a person of acting on a moral judgment can be framed this way: how does acting on a moral judgment affect a person spiritually, cognitively, behaviorally, physically, emotionally, or socially?

We have now looked at three factors influencing Christian moral judgment about sexual issues: beliefs about Scripture, an understanding of human nature (SCOPES model), and moral reasoning (six dimensional foundations). The fourth of four factors, beliefs about sexuality, is next.

Additional Resources

1. **Moral Development in Women.** Professor Carol Gilligan offers a woman's perspective on moral development and the problems with older stage theories. https://www.youtube.com/watch?v=2W_9MozRoKE
2. **Moral Values.** In this TED talk, psychology professor Jonathan Haidt offers a summary of his work showing differences between conservatives and liberals. https://www.youtube.com/watch?v=8SOQduoLgRw&list=PLkOT9jJaJha2nLGwVUrwbkltc5HeI8g1Q&index=2

3. **Moral Research Surveys**. Jonathan Haidt and his colleagues offer surveys related to morality online. You can explore these scales at http://www.yourmorals.org/explore.php

4. **Moral Tribes**. In a fifteen-minute talk at the 2014 meeting of the Society for Personality and Social Psychology, Professor Joshua Greene of Harvard University summarizes his perspective on moral conflicts: https://www.youtube.com/watch?v=9reBdFoIdY0&list=PLkOT9jJaJha2nLGwVUrwbkltc5HeI8g1Q&index=10

Discussion Questions and Topics

1. Suppose you and a friend decide to celebrate some good news. You choose a nice restaurant and the bill comes to over $70.00. According to World Vision in 2014, a gift of $35.00 would sponsor the needs of a child for such things as water, food, healthcare, and education for one month. Assume the information from World Vision is correct and that a failure to raise sufficient funds denies basic needs to a child. Is the decision to spend $70.00 on a meal a moral decision when you could have donated half that ($35.00) to care for one child for one month?

2. In the story at the beginning of the chapter, World Vision announced a policy change to permit people in same-sex marriages to work for them. In response to moral outrage and lost funds, World Vision undid their policy. How many of the six moral dimensions did President Mohler address in his blog post of March 25, 2014? http://www.albertmohler.com/2014/03/25/pointing-to-disaster-the-flawed-moral-vision-of-world-vision/

3. Psychologists have focused on the human disgust response as a basis for some rules about things that are wrong or immoral. What activities do you find disgusting that are also illegal or at least considered morally wrong by many people?

4. Consent is an important component of moral thinking. Laws declare when people can marry, drink alcohol, drive, enter into legally binding contracts, have consensual sex, obtain birth control without parent approval, and obtain an abortion without parent approval. Conduct an online search to discover the required legal age for two of these or similar activities where you live. Discuss or think about why the legal age restrictions may or may not make sense.

5

PSYCHOLOGY AND SEXUALITY

Bernadette and Alberto have been married six months. Life is good. They want to have children someday, but for now they are both devoting themselves to their careers and to each other. To prevent an unwanted pregnancy, Bernadette takes birth control, which she knows violates the teachings of her church. She and Alberto have discussed the matter with their physician, who assures them the contraceptive prevents pregnancy.

Beliefs can hinge on small details. Some religious groups oppose birth control methods that prevent a fertilized egg from being implanted in a woman's uterus. If a woman acts to block implantation then she has ended her child's life. Others believe life begins when an egg is implanted in a woman's uterus. Ending a pregnancy ends a child's life. From a doctor's perspective, abortion may only occur when a pregnancy has been terminated. As knowledge about sex and reproduction has increased, the opinions about morality have become more finely tuned. This chapter is about psychology and sexuality, and it is the first of two chapters providing information about human sexuality. The two chapters provide a foundation before considering Christian perspectives on morality in part 2.

Psychology and sex have been associated in people's minds at least since Sigmund Freud wrote about powerful Id impulses and psychosexual stages of child development. Although Freud's ideas rarely drive scientific investigations, they did stimulate an interest in the relationship between sexual development and psychological functioning. Given all the research and advice about sex in the past one hundred years, one would think we know most of what there is to know. Unfortunately, that is not the case. Folk beliefs and myths coexist with scientific findings. Self-reported sexual behavior remains suspect, and the scientific study of sexual functioning is appropriately limited by ethical considerations. Nevertheless, some contributions from psychological research are relevant to understanding the thoughts, feelings, behavior patterns, physiology, and social influences associated with Christian moral teachings about sexuality, which are the focus of this book.

The psychology of sex is a large and diversified field of study. In this chapter I will limit my scope to considering those findings and theories relevant to the sexuality topics evoking concern and provoking debate among contemporary Christians. Science can provide information about what can be observed and what people report. Science can inform about matters of harm and risk of harm. And an appreciation of harm is a factor in moral thinking. Ultimately, the decision about what is right and wrong or moral and immoral remains outside of science. And that's where religious leaders, theologians, philosophers, and others render opinions as to what is right and wrong. As we have already seen, many Christians turn to the pages of the Bible to understand God's perspective on morality. But as we will see in this chapter and those that follow, new discoveries about sexual attraction and reproductive processes along with new medical technologies have introduced a level of understanding and a measure of control over reproduction that were not possible when the biblical texts were written.

Sex and Love

The scientific study of love presents a particular difficulty because love includes emotion. Emotions are hidden from direct observation and must therefore be inferred. To psychologists, emotions are brain states. As observers, we can view behavior patterns associated with self-reported thoughts. That is, we can observe two people saying things and doing things with their bodies. And we interpret some of those actions as expressions of love. But we are dependent on the couple to tell us how much they love each other. Psychological scientists have measured biological correlates of self-reports of love, such as changes in blood flow, heart rate, and the digestive system. When we observe two people gazing at each other with the "look of love," we can measure their closeness and how long they focus attention on each other. Their smiles suggest a positive experience. At times these signs of love are obvious to friends even when the individuals seem to be unaware that they are in love.

Love is a complex experience and not merely an emotion. In addition to generally positive feelings, there is a pattern known as attachment.[1] The pattern of behaviors we observe in caring parents with infants provides evidence for a common emotional bond between parent and child in many

---

1. Bretherton, "Attachment Theory," 3–35.

species. In humans, the caring pattern is extended in time as children are dependent on their parents for years. Positive attachment is a loving, nurturing, and caring set of behaviors that indicate a warm and friendly bond between a parent and a child. Both parent and child experience distress when separated and are often anxious to know how the other is getting along, especially in hard times or when an adult child goes off to war. Attachment patterns continue to be evident in friendships and romantic relationships. People in love can be observed to be "all over" the loved one in a manifestly physical way as displayed on the lawns of parks and college campuses during warm weather. When separated, people in love miss each other. On social media sites, lovers picture themselves in each other's embrace and proudly declare their relationship status.

Researchers have found that parent-child attachment provides children with a basis for understanding relationships. By the time they are adults, people vary on how much anxiety they experience and how much they avoid others. I use the terms *anxiety* and *avoidance* because those are the terms researchers use. A state of low anxiety describes people who feel calm, able to feel loved, and not worried about rejection. People low in avoidance are able to enjoy close relationships, feel connected with others, and are capable of intimacy. The two dimensions of anxiety and avoidance can be combined to describe four ways (referred to as "attachment styles") people relate to others depending on how high or low the people are on anxiety and avoidance. These relationship factors can help us understand many adult relationships but are especially relevant to our understanding of healthy and problematic romantic and sexual relationships, so I will describe the four groups as summarized by Pamela Regan.[2]

1. **Secure Attachment Style**. People who are secure in their relationships report low anxiety and low avoidance. They are capable of enjoying close and supportive relationships. Compared to those having other attachment styles, people who feel secure report higher levels of satisfaction, trust, love, intimacy, and commitment. They are better at resolving conflicts and better at communicating.

2. **Preoccupied Attachment Style**. These people are high on anxiety but low on avoidance. They have a strong need for closeness but are constantly worried about being rejected or abandoned when in a relationship. Negative feelings are common in this style.

---

2. Regan, *The Mating*, 264–66.

3. **Dismissing-Avoidant Attachment Style.** This label applies to people who keep their distance from others and experience low anxiety. They favor being independent and self-reliant.

4. **Fearful-Avoidant Attachment Style.** People who are both high in anxiety and avoidance desire closeness but feel too fearful of rejection. Their avoidance of close relationships protects them from the pain of rejection and abandonment.

Sexual activity can occur within a love context or in other contexts. The whole idea of sex and love can be quite confusing because of the language we use. English speakers know that *making love* means having sexual intercourse. In pop music, phrases about love may intentionally be about sexual activity. Forbidden love conjures up stories of illicit sex. But of course people often speak about love without meaning sex. And casual sexual activity does occur between strangers or acquaintances—people in uncommitted relationships. The persons involved may know each other or experience a sexual attraction but not the other elements of love. There are of course sexual interactions that are abusive and destructive and not at all close to love.

To summarize, love is a multidimensional psychological construct. As we noted in the SCOPES model, there is an interweaving of thoughts, feelings, behavior patterns, and biological processes. Love has a social context too. The expressions of love vary with the time of day, the social setting, and the people present. Sex is often a part of what it means to be in love. Like love, sexual activity is linked to thoughts, feelings, behavior patterns, and biological processes. And sexual activity has a social context. In future chapters we will consider the spiritual framework that governs how people perceive the other five components of sexuality.

Sexual Arousal and Desire

Before discussing sexual arousal and desire, let me present a simple three-stage model that psychologists identify when describing sexual activity. Sexual activity is a basic instinctive response pattern. In humans, sexual activity has often been considered as having three stages. First, people develop sexual interest or sexual desire. Second, people experience sexual excitement when they are aroused by sexual stimulation. And third, people experience orgasm, which is the peak of sexual pleasure.

There are differences between women and men when it comes to patterns of sexual arousal and sexual desire. And researchers propose different scientific models to identify the sexual response process. In general, a woman's sexual response is less specific than that of a man.[3] And some think a woman's pattern of arousal does not follow the stepwise process commonly found in men. Richard Hayes describes the changes in modeling the human sexual response since the sexual research of William Masters and Virginia Johnson in the 1960s.[4] Masters and Johnson identified a progression of phases: excitation, plateau, orgasm, and resolution. A more recent approach to the process is the modified linear model characterized by sexual desire preceding sexual arousal. These stages may be followed by orgasm and resolution. Although the model seems to work well for men, it did not always describe a woman's sexual response pattern. Recently, researchers report that women are motivated to participate in sexual activity for many reasons in addition to sexual desire. When participation begins, sexual arousal might occur, which can increase sexual desire. So the pattern for a woman may involve some circularity rather than a straight linear progression from sexual desire to resolution.

Bancroft describes his view of the basic patterns of sexuality linked to reproduction as different for men and women.

> In the male this involves motivation for sexual stimulation and associated sexual pleasure that, via vaginal intercourse, can result in reproduction. Contrasting with this is the female "basic pattern," which involves motivation to be desired by a male partner and, in some sense, the ability to control the male's sexual behaviour, and which involves mechanisms, such as "automatic" vaginal penetration without discomfort. This can be manifested as a "desire to be desired", although research into these specific aspects of female sexual desire is at a very early stage . . . .[5]

Different summaries are given when researchers organize survey responses about reasons people desire sex. Some of the reasons people give for having sex include a desire for emotional closeness, increased commitment, bonding, and pleasure. A community study revealed a desire for sexual activity to express love, experience pleasure, relieve tension, and respond to a partner's wishes.[6] An older study of college students included such reasons as valuing a partner and feeling valued by a partner, experiencing relief

---

3. Chivers, "A Brief Update," 407.
4. Hayes, "Circular and Linear," 130–41.
5. Bancroft, "Sexual Desire," 167–68.
6. Cain, "Sexual Functioning," 266–76.

from stress, providing nurturance, increasing a sense of power for oneself and one's partner, experiencing pleasure, and procreation.[7]

Sexual Attraction

People invest considerable time and money to look attractive. And people pay close attention to the appearance of others. In addition to advertisements focused on an improved visual appearance, many commercials tout attractive fragrances. It appears that the brain's visual and smell (i.e., olfactory) systems are tuned to a quick analysis of cues linked to fitness. In this section, I am drawing on a recent summary of sexual attraction research by Jon Maner and his colleagues.[8]

The brain's attentional system is located in the posterior part of the parietal lobe. Normally functioning attentional processes focus on a salient stimulus, end that targeted focus, and subsequently orient toward another stimulus. For example, if you are planning on picking up a guest at an airport and have a picture of the person, you intentionally scan the crowd for faces similar to the one in your picture. You naturally orient from one face to another in search of a match. And you screen out other faces. Motivational processes guide the attentional system through the orienting processes by identifying key characteristics in the environment.

Both women and men search for mates who appear physically fit. In general, people with highly symmetrical characteristics are more attractive, and symmetry is linked to a strong immune system and overall genetic fitness. Women tend to select men who are socially dominant. Social dominance is linked to high levels of testosterone. The brain-linked bias toward attractiveness is not just based on what people say. Laboratory studies using eye-tracking technology identify how long men and women look at attractive faces. The bias is strongest for people who are single and interested in a sexual relationship. A difference between the sexes exists. Men tend to look longer at physically attractive women, and women tend to prefer men who display evidence of high social status. Both gay men and heterosexual men prefer sexual partners who are relatively younger than themselves, and they place an emphasis on physical attractiveness.

What might influence the motivation to focus on attractiveness? Researchers find that an almost magnetic property exists for attractive faces when people have a mating mindset. Here's an example of how the mindset is studied. A mindset can be created by giving people a short story to read

---

7. Hill, "Individual Differences," 27–45.
8. Maner et al., "Adaptive Relationship," 153–68.

or words about loving and kissing. Then a series of faces are presented and attention measured. In the blink of an eye (i.e., milliseconds), people who were primed by the mating mindset focused more on the attractive faces and sustained their attention on those faces longer than those who were not primed.

For women, psychological changes are linked to different points in the menstrual cycle. On days before and the day of ovulation, when the probability of conception is most likely, women show higher interest in their partners. The biological measure of interest is an increase in the diameter of the pupil. Also, using eye-tracking methodology, researchers find that women who were ovulating attended to more highly attractive men.

Because of the variations in the menstrual cycle and the obvious importance of timing to successful reproduction, researchers have focused attention on the time surrounding ovulation. Several findings describe commonly occurring behavior patterns linked to this time when fertility is optimal. Women report increases in self-stimulation, sexual desire, and sexual fantasies. They are more interested in social gatherings and wear more sexually provocative clothes. And they show a greater interest in men who appear fit.

Men appear biologically adapted to recognize the scent of a woman who nears her peak period of fertility. When men are presented with clothes worn by women at different points in their menstrual cycle, they preferred the clothes worn by ovulating women. And men biologically responded to the clothes as measured by higher testosterone levels compared to the men in a control condition who smelled similar clothes, which were not worn by ovulating women. The men were unaware of a woman's ovulation status when they were exposed to the scents in women's clothes. Also of interest, the men who smelled the clothes of an ovulating woman increased their responding to sexual words and ideas more than did men in other conditions. Other research, based on women's descriptions of their mates' behavior, indicates increased guarding behavior. An example of guarding behavior is actively becoming more possessive of a woman's time when she is ovulating. In experimental conditions, men displayed more risk taking when an ovulating woman was present suggesting an unaware effect of a woman's fertility status on how men behaved.

Women are also responsive to the scent of men. Women prefer men whose scents indicate genetic differences related to immune system functioning. They prefer the scent of men who appear highly symmetrical, especially when the women were ovulating. Women also prefer the scent of men with high levels of testosterone, as do gay men. But heterosexual men do not show a preference for the scent of testosterone.

In summary, men and women are largely unaware of how their brains are designed to focus attention on sexually attractive people. And people are largely unaware of how biological states or induced states motivate their attentional systems toward potential mates. When people decide on moral rules to govern sexuality, the level of awareness would seem to be important. We are only beginning to learn about the quick and automatic response patterns that prime sexual responding in people with heterosexual and other sexual orientations. Awareness is a factor in how early people can engage in control processes when it comes to limiting sexual responding. Many of the sex-related moral rules are focused on what to stop doing.

Sexual Responses

Some sex researchers present videos of sexual activity to volunteers in laboratory settings. They obtain physiological measures of sexual responding along with subjective reports of the experience. Information about sexual interest and visual responding can be obtained from eye-tracking technology and the time spent viewing a stimulus. Brain imaging can be used to identify which areas of the brain respond to sexual stimuli. Researchers measure the rigidity, circumference, and erection duration of a penis to determine variations in a man's physiological response to sexual stimuli.[9] A woman's genital response is taken from a probe inserted into the vagina, which measures vasocongestion.[10] The participants' subjective experience of sexual responses is based on self-reported ratings of items on questionnaires.

The relative specificity of the male response is illustrated in research reported by Meredith Chivers.[11] She and her colleagues found that men experience greater genital arousal and report greater subjective sexual responses when viewing increasingly sexualized content that included their preferred gender. The agreement between physiological arousal and subjective ratings is an average correlation of 0.66.

> Correlations range from -1.00 through zero to +1.00. Strong relationships are close to either -1.00 (strong negative relationship) or +1.00 (strong positive relationship).

---

9. Bancroft, "Sexual Desire," 167.
10. Chivers, "A Brief Update," 408–9.
11. Ibid., 407–14.

A woman's genital response also increases with sexual content, but there is a difference between heterosexual and lesbian women. Heterosexual women responded to both male and female sexual content. But lesbian women showed a stronger genital response to female stimuli. Subjective responses differed. The subjective arousal reports of heterosexual women did not closely match their genital responses. But there was a close match between subjective sexual arousal and genital arousal for lesbian women. The average correlation between physiological arousal and subjective reporting is 0.26, which helps demonstrate the considerably less obvious connection between the psychological or mental experience of sexual arousal and the measured genital response for women compared to the correlation for men (0.66).

Women and men respond differently to sexual stimuli. And same-sex oriented persons respond differently than do those attracted to persons of the opposite sex. The stronger connection for men might mean that sex-education and counseling programs need to be different for men and women and people of different sexual orientations.

Sexual Chemistry

Testosterone (T) continues to be a dominant factor in understanding male sexual response. When hypogonadal men are treated with testosterone, penile rigidity increases, and erections persist beyond the presence of a sexual stimulus. The role of T in women's sexuality is more nuanced. When given T, some women report increased sexual desire, but others do not. When women do respond to increased testosterone, the level of T is below the effective level for men.[12]

Sexuality and Self-Control

Bancroft and his colleagues have conducted research that leads to a dual control theory of sexuality. Two brain-based systems are at work—one is excitatory and the other inhibitory. Not surprisingly, people with low sexual inhibition are more likely to participate in high-risk sexual behavior, which is stronger in those with high levels of sexual excitation. People likely to experience sexual dysfunction were those with high sexual inhibition. And they may have low sexual excitation as well.[13] Self-control is a major factor

---

12. Bancroft, "Sexual Desire," 167–68.
13. Ibid., 168–70.

in morality. To be fair, moral rules require the same behavior of all persons. But people vary in their levels of sexual excitation and inhibition, which are the components of self-control. One may hypothesize that stricter moral rules will result in more noncompliance. Put another way, some people's biological status will make it easier for them to live a more saintly life.

Beginnings of Life: Contraception, Pregnancy, and Abortion

In Genesis, God tells the first couple to be fruitful and multiply. The joy of sex and the joy of welcoming children into the world are the themes of many stories. And such stories are common in the biblical narratives. In this section, I will review some of the facts about contraception, pregnancy, and abortion that can influence how Christians form moral judgments.

Contraception and Pregnancy

Since biblical times, people have sought ways to have children. In any given month, a woman attempting to get pregnant has, on average, a one-in-twenty chance of becoming pregnant.[14] Several factors affect the odds, such as age, regularity of menstrual cycles, frequency of sex, and various illnesses and medical conditions. In addition to praying for children, men like Abraham had sexual relations with other wives, concubines, slaves, or servants. Having an heir, and in some cases, a male heir, is still important in many cultures. Although many families pursue adoption, others seek alternative ways to enjoy having a family. Psychological stress will vary due to several factors, including the personal hopes and desires of the couple as well as pressure from family members and others within a given subculture. An additional source of stress for Christians can be their views about the ethical aspects of the available alternatives for reproduction and the consequences of some alternatives.

Alternative treatments for women and men include medication, surgery, and assisted reproductive technology (ART). The expenses of specialist treatments can produce considerable distress for many couples. In 2013, the cost in the United States for in vitro fertilization (IVF) was $12,400 for one cycle, and most require more than one treatment. The psychological cost to the woman can include uncomfortable symptoms of restlessness, irritability, and hot flashes along with headaches. IVF is a wasteful procedure. The production of eggs is boosted. To put matters in perspective, during IVF,

---

14. Speigelhalter, "Sex," para. 5.

about 90 percent of the eggs are not useful. Men produce vast quantities of sperm—some seventy-six million per ejaculation—but many sperm are not necessarily healthy. The procedure for determining healthy sperm appears primitive as it is based on visual inspection. When eggs are fertilized, the unused embryos are frozen. One moral decision is what should be done with unused embryos. The medical advances allow for the possible creation of a human life if further action is taken, but any given couple rarely pursues a large number of pregnancies.[15]

Other procedures may present a moral challenge to some individuals or couples. If a male partner has a low sperm count or a disease, sperm can be obtained from other men. Eggs can also be obtained from other women. If a woman cannot carry a pregnancy to term, she—or she and her partner—may choose a surrogate or gestational carrier.[16] Are these alternatives made possible by modern medicine similar to the ancient ways of men having sexual relations with other wives, concubines, and servants to obtain an heir? Was polygamy just about men having more sex, or were some of these relationships about the desire to have children and protect family wealth? I suspect that despite the immediate gratification of sex, ancient people were also concerned with having children to advance the general welfare of the family both in the short term and well into the future. They had little knowledge about reproduction. Drawing on farming analogies, women who did not bear children (or at least male children) were considered barren. Childless women may be seen as cursed or at least not blessed. It is not surprising that both men and women had the idea that a man's seed could be planted in another woman who might be more fruitful.

The decline in birth rates in Western cultures has been associated with the widespread availability of more effective methods of contraception. For various reasons people wish to limit the number of children they have. One method of contraception is also a method of controlling sexually transmitted infections (STIs). The long history of condoms and other methods of birth control indicate the importance of these products and the links these products have to morality.

There is some evidence that people in ancient cultures used various methods to limit contraception. Later Egyptians appeared to insert objects and compounds into vaginas to interfere with pregnancy. There are other references to condom use, but the mass production of condoms has been traced to 1844 in the U.S. following the invention of the vulcanization of

---

15. Kluger and Park, "Frontiers of Fertility," 50–54.
16 American Society for Reproductive Medicine, *Third-Party*, 3–16.

rubber by George Goodyear.[17] Various products were developed for several years until 1873, when Anthony Comstock led the charge to pass the Comstock Laws making all forms of contraception illegal in the United States.[18] To circumvent the restrictive law, people began to market the same products as feminine hygiene items.

War may have had an effect on condom use. During World War I, American troops were denied condoms. By the end of the war, they had high rates of STIs. By the 1920s, condoms along with other contraceptive methods were widely used. In the early years of the twentieth century, people continued to seek better ways of birth control.[19]

Researchers eventually developed the first birth control pill and received government approval in 1960. A few years later, in 1965, the U.S. Supreme Court ruled against the Comstock Laws that had limited the use of contraception.[20]

By 1968, an intrauterine device (IUD) was approved, but some women developed Pelvic Inflammatory Disease. The risk of disease outweighed the risk of pregnancy. By the 1980s better pills were developed. And in the 1990s the first long term injection, Depo Provera, was approved. Recent developments include the first emergency contraception, a slow release patch, an insertable ring, and a long-lasting IUD. Other improvements in pills developed, and in 2013, the morning after pill became available to teens without a prescription.[21]

Condoms offer protection against conception and sexually transmitted infections (STIs). Other methods offer varying degrees of protection against conceiving a new life. Protests by Roman Catholic Church leaders have made their perspective clear—that interfering with creating a new life is sinful—but data show a majority of Catholic women use birth control suggesting a possibility for feelings of guilt as these Christians violate religious teaching.

In recent years, beliefs about emergency contraceptives also called "Plan B" and "the morning after pills" added conservative Protestants to the ranks of those opposed to contraception. Many conservative Protestants oppose the use of emergency contraceptives because they believe that the morning after pill is a method of abortion rather than a method that

17. Gibson, "The Long," para. 4–8.
18. Coontz, *Marriage*, 193.
19. Planned Parenthood, "A History," 5.
20. PBS Online, "Timeline: The Pill."
21. Thompson, "A Brief History," para. 9–20.

prevents conception.²² Obviously, beliefs matter. In terms of psychopharmacology, there are no obvious negative effects on physical functioning attributed to the use of emergency contraceptives. Pharmacologically, Plan B pills appear quite safe, and they have been made available over the counter. In terms of pharmacokinetics, the pills, like common birth control pills, appear to prevent pregnancy in one of three ways. One, the menstrual cycle is changed and ovulation delayed. Two, eggs are not released from the ovaries. Three, a fertilized egg cannot attach to the uterus because the endometrium (i.e., lining) is irritated. The shared point of concern for Catholics and conservative Protestants is the possibility that a fertilized egg exists and that the egg will be removed from the mother, thus ending a human life.

The changing information about the advantages and disadvantages of the various forms of contraception requires constantly updating one's knowledge. Alexandra Sifferlin reported on the improvements in recent IUDs, which can last three to twelve years and are 99 percent effective. The failure rate for a shot lasting three months is typically 6 percent, and the rate is 9 percent for a patch and a ring. An implant may last three years and has a failure rate of 0.05 percent.[23]

Finally, outside the developed world, millions of girls become pregnant each year. And a substantial portion of these pregnancies are unintended. Paul Brandeis offered a summary of recent facts presented at the 2013 Women Deliver conference in Kuala Lumpur. The statistics are alarming: eight hundred women die during pregnancy and childbirth each day. By my calculations, approximately every two minutes a girl or woman dies during pregnancy and childbirth. For each of these 292,000 women who die each year, another twenty deal with related infections, disabilities, or injuries. The marital age is young in many parts of the world. For example, in Afghanistan, one in nine girls marries by age fifteen. There are about 210 million pregnancies each year. Of these, 33 million are unintended. Because about 90 percent of the world is associated with some religion, religious beliefs linked to pregnancy and abortion become highly relevant.[24]

Abortion

Abortion and mental health is the subject of much study by psychological scientists. According to Coontz, married women were seeking abortion

---

22. Moon, "Does Plan B," 15.
23. Sifferlin, "I Want," 19.
24. Raushenbush, "The Role."

with their husband's approval in the nineteenth century.[25] In the United States, the Supreme Court's 1973 decision in *Roe v. Wade*, resulted in legalized abortion.[26] In 1987, Surgeon General C. Everett Koop reviewed the scientific evidence and informed President Ronald Regan that the research was inadequate to address the psychological health of women who had an abortion. In later testimony before Congress, he reported no significant findings for physical health.[27]

In a review of the mental health research, Brenda Major and her team found that within the United States, some women who have had legal abortions experience mental health problems. But most women who terminate a pregnancy do not experience mental health problems. In their words,

> The most rigorous studies indicated that within the United States, the relative risk of mental health problems among adult women who have a single, legal, first-trimester abortion of an unwanted pregnancy is no greater than the risk among women who deliver an unwanted pregnancy.[28]

As with many studies dealing with sex and reproduction, ethical considerations and the difficulty in controlling so many variables make it difficult to establish causality. The best studies measure as many possible factors relevant to mental health and follow women before, during, and after pregnancy to understand the complex relationships that may be statistically linked to health status following an abortion. The effects of the situation that produced the unwanted pregnancy in the first place are another difficulty in discerning the effects of an abortion. There are many factors associated with an unplanned pregnancy. Some of those factors, such as substance abuse and high-risk sexual activity, are related to pre-existing health and mental health difficulties. Of course, abortion occurs within a social context, which includes religious and other cultural beliefs and attitudes, which may lessen or increase the personal conflict over the pregnancy and abortion experiences.

More recent work by Diana Greene Foster, associate professor of obstetrics and gynecology at the University of California, San Francisco, attempts to address some of the problems with previous research.[29] She has data on nearly one thousand women who either decided to have an abor-

---

25. Coontz, *Marriage*, 171.
26. Ibid., 255.
27. Major et al., "Abortion," 863–64.
28. Ibid., 863.
29. Lang, "What Happens."

tion or were turned away from an abortion clinic. Data about depression and anxiety indicated a similar status for both groups of women. Those turned away experienced more anxiety, but after six months, there were no significant differences between the groups. The two groups of women differed on general health and economic status. Those in the turnaway group had higher rates of hypertension and chronic pelvic pain. Also, adjusting for pre-event conditions, women who did not have an abortion were three times as likely to be below the federal poverty line compared to those who had an abortion.

The medical and psychological facts of abortion can contribute to a moral judgment, which depends on an analysis of care and harm. In other words, if one's morality involves a consideration of the possible harmful effects of an abortion on the unborn child and on the mother, then understanding the biopsychological impact of an abortion decision is relevant to forming a moral judgment about abortion. But a scientific understanding does little to inform the discussion based on other dimensions of morality, such as respect for authority or loyalty to a faith tradition.

Summary

In this chapter about psychology and sexuality, I reviewed some findings about sexuality that could have a bearing upon the moral issues that divide Christians. Science has its limits. Scientific evidence can inform a discussion about morality when moral arguments are based on observable evidence. But moral views derived from divine revelation are beyond the scope of scientific inquiry.

In romantic tales, sex occurs within the context of a loving relationship. There are many dimensions to a contemporary understanding of love. A psychological view involves an understanding of attachment theory. And researchers have found that the nature of attachment between parents and children has implications for understanding how Christians relate to God. The six dimensions of the SCOPES model can be applied to thinking about love and sexuality.

Sexuality can be viewed in distinct ways. For men and some women, sexuality begins with sexual desire. This stage is followed by sexual arousal, which leads to orgasm. For some women, sexual activity can begin for reasons other than sexual desire, but when arousal occurs, sexual desire may increase. So for at least some women, sexual activity may be more circular than linear.

Sexual attraction is an automatic process and includes a quick appraisal of features linked to physical fitness. People who are single and interested in a relationship are more attentive to attractive features of potential mates. Biology plays an important role in sexual desire, but we are usually not aware of the influence of biological and biochemical processes, such as the differential influence of time of ovulation on a woman's sex-related behavior or the impact of scents on sexual responsiveness.

Researchers find that men and women are different when responding to sexually stimulating imagery. Men are more aware of sexual arousal and link that arousal to subjective sexual responses, such as thoughts and feelings. The link between arousal and subjective responses is much weaker for women.

Self-control is an important component of morality. Research shows that people vary in their levels of sexual excitation and sexual inhibition. People with low inhibition are more likely to engage in risky sexual behavior. Those high in sexual inhibition are more likely to experience sexual dysfunction.

Scientific advances have made it possible to exert considerable control over becoming pregnant and sustaining a pregnancy. Women who could not become pregnant by natural means now have various options available. Women who become pregnant but do not wish to be pregnant have medically safe ways of ending the pregnancy. The procedures to control conception and terminate a pregnancy are generally medically safe. And the procedures do not appear to result in long-term negative psychological effects for most women. However, all of these procedures are matters addressed by Christian moral teaching.

Additional Resources

1. **The Fertilization Process.** A short video by Parent's Magazine illustrated the process of fertilization. https://www.youtube.com/watch?v=vFfqLs94iHc

2. **Sexual Attraction.** A series of videos from BBC Explorations answers the question, "What makes you sexy?" This link is to the series: https://www.youtube.com/playlist?list=PLA6210A383F643B1D

Discussion Questions

1. How can a consideration of using birth control influence the rightness or wrongness of a moral decision?
2. How might knowledge about the wellbeing of most women after an abortion influence moral thinking?
3. At what point in the process of reproduction should we consider a new life to have begun?
4. If life begins when a sperm fertilizes an egg, what should people do about unused fertilized eggs in laboratories?
5. What rights should unborn children have? What rights should women have to control what happens to their bodies?

6

SEXUALITY AND HEALTHY RELATIONSHIPS

Ted was the pastor of a large church in Colorado Springs, Colorado. And he was the president of the National Association of Evangelicals. In 2006, a sex and drug scandal broke. As a result, he resigned his positions and sought treatment. What was his problem? In 2013, Pastor Ted Haggard shared some thoughts on his blog. His reflections illustrate the problem of understanding the issue of sexuality, morality, psychology, and Christianity.

> I was so ashamed in 2006 when my scandal broke. The therapeutic team that dug in on me insisted that I did not have a spiritual problem or a problem with cognitive ability, and that I tested in normal ranges on all of my mental health tests. . . . Contrary to popular reports, my core issue was not sexual orientation, but trauma. I went through EMDR, a trauma resolution therapy, and received some immediate relief and, as promised, that relief was progressive. When I explain that to most Evangelical leaders, their eyes glaze over. They just don't have a grid for the complexity of it all. It is much more convenient to believe that every thought, word, and action is a reflection of our character, our spirituality, and our core.[1]

In this chapter I will review findings about sexuality following birth. I have chosen to present the topics in a general developmental sequence. For example, I begin with a review of circumcision, which is a decision parents commonly make close to the time a child is born. I then discuss sex education, which usually begins in childhood. Next I consider various health and mental health aspects of relationships, which first become issues involving sex during the adolescent years and continuing into adulthood. Finally, I

---

1. Haggard, "Suicide," para. 5–6.

turn to a discussion of sexual minorities who usually become aware of their differences from the majority during the adolescent years. I conclude with a brief discussion of some difficulties people face when it comes to sexual health. As with the last chapter, this chapter is not meant to be a comprehensive textbook on sexual health but rather a review of topics discussed in Part Two.

Childhood and Adolescence

Circumcision

Male circumcision is not an official part of Christian practices. Circumcision was the primary mark of the sacred covenant between God and Abraham and his descendants. Infant boys continue to be circumcised by most Jews and many people in other cultures. There is some evidence of benefits and evidence that some nonmedical circumcisions result in infections and death. Two moral issues for Christians include respect for a boy's right to make his own decision about an invasive and optional medical procedure and choosing to be involved in political activism to prevent harm to boys from unsafe procedures.

Female circumcision is a current topic of moral concern. Although the term *circumcision* is in common use, the term *female genital cutting* (FGC) has been used because the cutting is more intrusive than the cutting of a boy's foreskin. The different term, *female genital mutilation* (FGM), conveys the extreme cutting in some procedures. Carla Obermeyer reviewed evidence in 2005 and found some health consequences, but she noted problems in drawing firm conclusions because of the limitations in extant studies during the years of her review (from 1997 to 2005).[2] Although Christians do not practice FGM, a moral issue is the decision to act or stand by in cases where Christians are in a position to protect girls from harm.

Sex Education

Sex education has been a controversial topic in the United States. Most sex-education programs provide children ages nine to twelve with accurate information about puberty before their bodies begin to change. Sex educators teach more about anatomy and human reproduction as children age. Adolescents learn more details about healthy relationships, sexual health,

---

2. Obermeyer, "The Consequences," 443–61.

sexual attraction, sexual activity, and so forth. They also learn moral values by what is presented or withheld and how the information is conveyed. Of course, adolescents learn facts, myths, and values from peers, social media, and other readily available resources.

In recent decades, governments have provided sex information online. And schools have included various sex-education programs, which can result in protests when programs teach or fail to teach the sexual values held by the parents. Several components of the programs are controversial, including abstinence, contraception, masturbation, and abortion.

In 2004, Michael Young of the University of Arkansas reported that the first abstinence education grants were funded by the Office of Adolescent Pregnancy Programs about twenty years ago. He noted several problems with current programs. One, the definition used by the government to define the goals of abstinence-only programs is vague. Students were not informed about sexual activities that met the definition of being sexually abstinent. Two, Young observed problems in evaluating the effectiveness of the existing programs, though data indicate some programs yielded positive results. Three, he also identified problems in accuracy of information. For example, some programs do not include information about the value of condom use in preventing sexually transmitted infections.[3]

If scientists are funded to study the effectiveness of various sex-education programs, it will be possible to discover which components of which programs help adolescents make healthier choices. Beliefs about morality influence what is taught about contraception, abortion, and sexual activity. Even if it could be shown that programs that include teaching about contraception are linked to significant declines in teen pregnancy, Christian beliefs about the immorality of contraceptive use and premarital sex cannot be changed by scientific evidence unless programs are based on consequences rather than a biblical principle.

Premarital Sex

Western cultures have changed when it comes to attitudes toward unmarried persons having sexual relationships. Lawrence Finer reported that by age forty-four, most people in the U.S. have sex before they marry (96 percent of men, 94 percent of women).[4] Since most in the U.S. identify as Christians, it is obvious that most Christians do not adhere to the traditional moral beliefs of waiting until marriage before having sex.

3. Young, "What's Wrong," 148–56.
4. Finer, "Trends," 73–78.

Attitudes toward premarital sex changed toward a more permissive stance between the years 1972 and 2012. Survey respondents were given four attitude options regarding their opinions about sex before marriage: always wrong, almost always wrong, sometimes wrong, or not wrong at all. They could also choose "I don't know." In the following table, I summarized the data for just the two years—1972 and 2012.[5]

Answer	1972	2012
always wrong	34.2	21.3
almost always wrong	10.9	5.0
sometimes wrong	24.1	15.1
not wrong at all	26.5	56.0
don't know	4.3	2.6

The recent pattern of cohabitation and casual sexual relationships in Western cultures means that large percentages of persons do not follow traditional Christian moral teaching. A 2013 report from the U.S. Center for Disease Control and Prevention (CDC) revealed that 48 percent of women cohabited with a partner in their first relationship compared to 23 percent whose first relationship was a marriage. There seems to be an educational factor. Cohabiting was more common (70 percent) among those with less than a high school education compared to 47 percent for those with a college degree.[6]

Anthony Paik of the University of Iowa explored possible links between adolescent sexual activity and marital dissolution. He reviewed previous research indicating that since 1988, about a third of female teenagers have their first sexual intercourse between the ages of fifteen and seventeen. Four national studies found an association between premarital sex and increased risk of divorce. If the woman only had sex with her future husband, the risk of divorce was not increased. In Paik's study, age and desirability of premarital sex were significant factors. Women at higher risk for divorce had their first sexual intercourse before age sixteen or had sex that was not completely wanted. For those who wanted sexual intercourse, which began at ages sixteen and seventeen, other factors were important to understand the risk of divorce, such as the number of sexual partners. Paik opined that

5. Smith and Son, *Final Report*, 10.
6. Copen et al., "First Premarital," 1–6.

those who had early sexual relations experienced changes in beliefs and attitudes about marriage and relationships.[7]

Because more and more people are deferring marriage for years (discussed in the next section), the incidence of premarital sex is only likely to increase. Social attitudes are changing, but it is doubtful churches will change their official stance on the immorality of premarital sex. This widening gap between behavior and belief would appear to result in feelings of guilt, anxiety about having sexual activity become public, and possibly shame over engaging in forbidden behavior for those who are deeply committed to their faith.

Teen Pregnancy

Most U.S. teen mothers (almost 89 percent) were single when they gave birth according to 2013 data from the U.S. Department of Health and Human Services. The teen pregnancy rates have declined since 1991 but remain higher than those of many other developed countries.[8] The rates also declined in England and Wales.[9] Although the rate of teen pregnancy is improving, many young women face pregnancy with feelings of being overwhelmed.

Pregnancies can be difficult for women who wish to be pregnant and have a supportive partner. Most young single women face struggles to find spiritual, emotional, financial, psychological, and health care support. The trend in the U.S. is away from abortion options and toward caring for the mother and her unborn child. Although conservative Christians do not approve of sex outside of marriage, the web pages of conservative organizations such as Focus on the Family and Youth for Christ show sensitivity to the feelings and plight of teen mothers.[10] Teens who wish to consider abortion will find support from churches with prochoice positions such as the Presbyterian Church (USA), the Episcopal Church, the United Methodist Church, the United Church of Christ, and the Unitarian Universalist Association of Congregations.

---

7. Paik, "Adolescent Sexuality," 472–85.
8. "Teen Births," para. 1.
9. Trimmer, "Teen Pregnancy," para. 1.
10. FocusontheFamily.com; YFC.net

Marriage and Romantic Relationships

The concept of marriage is difficult to define if we look at how people married in different cultures throughout recorded history. There are examples of the obvious. A man and a woman live together for years and in the course of their relationship they have children and raise them together. Their relationship may be associated with some form of approval by a governing authority, in which case they are recognized as married. Although many Christians begin their marriage with a church wedding, marriages are governed by national or regional governments. For example, in the U.S., the states make the laws governing marriage. Challenges occur when state laws are considered to violate the U.S. Constitution.

Marriage and Relationships in Recent History

For most of human history, marriage has not been about love. People did not choose whom they would marry but followed the dictates of their parents. Deals were made that seemed to advance a family's standing within a culture or promote a better relationship between one group of persons and another. Tribes and nations have bonded together on the basis of an arranged marriage. New leaders emerged when a child inherited estates covering large swaths of land inhabited by a plethora of people. Marriages were made on earth and motivated by concerns for safety and wellbeing. As Western societies changed during the period known as the Enlightenment, individual rights appeared as a concern. Love-based marriage developed in the 1800s and reached prominence in the 1920s. By the 1950s, love-based marriage appeared to be normal.

In the nineteenth century, a syrupy sweet sentimental notion of a loving marriage emerged. Men and women had different cultural roles. Men "brought home the bacon," and women took care of home and hearth. Women were the "fairer sex" (likely a euphemism for weaker). And women cared for children. They were morally pure and superior. Men were to be strong and in charge of their wives and children, but they were expected to treat them kindly and lovingly. Yet churches and organizations would hold men responsible if their wives or children got out of line. Sex went undercover for the middle class and did not re-emerge as a public topic until the late nineteenth century.

In the first few decades of the twentieth century, women made great strides toward equality on an international basis. Women entered colleges and employment albeit at incredibly low wages compared to men. Eventually they won the right to vote. But they were still dependent on husbands in legal matters.

Sexual information became increasingly available, condoms were in use, but there was still no consistent and effective birth control method. Abortion was available. Young men and women increasingly went out together in urban settings to enjoy the silent movies where lessons in kissing were practiced in that "house of prostitution on wheels," the automobile. The Wall Street crash crashed many relationships. Marriages were deferred or canceled as some moved back with parents. The depression was long and hard on people in industrialized nations.

War followed the depression of the 1930s and brought with it new challenges to relationships. During the war years 1939–45, men fought and women remained at home caring for families until women were needed to support the war effort in factories and other key positions. The extreme demands of fighting such a massive war posed many moral challenges beyond the scope of this book. Clearly, there were many violations of the care-harm dimension. Let me identify a few relevant to changes in marriage, relationships and sexuality.

For the first time on earth, there was more mass destruction of human beings than ever before. Every loss of life represented a lost relationship. In some cases, a dead soldier or civilian meant many lost relationships if the person was married and had children. Also, the long separation of couples as a result of war meant many relationships were destroyed even when both spouses survived. Some relationships ended due to infidelity. Many relationships were strained as returning soldiers struggled to re-adjust to civilian life but women had little protection when it came to spouse abuse. The lack of equality for women also meant they had to give up their war time jobs when men returned from deployment. And many young women were suddenly widows at a time when women had few career opportunities.

I'll only mention a few other moral issues to illustrate the factors present before the appearance of an ideal life-long relationship between one woman and one man was to disappear as a norm in many Western cultures. During World War II many women became pregnant as the result of rape by occupying forces.[11] Some women had loving relationships with foreign soldiers. Many became "war brides"[12] and not a few were pregnant as they followed their husbands or boyfriends to new homelands.

---

11. Schuessler, "The Dark Side of Liberation."

12. According to Duncan Barrett writing in the L.A. Times, there were 70,000 women from Britain alone who awaited approval to join their U.S. husbands.

For a brief period of time during the 1950s and early 1960s, an ideal Christian marriage and family unit of a working husband, homemaker wife, and two children seemed to exist. Whether it actually existed is not our focus. The fact is, it would not be long before Western cultures entered the contemporary era where divorce, remarriage, and sex outside of marriage are common regardless of Christian affiliation.

Recent Relationship Data

In the United States, about half of adults are married, which is a historically low number. The average age of first marriage has increased for women (26.5) and men (28.7). About 72 percent of adults have been married at least once. Divorce rates have stabilized. About half of first marriages survive. Is marriage becoming obsolete? About 39 percent of Americans agree that marriage is becoming obsolete.[13] Despite the low marriage rates, many couples continue to marry, and many divorced persons remarry.

Regardless of marital status, people still enjoy intimate relationships. The incidence of cohabitation has increased for those never married as well as for those married. Cohabitation is one reason given to explain both the decline in first marriages as well as the decline in remarriage. Sharon Jayson of *USA Today* reported that the remarriage rate dropped more than 40 percent in the past twenty years. And 37 percent of those in cohabitation relationships have been married before.[14] Considering the rate of marriage and divorce, it appears Americans have multiple love relationships. This practice of multiple partners in a lifetime represents unstructured polygamy.

Plural Marriage

Plural marriage appears to be the norm throughout human history. First, let me clarify the terminology. The word *polygamy* is used as a generic term by many writers to refer to committed romantic relationships involving more than two persons. The most common form of polygamy has been polygyny. Polygyny means having many wives. Less common is polyandry—the practice of a woman having more than one husband. Polyamorous relationships are those involving multiple adult partners who may or may not be married. Because polygamy is not legal in the U.S. and other Western countries, it is

---

13. Cohn et al., "Barely Half."
14. Jayson, "Remarriage," para. 3–8.

likely best to refer to the polygamous-like units as polyamorous cohabitants, but writers have not been consistent in their use of terminology.

Most Native Americans practiced polygamy. Gizitdinov reported that polygamy is legal in at least forty countries, most of which are in Africa (e.g., South Africa, Kenya) and Asia.[15] According to Tsoaledi Thobejane and Takayindisa Flora, more than seventy percent of societies permit men to marry more than one wife.[16] And as noted previously, many instances of polygamy are illustrated among the patriarchs and kings in the Bible. In addition to the well-known reports of polygyny by nineteenth-century American Mormons, polygyny continues to be practiced in the United States by Fundamentalist Mormons and Muslims. Researchers estimate between fifty to one hundred thousand Muslims live in polygamous families in the U.S.[17] Considering Muslims and other ethnic groups, as many as five hundred thousand people live in polyamorous relationships. Interestingly, in terms of this book on morality, Goldfeder describes the relationship as "ethical non-monogamy." He attaches the following descriptive terms, which sound much like a moral justification: "loving, committed, concurrent, consensual relationships with multiple partners."[18]

Studying multiple relationships poses a challenge. In one study, participants were asked about need fulfillment in the first and second two-person relationships. They found that each relationship in a polyamorous family tends to be independent. Having an additional relationship did not have much of an effect on need fulfillment within the other relationship.[19]

A 2013 legal decision might affect the behavior patterns of polyamorous family groups in the United States of America. Judge Clark Waddoups of the U.S. District Court ruled against Utah State's law prohibiting cohabitation in a case brought by Kody Brown, Meri Brown, Janelle Brown, Christine Brown, and Robyn Sullivan. The decision refers to religious beliefs. They are members of the Apostolic United Brethren Church. The judge let stand the State's law against bigamy.[20]

15. Gizitdinov, "Polygamy," para. 6.
16. Thobejane and Flora, "An Exploration of Polygamous," 1058.
17. Hagerty, "Some Muslims," para. 2.
18. Goldfeder, "Polygamy and DOMA," paras. 2–3.
19. Mitchell, "Need Fulfillment," 329–39.
20. Schwartz, "A Utah Law," para. 1–6.

Relationships and the Welfare of Children

Most would agree that parents have a moral obligation to care for their children. Some relationships pose a challenge to identify lines of responsibility. It is not surprising to find children emotionally attached to a care giver who has functioned as a parent. Biological parents usually have a greater claim on their children than do others who have assumed the parent role. Difficulties can occur for children who experience the loss of a loving parent or parent figure due to changes in relationships regardless of how those changes came about. For example, caregivers may separate for a variety of reasons, new caregivers may appear in the child's life due to the decisions of one or more caregivers, and other changes may be ordered by courts that have identified the rights and duties of one or more adults in the child's life.

Divorce continues to be a common cause of disrupted relationships for children. The interests of the child are often considered but post-divorce parent-child relationships vary in the degree to which children fare in terms of the care versus harm dimension of morality.

Surrogate mothers play a helpful role for childless couples. But who are the legal parents of children born outside of a biological mother and father relationship? A 2013 legal decision might be relevant. In cases of egg donors and surrogate mothers, a child can have three natural parents.[21] Some couples that hire a surrogate mother are same-sex couples. In such cases, only one member of the couple may be the legal parent, which poses obvious legal difficulties for the other member who may be equally involved in the care of the child. Some of these issues may be clarified by new laws permitting same-sex marriage.

Sex in Relationships

Pamela Regan has summarized research on sex in relationships.[22] For the most part, despite changes in attitudes that approve of sex outside of marriage, both men and women believe sex should be reserved for people in committed, loving relationships. Most couples have sex two or three times per week. The frequency declines with age. A small percentage reports no sex in the past year. In one study, 7 percent reported sex four or more times per week. Cohabiting couples tend to have more sex than do married couples.

---

21. Goldfeder, "Polygamy and DOMA," para. 7.
22. Regan, "The Mating," 202–6.

In the U.S., the most common type of sex is vaginal intercourse as reported by 95 percent of people reporting about the last time they had sex. Oral sex is the next most common type reported by 24 percent of married men and 17 percent of married women. Other types of sex (e.g., anal) are quite rare.[23]

Expressed preferences for sex fit the pattern of reported sexual activity. Both young women and young men report the most appealing type of sex is vaginal intercourse. This holds true for older women and men as well. Most people in a relationship reported being satisfied with their sexual relationship and their overall relationship. Sexual satisfaction is highly correlated with relationship satisfaction. As Regan observes, the correlation does not indicate a causal relationship between relationship satisfaction and sexual satisfaction.[24]

Same-Sex Orientation and Relationships

There is some variation in terminology that can be confusing when reading about same-sex relationships. In this section I plan to address both the terminology used by scientists and relevant research findings.

Sexual Attraction

Sexual attraction is at least in part informed by prior attachment experiences and love relationships. People form friendships with same-sex and other-sex persons. Feeling sexually attracted to someone has a different quality that is hard to measure. Most men are either oriented toward the same sex or the opposite sex but some research suggests women are more flexible in their sexual attraction. It is probably best to view sexual attraction on a sliding scale from strong to weak where the focus of the attraction is a person of the same sex or the opposite sex. Clearly, some report feelings toward both sexes whilst a small percentage of persons do not experience sexual attraction to anyone.

In a simple scheme, people view sexual attraction as either toward one's own sex or toward the opposite sex. I have heard psychologists refer to a continuum from same-sex on one end, bisexual in the middle, and the opposite sex on the other end. But I don't think either approach fits the data. Sexual attraction is not just about the sex of the potential sexual partner,

23. Ibid., 206–7.
24. Ibid., 207–9.

but it is also about the strength of the sex drive. And, although rare, sexual attraction can be toward objects and animals.

Sexual attraction is not just an inner urge. Sexual attraction can vary in response to environmental variables, such as a person's view of a romantic evening. Of course sexual attraction can vary in response to medication or drugs that increase or decrease sexual desire. I think it best to think of typical sexual attraction on two simultaneous continua from none to strong. The feelings of a hypothetical heterosexual woman might be illustrated in the table below by placing an "X" under "None" for sexual attraction to Women and an "X" under "Strong" for sexual attraction to Men.

Sexual Attraction: Two Parallel Experiences

Attraction to	None	Weak	Moderate	Strong
Women	X			
Men				X

The above table of sexual attraction as two experiences can remind us that some people are asexual—they do not experience an attraction to either men or women. Other people may experience sexual attraction but at very low levels. Such people may say they "can take it or leave it" when it comes to having sex. Other people experience strong sexual urges many times a week. The parallel lines for women and men allow for an indication of relative strength in people of either biological sex who find themselves attracted to either or both men and women.

Understanding sexual attraction requires an understanding of both the focus of the attraction and the strength of the attraction. And it is important to note that sexual attraction does not indicate sexual activity, and it is not the same as sexual orientation.

Sexual Orientation

Sexual orientation is a subset of personal identity. When it comes to relating to others romantically, most people are sexually oriented toward the opposite sex, but some people are oriented toward both men and women while others are only oriented toward relationships with people of the same sex. Sexual orientation is not just about sex because it involves relationships with people found to be attractive and who share common interests and pursuits. Some are sexually active and some are not. Often not welcomed in conservative religious and other social contexts of the general population, sexual minorities have established their own churches, clubs, bars, and other places to hang out. When lived out, sexual orientation appears to evolve into alternative lifestyles. In the United States, sexual orientation is usually identified by one of four social labels: heterosexual, gay, lesbian, or bisexual. Sexual orientation emerges during early adolescence when feelings of sexual attraction are experienced toward members of one's own sex, the opposite sex, or both sexes. The causes of sexual orientation are unknown but seem to be a mix of biological and cultural factors. The experience of sexual attraction usually appears as a natural rather than a chosen experience. Bullying, discrimination, and rejection are reasons sexual minorities often do not reveal their sexual orientation as a part of their identity. In some parts of the culture, disclosing sexual identity comes at great personal cost.

Therapy and Sexual Orientation

Although some people report changing their sexual orientation as a result of psychotherapy, the preponderance of the evidence indicates such attempts can result in serious harm, including depression and suicide. Changing sexual orientation is not recommended by leading professional associations for mental health practitioners.[25] Mark Yarhouse at Regent University in Virginia Beach, a Christian psychologist, has proposed a form of therapy he calls "Sexual Identity Therapy," which focuses on helping people who question their sexual orientation.[26] This type of therapy is exploratory and does not guide the client toward a preconceived outcome.

Same-Sex Marriage and Relationships

Because same-sex marriage is a recent phenomenon, most people in same-sex relationships are unmarried. Although some census and other data are available, it is difficult to know how many people are in long-term or marital same-sex relationships. Based on survey data, the American Psychological Association estimated that 40 to 60 percent of gay men and between 45 and 80 percent of lesbians are in a romantic relationship. Between 18 and 28 percent of gay couples and 8 to 21 percent of lesbian couples have been together ten or more years. Many same sex couples are parents (33 percent of lesbian couples, 22 percent of gay couples).[27]

25. Serovich, "A Systematic," 227–38.
26. Yarhouse, "Narrative Sexual," 196–210.
27. American Psychological Association, "Answers to Your Questions," 4–5.

The status of children and their parents in family units involving LGBT persons can vary considerably due to applicable laws and how the children came into the family. For example, some children were born as the result of heterosexual relationships, some are born as a result of insemination, some are adopted, and some are foster children. The parents may or may not have a biological relationship to the children. In cases of gay and lesbian partners, those who are without a legal connection to a child may still have a considerable emotional connection but have no legal standing when relationships change. Some transpersons had children before transitioning, and some arranged to freeze eggs or sperm for use after transitioning. Some strategies for having children are very expensive; thus, socioeconomic status will have an influence on family relationships.[28]

Homosexuality and Mental Disorders[29]

Homosexuality is not a mental disorder. The issue is sometimes raised because, at one time, the *Diagnostic and Statistical Manual of Mental Disorders* (DSM) published by the American Psychiatric Association included homosexuality as a psychiatric disorder. Research has shown that experiencing same-sex attraction is a common experience of human beings. Katherine Milar credits psychological scientist Evelyn Hooker with the research that led to the removal of homosexuality from the DSM. In the early 1950s, Hooker used interviews and psychological tests to study homosexual and heterosexual men. People in both groups experienced a range of psychological adjustment; however, two-thirds of the participants in each group were considered to have average or better adjustment.[30] People who identify as having other than a heterosexual orientation often experience harassment, bullying, isolation, and discrimination if their sexual orientation becomes known; thus it is not surprising that they may experience high rates of emotional distress and suicide attempts as well as become involved in high-risk sexual activity and substance abuse.[31]

---

28. Mezey, *LGBT Families*, 71–112.

29. I used the term *homosexual* in this paragraph because of its historical reference. The word *homosexual* carries with it beliefs about mental illness and demeaning stereotypes.

30. Milar, "The Myth," 24.

31. Just the Facts Coalition, "Just the Facts."

Sex and Gender Differences

Although the observable anatomical differences between women and men are obvious, sex differences can be found in multiple dimensions of human functioning, including cognition, emotion, and behavior. The bases for sex differences are often attributed to the effects of hormones, genetics, maturation rate, and environment. Here are some examples. Androgens appear to have an organizing effect on the human brain during development. Sex hormones may also have effects on cognition later in life. Increased estrogen levels are linked to lower spatial ability and enhanced verbal and motor ability in women. Men with lower average testosterone levels do better on spatial tests and mathematical reasoning than do those with higher average levels. From a genetic perspective, the sex chromosomes (X and Y) are on the twenty-third pair of the twenty-three pairs of chromosomes in the human genome. If both chromosomes are X, then the person is genetically female. If there is one X and one Y chromosome then the person is genetically male. A genetic basis for differences in cognition has not yet been established.[32]

Research has documented consistent findings that girls mature sooner than boys. They develop larger vocabularies and use more complex linguistic constructions early on. They are generally better readers, and their speech is easier to understand. No doubt environment plays a role in the skills valued for men and women. Teasing apart the contributions from biological and environmental variables remains an ongoing process.

The study of epigenetics offers promise for expanding our understanding of genetics and environment. *Epigenetics* refers to gene regulation. The activation of a gene may take place due to environmental influences or other yet unknown factors. Research on identical twins documented differences with age. The differences were much larger for twins who had lived apart and developed different lifestyles than for those who did not live apart.[33]

Research into changes in sexual behavior associated with brain functioning has been limited due to the intrusive nature of such research. Reports have suggested some consistent findings. Orbitofrontal damage has been associated with reduced inhibitions resulting in public sexual behavior, such as masturbation. Dorsolateral lesions appear to reduce sexual interest.[34]

---

32. Kolb and Whishaw, *Fundamentals*, 316–25.
33. Ibid., 336.
34. Ibid., 455.

Gender

Gender refers to the personal identity people consider as true for themselves. The separation of gender from sexual identity occurred when clinicians became aware that the usual characteristics of sexuality such as genitalia and reproductive organs did not always match a person's identity as a girl, boy, woman, or man. Clinicians use the term *natal gender* to refer to the identity assigned to children based on their sex characteristics when they are born. This early gender assignment may not fit well with the person's self-perception later in life. Some other terms are probably worth noting. *Transgender* refers to a range of people who identify as different from their natal gender for brief to long periods of time. *Transsexual* refers to a person who has changed their sexual identity. This change includes a change in gender identity and often includes a change in biological characteristics by means of hormone treatment and sex reassignment surgery.

Primary Gender Roles

For most of recorded history until a few decades ago, women were expected to be mothers and homemakers. Their lives were focused on their husbands and their children. Those without children were expected to be devoted to their husbands and involved in charitable work. During World War II, the major parties to the conflict were sending millions of men into combat. But factory work was needed to produce weapons, ammunition, and the many things needed to run a contemporary society. It wasn't long before women were recruited into the war effort. My mother was hired to make radios. Some women were in paramilitary roles. And others served in the service as pilots, drivers, and a host of other roles. When times got tough, men discovered that women could perform a man's work. After the war, men came home and wanted their jobs back. Women returned to their homes. But it wasn't long before waves of social change washed across the Western democracies where most Christians lived.

In 2012 Pew Research reported that most Americans felt good about women at work. Here's a summary:

> In many ways a public consensus has developed around the changing role of women in society. Nearly three quarters of American adults (73%) say the trend toward more women in the workforce has been a change for the better. And 62% of adults believe that a marriage in which the husband and wife both have jobs and both take care of the house and children provides a

more satisfying life than one in which the husband provides for the family and the wife takes care of the home.[35]

Gender Dysphoria

Gender Dysphoria is a distressing condition brought about by the inner conflict between the gender with which one identifies in contrast to one's biologically linked gender. The clinical issue is the distress. As children grow they may reveal their differences from peers by preferring clothes and activities of the opposite sex. As they reach puberty, the sense of distress can increase. The risk of suicidal ideation, suicide attempts, and completed suicide also increases. Gender Dysphoria is rare and occurs in less than 1 percent of the population. Many continue to experience dysphoria into adulthood. Many of those who no longer experience dysphoria are sexually attracted to members of their own sex and self-identify as gay or lesbian.[36]

An understanding of gender implies an appreciation of both biological and cultural factors. The combination of these factors can be powerful in determining how individuals form their identities and relate to others. Morality requires a sense of choice. To hold people accountable for an act implies they are able to choose one act instead of another. Although all aspects of sex and gender roles cannot be understood in terms of biological processes within a person and cultural forces acting upon a person, it can be said that people have limited choices in the way they behave. The degree of freedom to choose is foundational to morality.

Other Topics

Bisexuals and Transpersons

Bisexual identity is complicated for several reasons. For one thing, being sexually attracted to people of both sexes does not mean a person has a sexual relationship with anyone. People may interact with bisexuals based on their presentation to others as gay, lesbian, or heterosexual. Their presentation may be inferred from their current relationship. A few terms can illustrate the variations in identity: *lesbian-identified bisexual, lesbian bisexual, gay bisexual,* and *heterosexual-identified bisexual.*[37]

35. Pew Research Center, "Women, Work," para. 2.
36. American Psychological Association, *Diagnostic,* 451–59.
37. Mezey, *LGBT Families,* 6–8.

Transgender, as mentioned previously, refers to a broad spectrum of persons who identify with a gender that is different from their natal sex. Those who wish to change their biological sex are known as transsexual. People with female bodies who live as men are known by various terms, such as *transmen* (female-to-male; FTM), *transgender men*, and *transsexual men*. And transwomen (male-to-female; MTF) may be identified as transgender women and transsexual women.[38] Transpersons may be involved in families in various ways. As noted, some do not choose to make a biological change.

Sex-Linked Fear and Disgust

Human sexuality involves bodily fluids. And many human beings react with fear and disgust toward blood and other bodily fluids. Paul Rozin of the University of Pennsylvania is known as Dr. Disgust. His interest in disgust was fueled by an awareness of its power.[39] Rozin explains that disgust is a biological response seen in humans and other animals in response to offensive-tasting food. The facial expression often with a tongue extended, wrinkled nose, and raised upper lip is linked to inner feelings of nausea and revulsion. The body prepares to reject the offending material. Cultural behavior patterns linked to this biological phenomenon emerge and expand. And eventually, that which is disgusting can become that which is wrong or immoral. Although psychologists are cautious about overgeneralizing research findings about behavior, some disgust responses are common, such as responses to vomit and feces.

Rozin and his colleagues found frequently occurring items that are deemed disgusting to people in several cultures.[40] They concluded that disgust-linked emotions functioned in four separate domains. Core disgust is a reaction to contamination that may be caused by food, contact with animals, and body products. Animal-reminder disgust seems to protect people from an awareness of their own animal nature and the fact they are mortal. This dimension includes feelings of disgust linked to sex, bad hygiene, death, and violations of the body (i.e., items that may enter the body). The third dimension is interpersonal disgust, which helps preserve society by rejecting contact with persons considered undesirable. Finally, moral disgust responds to moral offenses and also helps preserve the social order.

---

38. Ibid.
39. "Food for Thought."
40. Rozin et al., "Disgust," 757–76.

Haidt and his colleagues developed a Disgust Scale to discover how sensitive people are to various disgust scenarios.[41] A recent study identified three factors rather than the eight in previous studies.[42] Items measuring sexual activity and linked to social values and morality produced different results than did other items. People respond differently to thoughts about unacceptable sex than they do toward other disgusting items like rodents, insects, and feces.

Moral disgust has been found in response to incest scenarios. The best indicator of a strong negative response to incestual sex is the length of time close relatives had lived together. Also, women scored higher on sex-related disgust items when they were close to the point in their monthly cycle when the probability of conception is highest.[43]

Joshua Tybur and colleagues reviewed the problematic links of disgust responses to adaptation and found a basis for three types of disgust. They believe a sense of disgust to bodily fluids like blood and semen developed as a way of protection from infectious agents. Sexual disgust is a response to unwanted sexual activity or contact. Tybur and others find that sexual disgust helps people avoid problematic relationships. Researchers identify two quality dimensions of potential sexual partners: intrinsic quality and genetic compatibility. Intrinsic qualities are those physically attractive features like an attractive face and body. Genetic compatibility includes those characteristics that are suggestive of better reproductive success such as avoiding inbreeding. People with low intrinsic quality and low compatibility are poor choices for sexual partners and result in high levels of disgust, which serves to motivate avoidance. Moral disgust is the third type of disgust and relates to moral transgressions. These activities cause harm to oneself or members of our social groups. Many of these are antisocial acts, such as lying, cheating, and stealing. It may seem strange to link social acts and reactions to potentially contagious fluids as causing disgust, but brain research using an fMRI suggests a similar brain response for both kinds of disgusting items.[44]

To summarize, research on disgust has identified several common items that provoke the disgust response in people from many cultures. And relevant to this book, some items related to sex produce a disgust response, and these can be linked to morality. Specifically, sex and bodily fluids like semen and blood cause disgust in some people. People who are perceived as different provoke sexual disgust, which appears related to the idea of

41. Haidt, "Individual Differences," 701–13.
42. Olatunji et al., "The Disgust Scale," 281–97.
43. Haselton and Ketelaar, "Irrational Emotions," 21–40.
44. Tybur et al., "Microbes," 103–22.

selecting the best mates. But this disgust of people also keeps Christians at a distance from people engaged in sexual behavior identified as sinful or immoral. Sexual disgust might be a driving emotional factor linked to support for the rights of sexual minorities.[45]

Sexual Disorders

A sexual disorder is a condition that interferes with normal sexual functioning within one of the three stages mentioned above (i.e., desire, excitement, and orgasm) and causes distress for the individual. Current lists of sexual disorders can be found in a reference work, which clinicians refer to by its shortened name, DSM or DSM-5™.[46] The DSM is published by the American Psychiatric Association. The editions update mental disorders based on the most recent research reviewed by panels of experts. The DSM allows clinicians and scientists to communicate about conditions that have a common set of features. Four categories from the DSM-5™ are concerned with sexual conditions: Sexual Dysfunctions, Gender Dysphoria, Disruptive, Impulse-Control, and Conduct Disorders, and Paraphilic Disorders. Because sexuality is a large part of human functioning, other sections of the DSM-5 are relevant to other discussions. For example, the consequences of sexual trauma, such as rape or other forms of sexual abuse, are often post-traumatic stress disorder and depression.

Neuroscientists often learn a lot about human behavior when changes in behavior appear to be associated with a disease or brain damage. One such finding is a syndrome identified by the 1939 team of Heinrich Klüver and Paul Bucy.[47] The Klüver-Bucy syndrome is associated with no fear. Also, sexual behavior often increases and same-sex activity has been observed in people who were previously heterosexually oriented persons.

Changes in functioning associated with seizures are another phenomenon of interest. Of relevance to this discussion are changes in the regulation of sexuality, including both hypersexual and hyposexual behavior.[48] Also of relevance are findings of hypermoralism—attention to minor offenses and a strong desire to punish offenders. Religiosity and spirituality appear enhanced with multiple conversions, mystical states, and a strong

---

45. Richard Beck shows how disgust can interfere with the ability of Christians to show mercy to people considered unclean in his book titled, *Unclean.*

46. That is, *Diagnostic and Statistical Manual of Mental Disorders.* The 5 refers to the fifth edition.

47. Kolb and Whishaw, *Fundamentals,* 561–62.

48. Tatum et al., "Sexuality," 300–302.

sense of divine guidance. Another finding is hypergraphia, which can take the form of extensive diaries, detailed notes, and autobiographical writings. Those with more left-sided brain damage are more concerned with personal destiny whereas those with more right-sided damage appear to have more obsessions.[49]

Summary

This chapter is the second of two chapters about sexuality and relationships. The previous chapter examined sexuality with a focus on beliefs linked to reproduction, including such topics as contraception, abortion, and pregnancy. In this chapter, I began with a review of sexuality during childhood and adolescence. Then I looked at a variety of topics involving sexuality and relationships that are related to morality.

Although circumcision is not a Christian teaching, it has been a common practice in many Christian cultures. A recent change in morality favors the right of children to be free from genital cutting. Sex educators advocate that sex education should begin in childhood and include a great deal of detail before teens begin having sexual relations. Controversy arises as people debate what ought to be included with instruction about sex. For example, there is no need for birth control when people abstain from sex. Regardless of the programs, substantial percentages of teens and adults have sex before they marry. Of course, teen pregnancy occurs, and options for the young women will vary depending on the values of the community.

Social attitudes are changing when it comes to cohabitation, marriage, and divorce. These changes are fairly recent in the history of Western civilization. Although social values are trending toward more permissive norms, official Christian moral teaching continues to focus on limiting sexual activity to marriages that are between one man and one woman. Many churches have accommodated people who divorced and remarried. Polygamy is not part of Christian tradition, but a brief discussion was included to illustrate that polyamorous relationships were part of the pre-Christian biblical tradition and continue to exist throughout the world, including in the United States.

Differences between sexual attraction and sexual orientation were discussed in the context of same-sex relationships. There is little support for beliefs that people who experience same-sex attraction can change that orientation. Although many people with same-sex orientation experience emotional distress possibly linked to a range of hostile responses, there is

---

49. McNamara and Butler, The Neuropsychology," 215–33.

no reason to think of people with a same-sex orientation as having a mental disorder.

Finally, biology certainly plays a role in the development of sex-linked characteristics and gender roles. But experience also plays a significant role. Both biology and experience are factors in determining sexual identity and sexual health as well as sexual dysfunction and gender dysphoria.

Additional Resources

1. **Sex.** Several topics related to sex can be found on the topics page of the American Psychological Association. Here is that link: http://www.apa.org/topics/sex/index.aspx
2. **Therapy and Sexual Orientation.** This is the link to a report on therapies designed to change sexual orientation. *Report of the APA Task Force on Appropriate Therapeutic Responses to Sexual Orientation.* http://www.apa.org/pi/lgbt/resources/sexual-orientation.aspx

Discussion Questions

1. What topics do you think ought to be included in sex education programs for minors in different age groups? For example, you might consider these age groups: 8–11; 12–14; 15–18.
2. People usually think of sex education for children and adolescents, but what do you think people need to learn throughout the lifespan? For example, new methods of birth control might be developed, or new findings might discover ways to treat sexually transmitted infections.
3. What difference do you think it makes that homosexuality was once listed as a mental disorder?

PART II

*Christian Cultures
and Contemporary Sexuality*

Biblical Texts and Christian Perspectives

A Brief Introduction to Part II

In part two, I examine the moral issues that divide Christians into at least two moral tribes I identify as conservatives and progressives. As noted in the Introduction, I believe that Christian moral judgment about sex-related issues is based on four factors: Scripture, beliefs about human nature, multidimensional moral reasoning, and beliefs about sexuality.

In the chapters of part II, I discuss specific sex-related issues of concern to many Christians. Several of these issues are divisive. I discuss how Christians draw upon Scripture in different ways as part of their formation of moral judgments. I draw upon the six dimensions of functioning in the SCOPES model to identify aspects of wellbeing. I also review the contribution of the six dimensions of moral foundations to moral judgments. And I consider how acting on a moral judgment may impact one or more aspects of wellbeing. Not surprisingly, I will also draw upon information about sexuality, which may influence a moral judgment.

I will briefly review the points I made in Part I as a framework for Part II.

1. Most Christians form moral judgments by combining their understanding of Scripture, human nature, one or more reasons derived from six moral foundations, and an understanding of human sexuality.
2. Christians interpret Scripture based on several theological and psychological factors.
3. Christians reveal the moral foundations important to their moral judgment in the language they use. There are six moral foundations. Conservative Christians may draw upon all six foundations of care, equality, loyalty, authority, purity, and liberty. Progressive Christians tend to emphasize two or three foundations: care, equality, and liberty.
4. People understand sexuality and sex-linked issues differently. Some biological aspects of sexuality are relevant to questions about what is natural and the degree of choice a person has over sex-related functioning. I also considered factors relevant to understand sex-related harm.

5. It is possible that Christians will employ arguments derived from the same moral foundation but emphasize different aspects. This will be evident in several issues in Part II.

6. When Christians act on moral judgments, there may be an impact on one or more areas of a person's wellbeing. We can think about wellbeing in terms of six dimensions of functioning represented in the SCOPES model: spiritual, cognitive, behavioral, physical, emotional, and social.

7. We can analyze moral reasons by using two questions derived from the positive and negative dimensions of the six moral foundations. How does their language reveal concerns about care, equality, loyalty, authority, purity, or liberty? How does their language reveal concerns about harm, inequality, betrayal, disrespect, degradation, or oppression?

8. The impact of a moral judgment on wellbeing can be framed by using a question like the following: how does their language reveal concerns about harm, inequality, betrayal, disrespect, degradation, or oppression?

7

BEGINNINGS: FROM PREGNANCY TO ADOLESCENCE

Conflicting Christian perspectives on contraception were evident in the decision of the U.S. Supreme Court on 30 June 2014. At the time the case was heard, twenty forms of contraceptives were available to women, but four of these were controversial for conservative Christians who believe using those forms of contraception prevents a fertilized egg from developing. The U.S. government had granted exemptions to religious organizations from providing coverage for these forms of contraception. The issue in the case was whether private corporations could also be exempt from providing such coverage if the coverage violated the religious beliefs of the owners.[1] In a 5–4 decision, the U.S. Supreme Court supported the owners, but all of the women on the court disagreed. The vigorous dissenting opinion was written by Justice Ruth Bader Ginsburg.[2]

Beginnings: From Pregnancy to Adolescence

I now invite you to join me in a study of what Christians believe about sex and sex-linked topics. I divided this chapter into three major sections. First, I will offer an overview of how to understand Christian morality. Then we will begin at the beginning of life. That is, we will consider Christian perspectives on contraception, pregnancy, and abortion. Finally, in the third section, I will look at Christian perspectives on sex-related topics that first arise during late childhood and adolescence.

Officially, Christians get their understanding of what is moral and immoral from God. Most accept that the Bible is God's Word or at least

---

1. Liptak, "Supreme Court."
2. Liebelson, "The 8," para. 1.

that the Bible provides the primary basis for Christian morality. The official statements by Christian groups will vary based on how much weight they give to contributions from science and the role of reason in writing a position statement. In one way or another, most Christians turn to the Bible to decide what to do. And this is what Christians have been doing for close to two thousand years. Unofficially, many Christians make moral decisions based on feelings, personal beliefs, customs, traditions, and experiences. Unfortunately for those wanting to understand Christian morality, the task is complicated. Despite having a common Scripture, Christians reach different conclusions about what is right and wrong. And even the same group of Christians can change their official statements from time to time. How can we understand Christian morality?

In this book I have taken a pragmatic approach to understanding Christian morality. I will use a common distinction between what people say and what people do as a way to distinguish between official moral teaching and research reporting what people do. Official statements of morality are published by a church or organization and by recognized church leaders (e.g., popes, presidents, priests, board members). Churches and Christian organizations expect their leaders to follow church teaching as a condition of holding their leadership position. When data are available, I will also consider the difference between the official morality of a church group (e.g., Catholic, Presbyterian) and the morality of the people who are affiliated with a group (e.g., people who identify themselves as Catholics or Presbyterians). Understanding the official position of a church group is important, but so is an understanding of what most Christians believe and do.

I can illustrate this pragmatic approach to morality by using a grid. The belief column in the grid represents the beliefs held by a church and its people about a moral issue. The behavior column represents an indication of how important that belief is to the church leaders and the members. Let me illustrate by using an example from beliefs about marriage and divorce. For centuries, most Christian groups taught that when people marry they should remain together for life and that divorce was sinful. Most Christians accepted the official belief in the sanctity of marriage as their personal belief. People who were divorced could not be leaders in either the upper echelons of a church organization or in the local church. Married leaders who pursued a divorce lost their leadership position. Most members accepted the official church teaching about divorce. Many resigned themselves to live in conflicted or unhappy relationships to do the right thing or at least to avoid the social consequences of getting a divorce. But in recent decades, an increasingly larger percentage of marriages ended in divorce. And the social penalties have declined.

	Belief	**Behavior**
Church officials/ leaders	Official moral teaching of a church	Official church actions following a violation
Church members	Research reports on moral beliefs of Christians	Research reports on moral actions of Christians

I will look at the morality of marriage and divorce in a separate chapter. Church leaders and members have dealt with the problem of divorce in various ways. And in most cases, church leaders refer to the Bible as the basis for the official beliefs. But before discussing specific beliefs in more depth, I want to return to the analysis of Christian morality.

The value of the behavior column to this analysis of morality is its contribution to understanding the importance of a belief. If you look at the penalties for breaking various laws where you live, you will have a good idea of the seriousness of the law. For example, you may spend the rest of your life in prison for the crime of murder. If you violate a speed limit, you may get a warning or a fine. You can take this same approach to looking at the penalties for breaking the laws in the Bible. In ancient Israel, the laws could be enforced by the Israelite leaders. In the New Testament era, Jesus and the leaders (i.e., apostles or elders) who taught about morality were not in a political position to enforce their teachings. The importance of a moral teaching could be discerned by what they instructed a local church to do about a violation or by what they expected God to do if a person persisted in immoral conduct (i.e., sin). So to evaluate the importance of a moral teaching in the New Testament, we can evaluate the reported, proposed, or recommended consequences for the act. Sometimes people were to be warned or confronted about their sin (Matt 18:15–17; 1 Thess 3:14–15). At other times they were to be removed from fellowship (1 Cor 5:12–13). Sometimes people were punished by illness (1 Cor 11:30) or death (Acts 5). At other times, warnings were given about the eternal consequences of sinful conduct. At a simple level, the righteous gain eternal life, but sinners are damned to eternal punishment (Matt 25:46).

We can apply the same belief-behavior analysis to understand contemporary Christian morality. If a church teaches that premarital sex is sinful and immediately fires a leader (e.g., priest, pastor, or teacher) for a first offense of premarital sex, it is obviously a highly important belief. If, on the other hand, a leader is warned or given another chance, we may conclude the belief about premarital sex is of less importance than other beliefs that would result in immediate job loss.

On the personal level, Christians report their moral beliefs on surveys and in interviews. Thus, we can know that they believe a specific behavior is morally wrong, but we may also learn the value of that belief if we have data about how often they engage in the behavior. Using the same example, many Christians accept the traditional church teaching that premarital sex is sinful, but their high level of premarital sexual activity suggests the belief is not very important. Of course there may be other explanations about why premarital sex is so common despite church teaching. But in most moral matters, the assumption is that people have a choice about what they do.

In most cultures where there is separation of church and state, church leaders have very little authority over the lives of those who attend services. They can discipline or remove church employees, but if they were to discipline or remove those who attend a local church, the individual might just move on to another church or cease attending church altogether. Clearly, some acts rise to the level of importance such that the church leaders and the members agree to remove a person from fellowship or ask them to leave the church community. In many settings, the social psychological factors of gossip and fear of embarrassment work to restrain the actions of those who value their status in the church community.

To make the different Christian perspectives clear, I will need to refer to the biblical texts. Sometimes I will quote from various scholars or leaders to show how different Christians interpret the same texts and thus reach different official moral positions. I will also offer examples of what Christians believe and how they act with respect to those beliefs. Finally, following a discussion of the issues, I will apply the findings of moral psychology from part 1 to better understand how different Christian groups[3] can reach different conclusions about right and wrong.

Contraception, Pregnancy, and Abortion

Most conservative Protestants join with Catholics and Orthodox Christians to support a strong pro-life position. Children are viewed as a blessing from the Lord (Ps 127:3). And children are created by God for a purpose. Some conservative Christians consider any interference with reproduction to be a violation of God's plan for heterosexual couples to marry and have children; hence, contraception is sinful. The conservative Christian perspective on

---

3. I use the word group to mean a group of Christians sharing a common set of beliefs. Examples of groups include Roman Catholics, Presbyterians, and Methodists. Sometimes smaller groups agree to be a part of larger groups such as the National Association of Evangelicals in the U.S.

contraception, like many sex-related perspectives, begins with a reference to the first few chapters of Genesis. The specific verses are 27 and 28 of chapter 1, in which God created people as male and female and told them to be fruitful and multiply. I will look at these verses in more detail in the next chapter when I present different perspectives on marriage.

Contraception: Moral Teaching

For many Christians, life begins at conception, and that life represents a person. To destroy a fertilized egg is to destroy a new life. And the destruction of life is murder and thus a violation of God's law against murder (Exod 10:13).

Most conservative Christians favor abstinence as a means of birth control for unmarried persons. The Catholic tradition has a strong pro-life position, which includes a prohibition against the use of artificial means of contraception. The purpose of sex is to create new life; thus, any interference with that purpose is against God's will. Catholics are permitted to manage family planning through natural means.[4] As a general rule, non-Catholic groups are not opposed to contraception, but ultraconservative groups are opposed to forms of contraception that have the potential to end the development of a human being from a fertilized egg.

The idea of violating the natural processes that God created (i.e., natural law) can be a factor for some Christians. As noted above, conservative Christians believe that since creation, couples were designed by God to have children (Gen 1:27–28). When Onan spilled his semen rather than impregnate his brother's widow, he was not just shamed for his act, as would later be codified in law (Deut 25:7–10), but he was put to death (Gen 38).

The legal protection of a man's capacity to reproduce is also a part of biblical law. And this legal code is viewed as evidence against interfering with reproduction. An example of the importance of a man's right to reproduce might be seen in the penalty for a woman grabbing the genitals of a man attacking her husband: she was to lose her hand (Deut 25:11–12).

Progressive Christian groups support a woman's use of contraception for several reasons. Following Jesus' teaching about loving children and loving others, progressives believe couples should plan to bring children into a loving home where they will receive nurturance and care. Progressive Christians invoke concern for the total wellbeing of a woman and her children. In this view, birth control permits couples to exercise judgment about when they are ready to have children and when they can provide adequate

---

4. United States Conference of Catholic Bishops, *Marriage*, 11–21.

care for their children. The couple can also decide how many children they can reasonably care for. Progressives do not view the Genesis text to fill the earth as a literal commandment from God. The population of the world is large enough.

In addition to the principle of love, progressive Christians can point to the use of available means to control natural processes during the biblical era. For example, Jacob exercised judgment in controlling the breeding of animals (Gen 27–31). And Jesus observed the wisdom of counting the costs before carrying out a task such as beginning a building project (Luke 14:28–29). People also used available means to interfere with the natural course of illnesses and disease. The prophet Isaiah advised a king (Hezekiah) to apply a poultice to a boil (Isa 38:21). Jesus referenced the role of physicians in caring for the sick (Luke 5:31). When people use contraception, they use their God-given wisdom to control natural processes in their best interests and the best interests of any children they may have.

Progressive Christians also view contraception as a means of protecting women and children from some aspects of evil. Although contraception cannot protect women from the horror of sexual assault, effective contraception can protect women from also having to cope with an unwanted pregnancy. Also, some forms of contraception can offer protection against sexually transmitted infections. From the progressive perspective, the non-use of contraceptives by conservative Christian women places them at risk of harm in a world where so many girls and women are sexually assaulted.

Contraception: Beliefs and Practice

In 2014, Univision researchers asked 12,038 self-identified Catholics on five continents to respond to issues important to the church. Overall, 78 percent of Catholics support the use of contraceptives and only 19 percent were opposed.[5] Jones and Dreweke reported the results of a survey of 7,356 U.S. women aged fifteen to forty-four. Most sexually active women (99 percent) have used a contraceptive method of birth control aside from natural family planning. Although the official Catholic position opposes artificial contraception, 98 percent of Catholics have used artificial contraception—only 2 percent use natural family planning.[6]

For the most part, the prohibition against using contraception is a moral teaching of the Catholic Church. The available data show that most individual Catholics do not support that moral teaching in terms of their

5. Univision, "Voice of the People."
6. Jones and Dreweke, "Countering Conventional."

attitudes or, in the U.S., in terms of their behavior. And in the U.S., most women have used artificial means of birth control regardless of religious affiliation.

Pregnancy and Life

The desire to have children appears to be a strongly held desire in addition to the pleasure associated with having sexual relations. Individuals and couples have pursued many pregnancy options throughout history. Abraham and his wife Sarai hoped for a child, but Sarai did not become pregnant with Isaac until after they selected another option in which Abraham had a son by Sarai's maid. The stories of Isaac (Gen 25:21) and Hannah (1 Sam 1:11) are other examples of people making requests of God to bless them with children. Although most conservative Christians believe life is a gift from God that begins at conception, advances in medical technology offer new ways for Christian women to have children. Clearly, the creation of life in a laboratory is different from the natural process. The Bible does not speak directly about alternate forms of creating life and initiating a pregnancy.

One law (Exod 21:22-23) illustrates how Israelites were to handle harm done to a pregnant woman: "When people who are fighting injure a pregnant woman so that there is a miscarriage, and yet no further harm follows, the one responsible shall be fined what the woman's husband demands, paying as much as the judges determine. If any harm follows, then you shall give life for life...."

Because women belonged to their husbands, the person who injured the pregnant woman and caused the miscarriage was to compensate the husband and not the woman for the injury. But if there was more harm to the woman beyond the miscarriage, such as the death of the man's wife, then the person causing the harm was to die. The loss of the man's wife and not the unborn child was the focus of the death penalty. There are no laws regarding actions taken to end a pregnancy by a husband or by a pregnant woman. As Hornsby observes, this Exodus text does not identify the unborn child as a separate person.[7] But conservatives offer other lines of reasoning about personhood that are best discussed under the next topic—abortion.

---

7. Hornsby, *Sex Texts*, 128-29.

Abortion: Moral Teaching

Many Christians view the unborn child as a person and they view any act to end the life of the unborn child as a violation of God's commandment against murder found in Exodus 20:13. Two texts are often quoted by conservative Christians. The first is found in Jeremiah 1:5:

> Before I formed you in the womb I knew you,
> and before you were born I consecrated you;
> I appointed you a prophet to the nations.

An alternative view of this text is to consider it as a specific call on the life of the prophet Jeremiah, which does not apply to all persons.[8] Also, this poetic celebration of life does not present a moral argument about a woman's decision to end her pregnancy. The quote from Psalm 139:13-16 follows.

> For it was you who formed my inward parts;
>   you knit me together in my mother's womb.
> I praise you, for I am fearfully and wonderfully made.
>   Wonderful are your works;
>   that I know very well.
> My frame was not hidden from you,
>   when I was being made in secret,
>   intricately woven in the depths of the earth.
> Your eyes beheld my unformed substance.
>   In your book were written all the days that were formed
>   for me,
>   when none of them as yet existed.

The psalmist clearly celebrates God's work in his life since the very beginning of his life. The text refers to the psalmist's poetic praise and does not involve a commandment about managing pregnancies and decisions about abortion. Alternative views of this text note that it does not deal with matters of rape or incest—cases in which a woman has not become pregnant in accordance with God's plan for sexual relationships.

The previously quoted Scripture about miscarriage in Exodus 21:22-23 does not identify a sin against God for the death of the unborn child. Another passage that might refer to terminating a pregnancy can be found in Numbers 5:11-31. I will not include the lengthy passage, which describes the challenge by a jealous husband to a woman's sexual faithfulness. In the Numbers text, the husband brings his wife to the priest, who gives the

---

8. Ibid., 134-35.

woman a specially concocted drink with a curse. Here's that portion of the text (verses 27–28):

> When he has made her drink the water, then, if she has defiled herself and has been unfaithful to her husband, the water that brings the curse shall enter into her and cause bitter pain, and her womb shall discharge, her uterus drop, and the woman shall become an execration among her people. But if the woman has not defiled herself and is clean, then she shall be immune and be able to conceive children.

Hornsby suspects the woman is pregnant, but the husband is not sure he is the father.[9] In any event, the description of the effect of the drink and the curse on the woman suggest what happens during an induced miscarriage. This law and the procedure are not precise enough to derive a principle about abortion.

One difficulty in using selected texts from the Bible to support an antiabortion position as pro-life is the existence of biblical texts that suggest ancient people did not value life as highly as do some contemporary cultures. Two quotes challenge those who believe all biblical texts consistently place a high value on life in general and the life of children in particular. Psalm 137:8–9 offers a graphic picture of killing infants and children.

> O daughter Babylon, you devastator!
>   Happy shall they be who pay you back
>   what you have done to us!
> Happy shall they be who take your little ones
>   and dash them against the rock!

And in 1 Samuel 15:3 God commands the destruction of infants along with men and women: "Now go and attack Amalek, and utterly destroy all that they have; do not spare them, but kill both man and woman, child and infant, ox and sheep, camel and donkey."

How do Christians view abortion in the rare case when a mother's life is in danger? A case in point was the death of Savita Halappanavar, who was refused an abortion in Ireland on 28 October 2012. According to the story reported by Peter Taggart for CNN, Irish law permitted abortion if the mother's life was in danger but not if her health was at risk.[10] She was in pain and in the process of a miscarriage. Her husband asked doctors to expedite the miscarriage. The doctors understood the law to mean that they were not permitted to carry out an abortion as long as a fetal heartbeat was

---

9. Ibid., 132–33.
10. Taggart, "Woman's Death."

present. The pregnant woman developed septicemia and died three days later. A conservative perspective illustrated by the Irish law placed strong boundaries upon what a physician could do. Rather than actively ending any life, a conservative Christian approach seeks to protect the lives of mothers and their unborn children. A progressive Christian approach also seeks to protect the lives of mothers and their unborn children. But progressive Christians focus more on the wellbeing of the mother in conditions of high risk.

Abortion: Beliefs and Practices

The official statements of beliefs can be found on church websites. Here's a sampling of official positions for some of the largest groups. Catholics are officially opposed to abortion without exception. The Southern Baptist Convention is the largest U.S. Evangelical Protestant group. They view all human life as sacred and see all abortions as wrong "except to save the physical life of the mother."[11] Among mainline Protestants, the United Methodist Church is the largest. They oppose abortion and affirm their respect for both mother and child. The church sanctions legal abortions but rejects abortion as a method of gender selection or birth control.[12] A number of Evangelical Protestants are members of the National Association of Evangelicals. The NAE officially recognizes the sanctity of life and opposes abortion on demand.[13]

Catholics who responded to a worldwide Univision poll believed that abortion should be restricted. Only 9 percent believed abortion should be allowed in all cases. In contrast, 33 percent believed abortion should not be allowed at all, and 57 percent believed abortion should be allowed in some cases, such as when a mother's life is in danger.[14]

Each year the Marist Poll surveys Americans about their views toward abortion. The poll is sponsored by the Knights of Columbus, a Catholic organization. Their 2014 report was based on a poll of 2,001 adults surveyed between 10 and 15 December 2013.[15] In the report "Abortion in America," they found most (62 percent) in the U.S. believe "abortion is morally wrong." Only 2 percent considered abortion not a moral issue, and 36 percent reported abortion was "morally acceptable." As noted previously, a part of the

11. Southern Baptist Convention, "Resolution on Abortion."
12. United Methodist Church, "Abortion."
13. National Association of Evangelicals, *Theology of Sex*.
14. Univision, "Voice of the People."
15. Knights of Columbus, "Abortion in America."

moral issue is when life begins. The Marist Poll found that 53 percent believe life begins at conception, whereas 10 percent believe life begins at birth.

Data from the *Public Opinion on Abortion Slideshow* provided by PewResearch reveal variations based on religious affiliation.[16] Six-in-ten or more white Evangelical Protestants and Mormons think abortion should be illegal in all or most cases, as do about half (52 percent) of Hispanic Catholics. By contrast, nearly nine-in-ten Jews say abortion should be legal in all or most cases, as do about seven-in-ten Americans with no religious affiliation and 63 percent of white mainline Protestants. Among both black Protestants and white Catholics, about half say abortion should be legal in all or most cases.

In general, Christians officially view abortion as a moral issue. Catholics and some Protestants groups officially state that abortion is morally wrong in all cases. When surveyed, most Christians view abortion as a moral issue. And most want some restrictions on abortion. But many do not accept the official position of those Christian groups that believe abortion is always wrong under all circumstances. Few Christians seem aware that the knowledge we have of conception is of recent origin and therefore unknown to the people who lived when the Bible was written or during most of the centuries during which Christian traditions were formed.

Moral Perspectives on Contraception and Abortion

As you read through the analysis of the moral dimensions, keep in mind that other influences are at work. The understanding of when life begins is much more advanced in the last few decades than ever before in history. In addition, people viewed the idea of personhood and rights in different ways throughout history. Rights for women have only recently been recognized. The idea that an unborn child may have rights is relatively new and is not widespread. Consider some obvious cultural factors affecting the rights of the unborn and children. First, an official birth certificate is key to one's national identity, and the date of birth is tied to various benefits and privileges in many cultures. This type of cultural recognition does not occur for those lives unborn. Second, consider the high degree of control parents have over newborns. Parents have a moral duty to care for their children such that governments remove parental rights from those who fail to behave in certain ways. Third, as children grow, cultures gradually accord them more and more rights and considerations. The point is that rights and choices vary from conception to adulthood for children, and the rights of their parents

---

16. Pew Research Center, "Public Opinion."

change as well. People argue about the rights of the unborn, the rights of the pregnant woman, the rights of the father, and the rights of a society to set limits on the rights of its people.

Moreover, note that in some parts of the world, the investment of time, energy, and financial resources by Christians and non-Christians in matters of abortion laws and policies has been considerable. Thus, as predicted by the principle of sunk costs coupled with the principle that morality binds and blinds, it will be very difficult for Christians to take another point of view.

Finally, keep in mind the potential effects of a moral judgment, formed from one or more moral dimensions. The general question about the effects of acting on a moral judgment can be framed this way: how does acting on a moral judgment affect a person spiritually, cognitively, behaviorally, physically, emotionally, or socially?

1. Care versus Harm

In matters of caring, contemporary Christians do not disagree about the importance of protecting children and their mothers from harm. For ultraconservatives, the protection from harm begins before birth by ensuring there is no human interference with God's capacity to create a purposeful life by fertilizing a woman's eggs with a man's sperm. Other views are variations on when protection begins for cells with the potential to create a child or when a child's life begins.

Perhaps the most extreme view for some Christians is that protection should focus wholly on the woman, her rights, and her total wellbeing. A woman should be supported in her decisions about having a child (decisions about contraception) or maintaining a pregnancy (decisions about terminating a pregnancy). A special focus for progressive Christians is the compassion for a woman who has become pregnant as a result of rape or incest. This is not to say conservatives do not care; rather, it is a point to consider when analyzing the care-harm arguments provided by Christians.

2. Fairness/Reciprocity versus Cheating

Conservative and progressive views can diverge on how to fairly treat a woman and her unborn child. The stricter the law governing contraception and abortion, the less choice a woman has and the more weight people give to the life of the child over the life of the mother. Balancing the fair treatment of mother and child is a moral issue. And one can ask: what is fair in terms of the rights of the child's father? You might notice that conservative arguments tend to focus on biological life, whereas progressive Christians are more willing to consider all aspects of a woman's wellbeing.

3. Ingroup Loyalty versus Betrayal

Conservative Christians are loyal to the teachings of their tradition. To act against the conservative stance about contraception and abortion is to betray God as well as those who are designated to uphold God's Word. Progressive Christians are more likely to focus on God's love and compassion for the woman and her wellbeing. In this sense, progressives are loyal to the general principle of the law. Christians who fail to support a woman in need, regardless of her decision, may be considered to have betrayed their duty of love. In the case of a rapist or man who impregnates a woman and leaves her to cope with her pregnancy, moral betrayal is evident. The father has pragmatically abrogated his rights though various cultures and laws may approach the legal rights of fathers differently.

4. Authority/Respect versus Disrespect

Christians who make arguments emphasizing moral authority usually remind people that God is the ultimate authority who has made his commandments clear in the Bible. Progressive Christians emphasize the problems of various interpretations of biblical texts when arguing that people are not disrespecting God but rather disagreeing with the way Christian leaders interpret the Bible. As we have seen, the biblical texts do not specifically address contraception or abortion so Christians are left with prayerfully and carefully discerning principles.

5. Purity or Sanctity versus Degradation

"The sanctity of life" is a phrase full of meaning for conservatives faced with issues of contraception, pregnancy and abortion. Medical technology has worked in favor of conservative positions in the form of ultrasound images that show what fetal life looks like in the womb. The presence of a living and moving child is often a powerful emotional experience. Young couples eagerly share their pictures. In addition, images of the destruction of unborn children during middle and later pregnancies invoke a powerful disgust response accompanied by outrage, as in, "How could anyone do such a thing!"

For progressive Christians, the sanctity of the life of the mother is degraded when she is forced to have sex against her will. Progressives can point to the horrors of young girls carrying their father's babies as a result of incestuous rape. A girl's sacred status is degraded when she is forced to bear the burden of man's sin, recover from the sexual abuse, and discover that many people are unwilling to treat her with respect. Some progressive Christians also respond with outrage toward the callous response of conservatives who seem to ignore the trauma of rape in their requirement that a woman give birth to their rapist's child. Progressive Christians view conservatives as adding one degradation (i.e., rape) to another (i.e., carrying the rapist's child). And some progressive Christians see this degradation in the context of a long history of the degradation of women by male-dominated Christianity.

6. Liberty versus Oppression

Conservatives value their religious freedom and respond with righteous anger when government laws and regulations interfere with their perceived right to follow their view of God's teaching about contraception and abortion. Progressive Christians focus on the freedom of all persons from the tyranny of laws that restrict individual freedoms to follow their understanding of God's law. They view the restrictive interpretations of Scripture as man-made doctrines designed only to oppress and control women.

Consent and Choice

It is difficult to find a basis for the contemporary notion of consent as a moral foundation in biblical laws or texts that could relate to matters of conception and abortion. Some texts considered in future chapters document that fathers had the right to consent to the marriage of their daughters. And a father had the right to be compensated if a man had sex with his daughter. Conservative Christians do not frame moral arguments about contraception and abortion using the language of consent. But they do work for laws that require parents to grant consent before their daughters can use birth control or obtain an abortion. Progressive Christians tend to support a woman's right to make her own decisions in consultation with a medical provider even if she is an adolescent.

Childhood and Adolescence

Understanding human sexuality in the context of relationships begins soon after birth in simple ways as infants learn to trust parents and caregivers to feed them, change their clothes, interact in closely personal ways (e.g., parents vary in the type and frequency of kissing), and teach them the names for body parts. Children observe others and see how family members and friends show love and affection. Parents and caregivers send moral messages when they teach or do not teach their children medically accurate information about the names for their sex organs, provide examples about how much of their naked bodies to cover with clothes, and show them by example how to relate to others in romantic relationships.

Circumcision

Biblical circumcision began with Abraham, who circumcised himself and his son Ishmael on the same day (Gen 17:26). When Isaac was eight days old, Abraham circumcised him following God's command (Gen 21:4). Since then, male circumcision has been a common religious practice within Judaism and a common cultural practice in the West for infant boys. It has been argued that male circumcision was ordered by God for a practical matter of good hygiene.

For Christians, the commandment about circumcision ended in the first century. Apparently there was a conflict in the early church when gentiles converted to Christianity and had not undergone circumcision. After some debate, the Jewish leaders of the Jesus movement decided against requiring physical circumcision of gentiles, which then became symbolic—a matter of the heart (Rom 2:25–29).

The contemporary practice of male circumcision has been called into question especially when problems occur. Although this is more of a concern for those Jews who continue to practice male circumcision, many Christian parents have their boys circumcised as well. Circumcision at least becomes a moral issue when harm is done. Others contend that the lack of the ability of the child to grant consent makes circumcision a moral issue. That is, it is immoral for parents to decide to cut a boy's penis when this procedure is clearly optional. Philosophically, if a child is a person with rights, then he has the right to decide to cut his body or not. Female circumcision or genital cutting is not part of Christian tradition or teaching.

Sex Education

One way or another, children learn about the biological changes in their bodies. Many learn from parents and friends. Some learn as participants in formal sex-education programs. Learning to abstain from sexual activity during adolescence is a mainstay of conservative Christian sex-education programs. Abstinence programs will vary in terms of their components, which allows for an understanding of how social conservatives and progressives hold different views about sexuality. A common categorization of sex-education programs is offered by Ruth Franklin and Sharon Dotger.[17] Some students receive no sex education while others receive comprehensive programs or two forms of abstinence programs: abstinence-only and abstinence-plus. Abstinence may be the only approach to sexual activity or abstinence-plus programs may include information about contraception and abortion.

One way to identify what Christians believe about sex education is to ask about their experience. On the one hand, we understand the official teaching of the Christian traditions. Data from youth in a conservative sample (151 Southern Baptists) indicate limited sex education. About half did not learn about key sex-education topics from their families. And one quarter reported no sex or sex-related moral education. Most said they got their information about vaginal and oral sex from friends.[18]

How did the conservative Christians live out their sexuality compared to those in the general culture? It turns out, the Christians in the sample were not very different from people in other studies. Lawrence Finer reported that most adolescents (75 percent) will have sexual intercourse by age twenty-one.[19] The participants in the Southern Baptist sample, America's largest conservative Protestant Christian denomination, revealed that more than 70 percent had vaginal or oral sex before they married. For those who married after age twenty-five, more than 80 percent had premarital sex. At the time of the survey, 82.7 percent regretted not waiting to have sex until they married.

A study of adolescent sexual behavior reported by Jeremy Uecker was based on a U.S. sample. The survey included information about religious affiliation, premarital sex, and virginity pledges. Overall, most young adults had premarital sex. About 11 percent were sexually abstinent until marriage. Most (67 percent) had sex with someone other than the person they

---

17. Frankilin and Dotger, "Sex Education," 199–213.
18. Rosenbaum and Weathersbee, "True Love," 263–75.
19. Finer, "Trends in Premarital," 73–78.

married. A small percentage (about 22 percent) exclusively had sex with the person they married. Those who were affiliated with a religious group had significantly less premarital sex than did the unaffiliated, but religious leaders would not likely find the data reassuring. The most conservative rates of abstinence were found for Mormons (43 percent).[20]

The idea of a virginity pledge has become popular among U.S. Christians. The movement took off after the beginning of a 1993 Southern Baptist initiative called "True Love Waits."[21] Those who reported pledging to remain a virgin until they married were significantly less sexually active than those who did not take such a pledge. Those who honored their pledge to remain a virgin until marriage represented a little more than 25 percent of the sample. When those who pledged had premarital sex, they were more restrictive in their sexual partners than were those who did not pledge. About 72 percent of nonpledgers had sex with people other than the one they married compared to 41 percent of those who took the pledge. Uecker's analysis indicated that a person's Christian spirituality and making a pledge was linked to lower rates of premarital sex.

In summary, most Christians officially believe and educate their youth that people should only have sex when they are married (abstinence). Although there is some evidence that religious affiliation and pledging abstinence influences premarital sexual behavior, substantial numbers of Christians have premarital vaginal and oral sex. A cause-effect relationship between sex education and premarital sex has not been established.

Masturbation and Self-Pleasuring

Children explore their bodies, which includes touching their genitals. The scientific study of sexuality during childhood is limited for ethical reasons. Reports from parents offer one source of information. A questionable source of child sexuality is the report of childhood memories offered by adults in response to interviews or surveys. What data are available suggest that some prepubertal children manipulate their genitals. This autostimulation increases during adolescence to the point that almost all boys and most girls masturbate. Masturbation continues into adult life.

Some Christian groups taught that masturbation is wrong, but teaching against masturbation has not been a significant issue in recent decades for most Christian groups except for teaching that lustful thoughts are sinful. In Christian tradition, masturbation was called "Onanism." In the past, some

---

20. Uecker, "Religion, Pledging," 728–44.
21. Ibid.

argued that the sin of Onan (Gen 38:9–10) was spilling his semen, which was used to condemn masturbation; however, most contemporary scholars interpret the story to mean that Onan's sin was the failure to fulfill his duty toward his brother's wife. The story has nothing to do with masturbation.[22]

The Song of Songs is a biblical book with much sexual imagery. In chapter 5, the woman lies on her bed and reports a sexual fantasy. Some have considered this as possibly referring to female masturbation.[23]

The prophet Ezekiel warned the Israelites about their behavior. A couple of verses suggest female masturbation with phallic objects. Here's a quote from Ezekiel 16:17 (ESV): "Then you took your beautiful jewelry that I gave you, and you used the gold and silver to make statues of men, and you had sex with them too!"

Essentially, there is not much in the Bible related to masturbation. And there is no biblical law or teaching specifically prohibiting masturbation. The contemporary moral concern comes from the interpretation of biblical texts prohibiting lust.[24]

Pornography

U.S. Attorney General, John Ashcroft, widely known as a conservative Christian, was widely panned when, he appeared at a Department of Justice press conference in front of naked statues that were partially covered with cloth.[25] Three and a half years later, the blue drapes were removed.[26]

Pornography is a matter of concern to many people. Christians have warned about the harm caused by an increasingly sexualized society in Western cultures.[27] Defining pornography is the key problem. Western cultures value freedom of expression. For some Christians, nudity is forbidden and counts as pornography. For others, pornography involves depictions of sexual activity. And others may use more refined definitions of pornography.

Nudity has been a commonplace in public art work for millennia. There are a number of verses referring to nakedness in the Bible. In the origin narratives from Genesis, the first couple was naked and not ashamed (Gen 2:25), but after eating the forbidden fruit, they were ashamed, and

---

22. For example: Friedman and Dolansky, *The Bible Now*, 11; Hornsby, *Sex Texts*, 88–89.

23. Hornsby, *Sex Texts*, 90–91.

24. Graves, "Getting to the Root," 1–3.

25. "Justice Department Covers."

26. "Drapes Removed."

27. United States Conference of Catholic Bishops, *Marriage*, 50.

God is seen as providing them with clothing. When Noah was drunk, two of his sons covered him up and walked backwards to avoid looking on his naked state, which on the surface revealed a prohibition against children seeing their fathers naked (Gen 9:20–29). However, biblical scholars often interpret this reference to nakedness as a euphemism for sex. But scholars disagree on exactly what the sex might entail. For example, to uncover a father's nakedness could be taken to mean having sexual relations with a father's wife.

Nudity is not necessarily sexually attractive. Within any given culture, certain persons are considered sexually attractive. And people desire to see them naked. Those who are unattractive are sometimes told in a callous way to "cover up." Within medical contexts, nudity is a commonplace, yet most providers offer some ways (e.g., gowns, curtains) to minimize exposing the genitals to those not involved in direct care.

As to pornography, there are no direct biblical references available. However, the apostle Paul's general warnings against sexual immorality (e.g., 1 Cor 6:9–10, 13–20, 18; 7:2; 10:8; 2 Cor 12:21; 1 Thess 4:3–5; Eph 5:3–5; Col 3:5; Gal 5:19) allow Christians to include prohibitions against creating or using sexual content that could be identified as immoral.

As noted above, the problem for those attempting to create a biblical basis for prohibiting the use of pornography will be reaching a conclusion about what constitutes pornography. At a minimum, Christians would be expected to obey civil laws about pornography. In addition, works that could be judged as degrading people could also be considered a violation of God's teaching. Admittedly, the concept of degrading is also vague.

The problem of lust is also nuanced. Human beings automatically notice sexually attractive persons. Human brains quickly scan and process information about sex characteristics. Presumably, lust involves a persistent focus on desiring sexual relations with someone. A conservative approach focuses on restricting sexual desire to one's spouse. A progressive approach focuses on faithfulness toward one's spouse and does not address the status of the unmarried. To control this natural process of focusing on sexually attractive persons requires cognitive effort. The ability to exert self-control naturally varies from person to person, and it varies throughout the day.

Teen Pregnancy

For Christians, teen pregnancy becomes a moral issue when a young woman is unmarried and in the legal custody of her parents. Conservative Christians draw on the same Scriptures as they would for other sexual issues to affirm that sex outside of marriage is immoral. And conservative Christians support the rights and responsibilities of parents to govern the life decisions of their minor children. Conservative Christians also consider abortion to be sin as noted previously; therefore, the young woman is expected to give birth to her child regardless of how she became pregnant.

In years past, a young man would be expected to marry his pregnant lover and provide for her and their child. Today, even conservative Christians are less willing to require a marriage under such circumstances. Some conservative Christian groups offer assistance with pregnancy care and adoption services if the mother chooses to place her baby up for adoption.

Progressive Christians are more likely to focus on the values and needs of the young woman when offering supportive services. Because there are several factors to weigh, progressive Christians are less likely to follow a strict protocol when it comes to helping the young woman select the best course for her life once she is pregnant.

Moral Perspectives on Sexual Issues during Childhood and Adolescence

In this analysis of moral perspectives, I will address the salient concerns of conservative and progressive Christians about the sexual issues of those who are legally in the care of a parent or guardian. Recall that there can be up to six moral perspectives derived from one or more of the six moral foundations. A moral judgment is usually formed on the basis of more than one moral dimension. I will not consider additional concerns about circumcision because the practice is not part of the Christian tradition. As you review the moral analysis, consider the impact on the child or adolescent in terms of the six dimensions of the SCOPES model. More specifically: how does acting on a moral judgment affect a child or teen spiritually, cognitively, behaviorally, physically, emotionally, or socially?

1. Care versus Harm

Conservatives and progressives can agree with secularists that sex education is important. Disagreements arise about the content of the programs and the importance of a Christian moral context when presenting the information. Conservatives see harmful consequences of programs that fail to teach abstinence until marriage. The physical effects of infections and the stress of coping with infections and pregnancy can be avoided by abstaining from sex. Abstinence is protective. Conservatives are also aware of the harmful emotional effects—as one pastor told me, "You can't put a condom on the heart." Notice the implied failure of condoms—they protect against pregnancy but do not protect against spiritual and emotional harm.

Progressive Christians focus on the same harmful consequences as conservatives do but express concern that abstinence programs do not work for most people. Most Christians have sex outside of marriage. Effective programs must include information about contraception. They also note the harm done to young women who are often unprepared for parenting.

In recent years, most Christians have ceased condemning masturbation. But conservative Christians do focus on the common use of pornography during masturbation and condemn the sin of lust as harmful, noting the damaging potential of desiring sexual relationships with someone other than one's spouse. Progressive views consider the lack of biblical condemnation of either masturbation or sexual imagery. Progressive Christians join with others in condemning sexually explicit material involving the harm and exploitation of children.

Although some teen mothers can experience joy in giving birth to a child, many struggle with poverty and suffer from lack of familial and other social support. Those who became pregnant as a result of incest or other forms of rape have psychological and sometimes physical pain and distress to endure in addition to coping with an unplanned pregnancy. Conservative and progressive Christians focus on the sanctity of life. Conservatives generally hold to a hard line on prohibiting abortion. Progressive Christians affirm restrictions on abortion but are willing to consider the total wellbeing of the mother.

2. Fairness/Reciprocity versus Cheating

Conservative Christians observe that there are natural and spiritual consequences that people suffer when they choose to sin. Sex-education programs should emphasize the life problems that can follow the failure to choose abstinence from sex outside of marriage. Teen pregnancy with its attendant struggles is an example of what can happen when people choose to disobey God's laws. Nevertheless, conservative and progressive Christians alike believe in forgiveness and the redemption of all persons.

Progressive Christians are less likely to focus on perceptions of fair and just punishment following personal choices and are more likely to consider various life factors in addition to personal choice that could have led to a distressing situation such as a teen pregnancy. Progressive Christians are mindful that too often women have been treated unjustly by those who blame women for being raped and simultaneously excuse men for failing to control their sexual desires.

3. Ingroup Loyalty versus Betrayal

Conservative Christians encourage young persons to be loyal to God's Word and the teachings of the church in regard to sexual activity. From this perspective, loyalty is rewarded with a happy marriage where the gift of sex can be enjoyed the way God intended sex to be enjoyed. When people betray God, there are consequences to be paid. Progressive Christians view loyalty and betrayal in terms of interpersonal relationships. Although agreeing with conservatives that limiting sexual activity within the bounds of marriage is ideal, the principle of being loyal and trustworthy in a committed romantic relationship and not betraying each other is at the heart of marriage.

4. Authority/Respect versus Disrespect

Conservative Christians expect people to submit to the authority of God's Word. Teaching anything contrary to God's plan for sex within marriage is a subversive activity. Any government policy or program that intrudes on the rights of a father to govern the members of his household violates God's plan for an orderly society. In this view, fathers, or at least parents, must approve sex-education programs and must be consulted in matters of birth control and pregnancy. Progressive Christians sometimes disagree on the way conservative Christians interpret the Bible. They view conservative appeals to authority as expectations to follow a group's teaching. Like conservatives, progressive Christians affirm the importance of strong families. But they are mindful that substantial numbers of children have only one parent and some have no parents; thus, partnering with government is important.

5. Purity or Sanctity versus Degradation

Sexual purity and the sanctity of life are key concerns during childhood and adolescence. Whether the topic is sex education, pornography, or sexual activity, conservative Christians focus on a holy life, which means not just avoiding sexual activity but guarding one's mental life from impure thoughts stimulated by sexually explicit materials, jokes, or personal imagination. Conservative Christians emphasize the importance of virginity as the godly ideal. Progressive Christians recognize that so many people are involved in sexual activity outside of marriage, often through no personal choice. Most people are not virgins when they marry. To focus on virginity is to miss the point of redemption, which allows people to be fully restored in God's eyes regardless of their past.

The psychology of virginity is linked to the psychology of disgust. People reject food and drink if a disgusting insect has come into contact with it—even if the insect was sterilized. Conservative Christians have linked sexual purity to virginity. In this scenario, having sex outside of marriage is linked to being dirty, impure, and unholy. Christian men are advised to steer clear of such women. Some Christian parents still cover up the shame of premarital sex when their pregnant daughters are hastily married. Tragically, even rape victims have been rejected because they are no longer virgins. It should also be noted that even though Christians expect young men to abstain from sex, the focus has long been on preserving the virginity of women. Even though Christians believe in forgiveness, an unmarried nonvirgin woman will always be viewed as morally suspect by some.

Moral purity has the potential to impact many aspects of a young person's functioning. Again, looking at the SCOPES model, we can consider how their spirituality—their relationship with God is marred when actions are condemned as impure. Their memories will store the condemned experiences and the critical words leading to low self-worth as a moral failure. If they violate their parents' moral teaching for long, they will develop persistent behavior patterns. Risky sexual behavior carries a real risk of physiological harm in the form of disease. And social relationships are often impacted when the sexual component is considered dirty, unclean, or disgusting by influential people in the adolescent's life.

6. Liberty versus Oppression

Conservative Christians wish to be free from government intrusion in terms of sex education and laws allowing contraceptive use and abortion. They seek religious liberty to follow God's law in matters of sex and view government intrusion as oppressive regardless of the possible merits of a program. Progressive Christians affirm the importance of freedom and individual liberty but weigh that concern against the plight of so many people who are the victims of rape and sexual exploitation. The problem is too widespread to take a "hands-off" stance. Both conservative and progressive Christians may be politically active in attempting to change laws to represent their views, which may have the effect of restricting the liberty of other persons.

Consent and Choice

Conservative Christians believe consent in matters of sex education, birth control, and the care of an underage pregnant teen resides with a child's father or at least with a parent. Progressive Christians tend to give more weight to the participation of an adolescent in decisions about personal sexuality. The needs and opinions of the adolescent should be considered when she or he must bear the consequences of a life-altering decision such as birth control or abortion.

Summary

I divided this chapter into three major sections. First, I presented information on how to view Christian morality. I offered two perspectives. We can learn about Christian morality from the official statements of Christian groups, which quote biblical texts and offer their interpretation of those texts. We can also learn about Christian morality from research, which provides data about the beliefs and behavior patterns of people who identify themselves as Christians.

The second section covered topics dealing with the beginning of life. Christians view life as a gift of God, and most view life as beginning at conception. Life is sacred. The sacredness of life guides most Christians toward a strong pro-life position when it comes to abortion. A strong conservative position officially held by Catholics and some Protestants does not allow for the use of contraception, which interferes with God's plan for couples to have children. The strong pro-life position also declares all abortion to be immoral. Progressive Christians support the use of contraception. Progressive Christians affirm the sacredness of life and the importance of the lives of mothers and children but strongly consider the mother's wellbeing in decisions to terminate a pregnancy, especially in cases when a woman has become pregnant as a result of incest or other forms of rape.

In the third section, I reviewed sexual issues, which emerge during the course of childhood and adolescence. Although circumcision is not a Christian practice, some Christians practice male circumcision. The moral objection to medically safe procedures is the unnecessary pain to the boy and his inability to give consent. Sex education is controversial because there are value conflicts. Conservative Christians teach the importance of abstinence until marriage, and some programs ask teens to pledge that they will remain virgin until marriage. If people are abstinent, there is no need to use contraception. And abortion is not a viable option because it constitutes murder. Progressive Christians include teaching about contraception because of the importance of protecting youth from unplanned pregnancies given evidence that substantial percentages of Christians have premarital sex. Progressive Christians also advocate condom use to protect youth from sexually transmitted infections.

Masturbation used to be condemned by Christians, but the Scriptures on which the condemnation was based are no longer considered to be about masturbation. In fact, there is some evidence that masturbation was celebrated as a part of sexual activity. One problem related to masturbation is the use of pornography. Conservative Christians are concerned to protect children and adolescents from exposure to immorality found in pornography. Christians vary in how they define pornography. Conservatives and progressives agree that depictions of sexuality that demean and degrade human beings are immoral as are any acts that exploit vulnerable persons.

The problem of teen pregnancy represents a significant moral challenge throughout the world. Christians differ on how to reduce teen pregnancy because of differences of opinion on acceptable practices of birth control and the termination of pregnancies. Most Christians offer support for pregnant teens and their newborns.

Following each section, I looked at how Christians might view the moral issues in terms of the six moral foundations proposed by Haidt and his colleagues along with the moral issue of consent.

Additional Resources

1. **Education about Sex.** A fact sheet is available from SIECUS (Sexuality Information and Education Council of the United States.) http://www.siecus.org/index.cfm?fuseaction=Page.ViewPage&PageID=1193

2. **Consent.** What does it mean to consent to sexual activity? A recent emphasis has been to increase safety for students on college campuses. An NPR story addresses this problem. http://www.npr.org/2014/06/13/321677110/a-campus-dilemma-sure-no-means-no-but-exactly-what-means-yes

3. **Teen Pregnancy.** The Center for Disease Control and Prevention offers information about Teen Pregnancy and related topics on reproductive health. http://www.cdc.gov/TeenPregnancy/AboutTeenPreg.htm

Discussion Questions

1. If a fertilized egg is considered a person, what kind of rights does this person have?
2. Does quality of life of the mother count as a moral consideration when a girl becomes pregnant as the result of rape?
3. How would you define pornography? What kinds of things do you consider too indecent for humans to view or experience? How do you make that decision about indecency? How much of a role do feelings play in decisions about pornography?
4. If sex-education programs that focus on abstinence fail to significantly prevent teen pregnancy and the spread of sexually transmitted infections, are those programs unethical? Is it morally wrong to ask people to participate in and pay for programs that do not work?

8

MARRIAGE, DIVORCE, AND SEXUAL RELATIONSHIPS

On a beautiful Spring Saturday afternoon, June glances in the mirror to have one last look at her hair, face, and gown. The perfect marriage is about to begin at the church she and her family attended for the past twenty-two years of her life. She met Doug at a Christian College. He grew up in a small town some one hundred miles away, but they share the same conservative Christian faith—the faith of their parents and the school they attended. The sanctuary is full of guests—family and friends with wide smiles. June's father meets her in the foyer. They step forward as people rise, and all eyes turn to admire June's beauty. Women compare her dress with the one they wore. Men assess her appearance—but not the dress. Doug's eyes meet June's. The whole ceremony is a blur. They hear words, exchange rings, kneel to take communion, and kiss before the cheering crowd. All rise to the pronouncement, "I now present you . . . ."

Storybook weddings still happen in conservative Christian enclaves around the world. A new marriage begins with a lifetime commitment witnessed by church members. Within a few years, family and friends will wonder when the young couple will have children. It's expected. But even in the U.S. "Bible Belt," Christian marriages reveal some variations unimaginable several decades ago.

This chapter is about marriage. Because many Christians associate sexual relationships with marriage, it is also about sexual relationships. Because marriages have a beginning and an end, it is also about divorce. It is not just about any form of marriage. It is about Christian marriage. But the perspectives on what constitutes a Christian marriage have changed. To understand Christian marriage and the church's teaching about sex and divorce, I will present the passages of Scripture typically referenced by Christian leaders. I will also look at the social challenges to contemporary teaching and how Christians respond to those challenges. I decided to break the discussion about sexual relationships and marriage into two chapters. This chapter contains a general framework for discussions about marriage, divorce, and sexual relationships. I have focused on heterosexual relationships. In the next chapter, I look at relationships among sexual minorities, including same-sex marriage.

Roman Catholics and Evangelicals agree that marriage is between one man and one woman and that sexual activity is only acceptable within a marriage.[1] Contemporary Christians often long for the old days when things were different. Older Christians—and there are many of them due to the post-war baby boom—recall an era when marriage boomed, divorce rates were low, men were the breadwinners, and women raised their children in a godly home. Most people went to church on Sundays, which was a day of rest—a day when only vital activities took place so Christian families could worship together. That era, known as "the long decade," ended in the early 1960s.[2] In the history of marriage, the era represented a peak for love-based heterosexual marriage freely entered into by two adults and supported by governments and churches in Europe, the United States, and other parts of the world where Christianity held sway.

In the Beginning: The Model Marriage

Do you have an image of Eve in a flowing white gown walking down the aisle of a stately temple to meet Adam, dressed in a tuxedo and standing before God, who looks like a priest in white robes? Of course the image is ridiculous. But when Christians write and speak about marriage, they often take us back to the union of Adam and Eve in the Garden of Eden. For many Christians, both Catholic and Protestant,[3] the Genesis Scriptures represent God's plan for marriage. Jesus' comments do suggest that, by his time, at least some Jews agreed that the joining together of man and woman was God's plan for relationships and that divorce was not part of the original plan (Matt 5:32; 19:1–12). In addition to the teachings, we have an image of Jesus celebrating at a Jewish wedding feast and helping with the wine supply (John 2). Before we go further, let us begin our discussion of marriage by

---

1. United States Conference of Catholic Bishops, *Marriage*, 2–17; NAE, *Theology of Sex*, 2–8.

2. Coontz, *Marriage*, 226.

3. Francis, "General Audience," para. 1; see Graham, "A Sacred," para. 1, and Humphrey, "Recovering Christian," 36–41.

reading excerpts from the two creation narratives. The creation of human beings is the final act in the Genesis 1 creation sequence.

> Then God said, "Let us make humankind in our image, according to our likeness...." So God created humankind in his image, in the image of God he created them; male and female he created them. God blessed them, and God said to them, "Be fruitful and multiply, and fill the earth and subdue it...." (Gen 1:26-28)

The second story comes from Genesis 2 verses 18 through 25.

> Then the Lord God said, "It is not good that the man should be alone; I will make him a helper as his partner." So out of the ground the Lord God formed every animal of the field and every bird of the air, and brought them to the man to see what he would call them; and whatever the man called every living creature, that was its name. The man gave names to all cattle, and to the birds of the air, and to every animal of the field; but for the man there was not found a helper as his partner. So the Lord God caused a deep sleep to fall upon the man, and he slept; then he took one of his ribs and closed up its place with flesh. And the rib that the Lord God had taken from the man he made into a woman and brought her to the man. Then the man said, "This at last is bone of my bones and flesh of my flesh; this one shall be called Woman, for out of Man this one was taken." Therefore a man leaves his father and his mother and clings to his wife, and they become one flesh. And the man and his wife were both naked, and were not ashamed.

I also recommend you read Genesis chapters 1 through 3 so you have a richer context for the frequent references to the first relationship. Genesis 3 contains the story of what happened when Eve and Adam ate forbidden fruit. After eating, they realized they were naked, so they wore fig leaf clothes. This story of violating God's rule in the Garden of Eden is known as "the Fall" in traditional Christian theology. When God confronted them, Eve blamed the serpent, and Adam blamed Eve. Each received a specific curse. Eve's curse is about hard labor in childbirth and submission (Gen 3:16): "To the woman he said, 'I will surely multiply your pain in childbearing; in pain you shall bring forth children. Your desire shall be for your husband, and he shall rule over you.'" And Adam is cursed because he listened to his wife and because he ate the forbidden fruit. He is cursed to hard labor in fieldwork. God gives them clothes but bars them from the garden so they will not have eternal life.

Conservative Perspectives on the Creation Verses

Many interpret the statement that Adam and Eve were created in the image of God (Gen 1:31) to mean human beings have a God-endowed dignity. Here's a quote from Mark McMinn and Clark Campbell: "Perhaps the most exceptional thing about creation is the biblical assertion that humans are created in the image of God (or, *imago Dei*). This means that humans reflect something about God that is not revealed in the rest of creation . . . ."[4]

In a series of articles, Gangel summarized the Genesis verses this way: "So, two patterns emerge early in God's revelation. One is the pattern of monogamy, voluntary union, love, and marital fidelity, obviously God's pattern from the very first."[5]

Most conservative Christians offer Genesis 2:24 as evidence that God meant for one woman and one man to be joined together as one.[6] Also, most conservatives reference Genesis 1:28 in conjunction with the sexual union. That is, a reason for sexual intimacy was procreation.[7] Conservatives observe that sex was created by God, but only sex within a marriage is good.[8]

The formation of Eve from Adam's rib to be a helpmate has often been interpreted by conservative Christians as evidence of God-ordained sex-role differences in marriage. And the man's preferential first appearance in the order of creation means that a man is the leader in such relationships.[9] The rule of Adam over Eve identified the beginning of the patriarchal family pattern in which women were subordinated to men.[10] As noted above, the fact that Jesus referred to these Genesis verses highlights the importance of God's plan for marriage (Matt 5:32; 19:9).

The story of the fall of humanity in Genesis 3 also factors into conservative views of marriage. Attributions of blame toward Adam and Eve, in addition to God's curses, have been seen as a basis for at least three ideas about relationships.

---

4. McMinn and Campbell, *Integrative Psychotherapy*, 26–27.

5. Gangel, "Toward a Biblical," 56.

6. For example, Francis, "General Audience," para. 1; Humphrey, "Recovering Christian," 36.

7. For example, Goldingay et al., "Same Sex," 25; NAE, *Theology of Sex*, 4.

8. For example, Graham, "God's Best," para. 2.

9. Knight, "The New Testament," 216–29.

10. Coogan, *God and Sex*, 54–55.

1. Women are to be under the authority of men.
2. A woman's sexual desire is focused on her husband.
3. Women and men have different roles in a marriage.

Here's an example from Stanley Grenz: "The man and the woman were created in order to supplement each other. But after the Fall, mutuality digressed into competition. Now the desire of the woman is directed toward her husband, but he exercises rulership over her."[11]

To close this section, I offer two comments from different conservative leaders who emphasize the role of God and love in marriage. Billy Graham, the well-known U.S. preacher who dominated Evangelical Christianity for many decades of the twentieth century, invoked an image of a tripartite relationship by including God as part of the marital relationship: "The perfect marriage is the uniting of three persons—a man and a woman and God. This is what makes marriage holy. Faith in Christ is the most important of all principles in the building of a happy marriage and a successful home."[12]

Finally, Pope Francis offered a detailed teaching on marriage in 2014. He reminds his audience of the Genesis union and ties this relationship to an understanding of love and God.

> The image of God is the married couple: the man and the woman; not only the man, not only the woman, but both of them together. This is the image of God: love, God's covenant with us is represented in that covenant between man and woman. And this is very beautiful! We are created in order to love, as a reflection of God and his love. And in the marital union man and woman fulfil this vocation through their mutual reciprocity and their full and definitive communion of life.[13]

Alternative Perspectives on the Creation Verses

Christians from various traditions agree that God views people as having dignity and worth. Several scholars make the point that the first two chapters of Genesis are about the origins of things important to the ancient Israelites. The biblical words should not be taken as laws or commandments. Although Genesis 2:24 has been quoted to support marriage between a man and a woman, it is not a commandment and does not prohibit a man from

---

11. Grenz, *Sexual Ethics*, 53.
12. Graham, "A Sacred," para. 1.
13. Francis, "General Audience," para. 1.

having other wives, as was evident in other chapters of Genesis. Similarly, the other Genesis stories explain where people come from, why men and not women have leadership roles, why childbirth is so hard, why people work hard, and why people should cover their genitals (i.e., nakedness).[14]

Jennifer Knust and others have noted a distinction in the forming of humans between the two creation accounts in Genesis 1 and Genesis 2.[15] First a human is created. God looks for a mate for the man and finds none among the animals. God then creates a helper from the side of the first human. Humankind becomes separated into male and female. They are joined together when a man cleaves to a woman when having sex. Menn opined that originally the two sexes were equal but after the Fall, a hierarchy developed in which men were the head of the relationship.[16]

The gender roles in the verses appear to indicate ancient customs. At the time, men were bound to the land in agricultural activities; hence, Adam is made of the land. There's a play on words and images here. Women are like land. Some are barren and some are fertile. In ancient views of sex, men planted seeds in the ground and in women. Seeds were precious as was land. And by extension, fertile women were also precious.

Jesus' reference to the Genesis verses supports the long-term importance of the binding together of people in marriage before God and the seriousness of divorce. The presence of other teachings and examples of marriage and divorce in the Bible allows for consideration of other forms of relationships.

The Genesis chapters illustrate marriage customs in a male-dominated society. The superior role for men above women is found throughout biblical narratives. The man is created first, and the woman is second. The man cleaves, but the woman does not. Following the advice of women can be dangerous because of the woman's susceptibility to sin. These Genesis verses reflect ancient customs and are not necessarily the way people must live in contemporary society.

In these Genesis verses and elsewhere in the Bible, there's not much to suggest a beautiful wedding ceremony taking place in a house of worship. Commenting on Genesis 24:63–67, Menn observed, "Apparently it was easier to get married in those days. All one had to do was to have sexual relations . . . ."[17] Perhaps, as Rob Bell wrote in a popular book, *Sex God:*

---

14. For example, Knust, *Unprotected Texts*, location 973; Friedman and Dolansky, *The Bible Now*, 81–82.

15. Knust, *Unprotected Texts*, locations 895–920; for example, Snyder and Shaffer, "On Male," 108–13.

16. Menn, "Sexuality," 37–45.

17. Ibid., 39.

Exploring the Endless Connections between Sexuality and Spirituality, when a man had sex with a woman, he sealed the marriage.[18] The Genesis verses indicate the importance of a committed relationship, not how contemporary people establish such a relationship.

Lessons from the Apostles

Because the apostle Paul wrote so much of the New Testament, his perspective on marriage and divorce are often quoted by Christian clergy. There is more than one text to examine, but let's look at Paul's first letter to the Corinthians. In the first verse of chapter 7, it is clear Paul is responding to things the Corinthians asked about. Here's what he wrote through verse 9:

> Now concerning the matters about which you wrote. It is well for a man not to touch a woman. But because of the temptation to immorality, each man should have his own wife and each woman her own husband. The husband should give to his wife her conjugal rights, and likewise the wife to her husband. For the wife does not rule over her own body, but the husband does; likewise the husband does not rule over his own body, but the wife does. Do not refuse one another except perhaps by agreement for a season, that you may devote yourselves to prayer; but then come together again, lest Satan tempt you through lack of self-control. I say this by way of concession, not of command. I wish that all were as I myself am. But each has his own special gift from God, one of one kind and one of another. To the unmarried and the widows I say that it is well for them to remain single as I do. But if they cannot exercise self-control, they should marry. For it is better to marry than to be aflame with passion.

Now let's look at the verses in Ephesians 5:21–33. I should point out that although conservative scholars accept the tradition that Paul wrote Ephesians, other Bible scholars think another person wrote this letter and other letters called "Pastoral Epistles."[19] Attributing a document to a famous author was not uncommon.

> Be subject to one another out of reverence for Christ. Wives, be subject to your husbands, as to the Lord. For the husband is the head of the wife as Christ is the head of the church, his body, and is himself its Savior. As the church is subject to Christ, so let

18. Bell, *Sex God*, 130.
19. Furnish, *The Moral*, 12.

> wives also be subject in everything to their husbands. Husbands, love your wives, as Christ loved the church and gave himself up for her, that he might sanctify her, having cleansed her by the washing of water with the word, that he might present the church to himself in splendor, without spot or wrinkle or any such thing, that she might be holy and without blemish. Even so husbands should love their wives as their own bodies. He who loves his wife loves himself. For no man ever hates his own flesh, but nourishes and cherishes it, as Christ does the church, because we are members of his body. "For this reason a man shall leave his father and mother and be joined to his wife, and the two shall become one flesh." This is a great mystery, and I mean in reference to Christ and the church; however, let each one of you love his wife as himself, and let the wife see that she respects her husband. (Eph 5:21–23)

Referring to the Genesis verses, the author of 1 Timothy offers guidance in 2:11–15:

> A wife should learn quietly with complete submission. I don't allow a wife to teach or to control her husband. Instead, she should be a quiet listener. Adam was formed first, and then Eve. Adam wasn't deceived, but rather his wife became the one who stepped over the line because she was completely deceived. But a woman will be kept safe through childbirth provided she continues in faith, love, and holiness, combined with self-control.

Now a few words from the apostle Peter found in 1 Peter 3:1–7:

> Likewise you wives, be submissive to your husbands, so that some, though they do not obey the word, may be won without a word by the behavior of their wives, when they see your reverent and chaste behavior. Let not yours be the outward adorning with braiding of hair, decoration of gold, and wearing of robes, but let it be the hidden person of the heart with the imperishable jewel of a gentle and quiet spirit, which in God's sight is very precious. So once the holy women who hoped in God used to adorn themselves and were submissive to their husbands, as Sarah obeyed Abraham, calling him lord. And you are now her children if you do right and let nothing terrify you. Likewise you husbands, live considerately with your wives, bestowing honor on the woman as the weaker sex, since you are joint heirs of the grace of life, in order that your prayers may not be hindered.

Conservative Perspectives on the Apostles' Letters

The consistency from Genesis to Jesus to Paul makes it clear that God has a plan for marriage as a God-ordained relationship between one man and one woman. The marriage of a man and a woman represents the marriage-like relationship of God and his bride, Israel. And in the new covenant, the marriage is between Jesus, God's son, and his bride, the church. The organization of a marriage places man as the head of the relationship just like Jesus is the head of the church. Men and women submit to each other and are to treat each other with love and respect. A quote from Baptist preacher and author, John Piper, illustrates a complementary approach to marriage: "The Bible really cares about the dynamic between men and women. It has nothing to do with a woman's incompetency. . . . This has to do with God's created dynamic of what a man is and what a woman is in their gut with regard to the ballet of leadership and submission."[20]

Ultimately, the woman submits to a man's authority because Eve and not Adam was deceived. Conservative Christians view marriage as a covenant relationship that mirrors the relationship between God and humankind.[21] In the marriage relationship, the husband is the head of the relationship.[22]

The biblical teachings about washing and holiness—as well as the phrase "without blemish"—indicate God's concern for purity in the relationship. Christians write about the sanctity of marriage and use the word *undefiled* to refer to sex within a marriage in contrast to other sexual activity, which defiles. A quote from Don Wilton in *Decision Magazine* offers an example.

> When God spoke the words "Do not commit adultery," He was establishing the fact that any sexual activity between a man and a woman outside of marriage is adultery. In so doing, God affirmed three very important things. First, He affirmed that marriage was to be only between a man and a woman. Second, He affirmed that this relationship was to be monogamous and permanent. Third, He affirmed the sanctity of the marriage relationship, which was to be undefiled. The marriage relationship was to be sacred.[23]

---

20. Kumar, "John Piper," para. 2–4.
21. Foster, "Covenant," para. 1–2.
22. For example, Sun, "Mark Driscoll," para. 1–2.
23. Wilton, "You Shall Not," para. 17–18.

Sex is restricted to the husband-wife relationship. They should come together to avoid seeking sexual satisfaction outside of marriage, which would be sexual immorality. A quote from Billy Graham illustrates a common conservative perspective:

> The Bible teaches that God created sex. He made "male and female." Then it says, "God saw everything that He had made, and behold, it was very good." This included the natural sexual attraction between the man and woman He had created. Therefore, sex is not sin! It is God's gift to the human race. It is for procreation; for enjoyment within the bonds of matrimony; for the fulfillment of married love.[24]

Women should focus on their family role as wives and mothers. This view fits with the beliefs of many contemporary U.S. women. For example, a Barna survey revealed that more than half (53 percent) of Christian women indicated family as the most important priority.[25]

The idea that women are weaker than men comes from 1 Peter 3:6–7. The idea that women need male protection has been a generally accepted idea in Christian history. And contemporary sermons still advocate that women should be under the authority of men.[26] The theme of this section clearly emphasizes the authority dimension of morality. God's words and actions recorded in the Bible prescribe the moral foundation for marriage. The authoritative position for men derives from God himself. When challenged by modern notions of equality, conservatives sometimes respond that *equal* does not mean the *same*. An equal partnership can mean different but equally valuable contributions to a relationship.

Progressive Perspectives on the Apostles' Letters

The New Testament letters reveal the importance of marriage as a relationship blessed by God. The loving and respectful relationship stands out as a model for caring and consideration of the others' wellbeing. The pattern of Scripture places women in a subordinate role. For millennia, most cultures limited women's opportunities for education and employment. Principles governing contemporary marriages include extending the New Testament

---

24. Graham, "God's Best," para. 2.
25. Barna Group, "Christian Women," para. 4–5.
26. Hyatt, "Why the 'Woman,'" para. 1–2.

principles of love and respect but need not retain the ancient cultural values placing a man above a woman.[27]

Women and men are equal when it comes to a person's relationship with God. Women and men have the same responsibility for the way they live their lives before God and others. In this view, authority within a marriage can be shared, and the issues of authority and inequality emphasized by conservative perspectives are based on cultural customs rather than the principles of love and mutual respect, which call for a recognition of the different strengths each person brings to a marriage.

Other Comments about the Apostles' Letters

Comments by Jesus and Paul appear to place marriage in a subordinate role to singlehood. Jesus seems to say some are called to a life of singlehood without sex for the sake of the kingdom of God. Paul considers marriage a practical option for those who lack self-control over their sexual desires. Whatever these verses may mean, they do not support the contemporary elevation of marriage with the concomitant disfavoring of singlehood many experience in Christian churches.

The idea of a woman's being saved through childbirth has led many women to believe they are cursed if they cannot become pregnant. Christian women have searched for supernatural reasons. Some wonder if they lack faith or demurely think, "God must have a reason." Churches often complicate the matter by celebrating growth in the number of infants in their nurseries and focusing great attention on Mother's Day or special mother-daughter events—but all of these exclude the childless woman or couple.

Sex and Marriage

An example of a strict boundary on premarital sex identified as fornication can be found in H. Norman Wright's advice. He asks couples "to stop having complete sexual relations for two basic reasons. One reason is to find out if their relationship is built on something other that [sic] just the physical. . . . The second major reason . . . is based on Scripture. The New Testament teaches that we are not to engage in premarital relations. The Scripture calls that fornication."[28]

---

27. Hyatt, "Why the 'Woman,'" para. 3.
28. Wright, *The Premarital*, 148–49.

The containment of sexual relationships within a marriage was affirmed by the prohibitions against adultery in the laws of Israel and numerous stories illustrating punishment for adultery. Jesus refined the teaching on adultery by equating thoughts of lust with adultery. The importance of sexual faithfulness in marriage was evident by his strong stance against permitting divorce in Mark 10:1–12 and Luke 16:18. Christians affirm the importance of sexual faithfulness within a marriage. Differences will come in why faithfulness is important. A conservative approach argues based on the authority of God's Word, but progressives see a principle of love that is destroyed when people are sexually unfaithful.

Christians differ on the morality of sexual relationships among unmarried persons. Conservative perspectives on sexual relationships emphasize matters of holiness and purity. Sexual activity outside of marriage is condemned as fornication and immorality.

Alternative views focus more on a person's current relationship status. In a love-focused theology, all persons are welcome. And the emphasis is on creating healthy relationships. One alternative response to sex among unmarried couples is by a well-known Evangelical pastor, Rob Bell. Bell discusses the unusual verses in Exodus 22 and Deuteronomy 22 suggesting that when a man raped a woman he was to treat her as a wife. Sexual intercourse appears to be a primary or even exclusive criterion of marriage in the ancient biblical world.

Here's the Exodus 22:16–17 text:

> When a man seduces a young woman who isn't engaged to be married yet and he sleeps with her, he must marry her and pay the bride-price for her. But if her father absolutely refuses to let them marry, he must still pay the same amount as the bride-price for young women.

And here's the Deuteronomy 22:28–29 text:

> If a man meets up with a young woman who is a virgin and not engaged, grabs her and has sex with her, and they are caught in the act, the man who had sex with her must give fifty silver shekels to the young woman's father. She will also become his wife because he has humiliated her. He is never allowed to divorce her.

Now here's a quote from Rob Bell related to the texts: "The point of the Deuteronomy and Exodus passages? Sex, in the ancient world, was marriage. If you had sex, you were married. All that needed to be worked out was the legal and financial consequences of what this man and this woman had just done."²⁹ Bell also opined, "But maybe it's already a marriage in God's eyes, and maybe their having sex has already joined them as man and wife from God's perspective."³⁰

As with any such small quote from a book, it's important to read the author's context. No Christian leaders favor sexual promiscuity. Alternative voices like Bell find a close connection between sexual union and the idea of establishing a husband-wife relationship.

Divorce and Remarriage

Conservative Christians view marriage as a lifelong commitment. Jesus offered the strictest guidelines prohibiting divorce in Mark 10:1–12 and Luke 16:18. However, Evangelicals point to Matthew 19:9, where Jesus is said to have made an exception, which allows a man to divorce a woman if she commits adultery. Here's Jesus' teaching on divorce from Matthew 19:1–12:

> And Pharisees came up to him and tested him by asking, "Is it lawful to divorce one's wife for any cause?" He answered, "Have you not read that he who made them from the beginning made them male and female, and said, 'For this reason a man shall leave his father and mother and be joined to his wife, and the two shall become one'? So they are no longer two but one. What therefore God has joined together, let not man put asunder." They said to him, "Why then did Moses command one to give a certificate of divorce, and to put her away?" He said to them, "For your hardness of heart Moses allowed you to divorce your wives, but from the beginning it was not so. And I say to you: whoever divorces his wife, except for unchastity, and marries another, commits adultery; and he who marries a divorced woman, commits adultery." The disciples said to him, "If such is the case of a man with his wife, it is not expedient to marry." But he said to them, "Not all men can receive this precept, but only those to whom it is given. For there are eunuchs who have been so from birth, and there are eunuchs who have been made eunuchs by men, and there are eunuchs who have made themselves eunuchs for the sake of the kingdom of heaven. He who is able to receive this, let him receive it."

---

29. Bell, *Sex God*, 130.
30. Ibid., 132.

Other references to Jesus' teachings include Matthew 5:32, Mark 10:11–12, and Luke 16:18. The apostle Paul offered advice in 1 Corinthians 7:10–16:

> To the married I give charge, not I but the Lord, that the wife should not separate from her husband (but if she does, let her remain single or else be reconciled to her husband)—and that the husband should not divorce his wife. To the rest I say, not the Lord, that if any brother has a wife who is an unbeliever, and she consents to live with him, he should not divorce her. If any woman has a husband who is an unbeliever, and he consents to live with her, she should not divorce him. For the unbelieving husband is consecrated through his wife, and the unbelieving wife is consecrated through her husband. Otherwise, your children would be unclean, but as it is they are holy. But if the unbelieving partner desires to separate, let it be so; in such a case the brother or sister is not bound. For God has called us to peace. Wife, how do you know whether you will save your husband? Husband, how do you know whether you will save your wife?

Ultraconservative Views on Divorce and Remarriage

Divorce must be viewed in the context of marriage, which is a sacred agreement made before God and between a man and a woman and meant to last a lifetime. God's relationship to his people was like a marriage. God often warned his people about pending punishments for those who would violate the agreement. Divorce is simply not part of God's plan. Jesus' teaching supersedes other teachings. There is no basis for a just divorce. If a person has been divorced, then he or she must remain single. There is no justification for remarriage. If a man marries a divorced person, he has committed adultery.

Conservative Views on Divorce and Remarriage

The conservative view is similar to the ultraconservative view but with a bit more leeway when it comes to divorce. Again, divorce must be viewed in the context of marriage, which is a sacred covenant between a man and a woman in the presence of God and meant to last a lifetime. Christians have recognized adultery as a legitimate reason for divorce. For much of history, divorce was granted by the Church. Divorce issues became a part of the major divisions within Christianity. In the 1500s, King Henry VIII of England wanted a divorce because he did not obtain a male heir from Catherine of Aragon. The Pope denied the request. King Henry reformed the Church in England, setting himself up as head. He pressed for and received permission to divorce his wife from the Archbishop of Canterbury in 1553.[31]

Christians are not to seek divorce, but in cases of adultery, and when a non-Christian spouse leaves a Christian spouse, the Christian spouse is permitted, but not required, to divorce. In recent years, Evangelicals have expanded the basis for divorce to include physical abuse and the unwillingness of the abuser to change.[32] But a biblically justified basis for divorce does not require the wronged spouse to seek a divorce. Christians are to prayerfully consider forgiveness and reconciliation.

Remarriage is permitted for a biblically justified divorce. But some conservatives do not allow remarriage for clergy based on the letter to Timothy stating that pastors must only have one wife (1 Tim 3:2, 12). In other words, clergy are held to a higher standard than are the laity. Some churches have a procedure called "annulment" that essentially declares a relationship as not a legitimate marriage in the view of the church.[33] Following an annulment, people are free to marry as if they were entering a first marriage.

Alternative Views on Divorce and Remarriage

Progressive Christians agree that marriage is a sacred covenant that should be held in high esteem. There is biblical evidence of divorce in law (e.g., Deut 24:1–4) and when Abraham sent Hagar away with his firstborn son, Ishmael (Gen 21:8–21). Hornsby points out that the large-scale ending of Israelite marriages counseled by the prophet Ezra (10:3) was based on commandments against marrying people who worshipped other gods.[34]

Jesus' teaching on divorce and remarriage affirms the value of the people in the relationship. They are to treat each other with ultimate respect. When the partners in a marriage act in ways to harm the other by adultery, failing to meet the needs of or harming the other, the marriage agreement is destroyed. Divorce may be the best way to legally end a relationship that has ended in other ways. Divorce can allow injured parties to heal. A divorce

---

31. The BBC, "Divorce in Christianity," para. 3.
32. For example, Alsdurf and Alsdurf, *Battered into Submission*, 153–58.
33. Rapp, "Catholic Marriage," para. 14.
34. Hornsby, *Sex Texts*, 38.

frees a person to live singly or remarry. A remarriage involves the same commitment to each other as any other Christian marriage.

Additional Perspectives on Marriage and Divorce

Over the years, I have come across other comments on these verses, which reveal a bit more diversity when considering what Christians believe. I will just list them, as I believe they are self-explanatory.

1. Jesus considered a single life devoted to God as a better state than marriage. Paul offered a similar opinion in 1 Corinthians 7.
2. Jesus contrasted the law attributed to Moses with God's original plan, implying that at least some of the laws attributed to Moses were not attributable to God.
3. The exception for adultery reported by Matthew only applied to men. Women did not have the right to seek divorce within that culture.

Plural Marriage

Christians traditionally do not view plural marriage as a viable option; therefore, there is nothing to discuss as a difference between conservative and progressive Christians. Polygamy is, however, a contemporary social issue and a relationship that was part of biblical history. Leaders in the Old Testament had many wives and concubines (e.g., Abraham, Jacob, Moses, Gideon, David, Solomon). The story of Tamar and Judah in Genesis 38 illustrates an expectation that when a woman's husband died without leaving a child, his brother was expected to have sexual relations in order for her to have a child, who would be named for the deceased brother and protect the family's wealth. Later, in Deuteronomy 25:5–10, the rules about the relationship are recorded. The penalty appears to be public shaming if the brother-in-law refused, but the Tamar story suggests the obligation was much stronger at that point in Jewish history. In any event, there is no evidence the brother-in-law had an obligation to marry his brother's widow. These Genesis and Deuteronomy verses are sometimes cited when discussing levirate marriage.

Do Christians practice polygamy today? The short answer is yes. The polygamy that was part of the Mormon Church in the U.S. is fairly well known, but of course the primary group of Mormons disavowed polygamy (actually, polygyny—many wives) in the 1800s.[35] A few Fundamentalists continue the practice, as illustrated in a *Time* article by Belinda Luscombe.[36] In 2013, the National Geographic channel aired a feature titled "Polygamy USA" describing the lifestyle of an Arizona group practicing polygamy as part of their Mormon beliefs. Christian missionaries to countries where polygamy was legal were divided on what to do when people in polygamous relationships converted to Christianity. Some believed the polygamous marriages should end, but others did not.[37] Following the Apartheid Era in South Africa, branches of the Apostolic Faith Mission Church united. One branch included pastors in polygamous relationships. The fellowship decided against breaking up existing polygamous families.[38]

One Christian group, the Truthbearers, founded by Mark Henkel, argues for the legitimacy of Christian polygamy.[39] The group references the biblical basis for polygamy and insists on consensual relationships. Although it has been argued that early Christians had more than one wife—hence, the apostle Paul's responding to polygamy among early Christian by requiring leaders to have only one wife (1 Tim 3:2, 12)—the interpretation is not widely accepted.[40]

Moral Perspectives on Marital Issues

In this section I review the six moral dimensions previously discussed along with the role of consent. Recall that Christian moral judgment usually includes references to Scripture along with arguments based on one or more moral foundations. As you consider the six moral foundations, note how the moral analysis relates to various dimensions of human nature illustrated in the SCOPES model. Clearly, marriage and relationship issues are social context issues so we will look at the impact on the couple. But we also want to examine the individual issues as well. Here's how we can frame a question: how does acting on a moral judgment affect a couple spiritually, cognitively, behaviorally, physically, emotionally, or socially?

---

35. Hansen, "Mormonism," 142–59.
36. Luscombe, "I Do," para. 1.
37. Holst, "Polygamy," 205.
38. Johan Mostert, face-to-face conversation, April 11, 2015.
39. www.truthbearer.org
40. Holst, "Polygamy," 210–12.

1. Care versus Harm

In matters of caring, contemporary Christians do not disagree about the importance of marriage and the importance of treating each other with respect and honor. Also, most Christians consider divorce to be a moral concern that deserves attention by church communities.

Ultraconservatives place heavy emphasis on the God-ordained concept of the marriage covenant, which can be interpreted to mean that a marriage relationship cannot be broken, regardless of the harm to the people in the relationship. Some conservatives hold more moderate perspectives and allow divorce in cases of adultery. The harm done is viewed as breaking an agreement with God with implied disastrous consequences to the husband and wife who would consider breaking their agreement.

Progressive Christians focus on the harm done to the persons in the marriage. They are more willing to consider divorce the most moral action when at least one partner is abusive. Progressives view marriage as made for the benefit of people. When a marriage appears to harm rather than promote wellbeing, the marriage ceases to be a moral good and becomes a curse that can be ended by dissolving the relationship. Think of the SCOPES model for this and other moral dimensions. Harm can be spiritual, emotional, physical, and social. Constant criticism is stored in memory and those negative thoughts destroy self-esteem and self-confidence. Psychological abuse can take many forms, such as insulting language, false accusations of infidelity, and abusing financial or other resources leading to poverty. Over-controlling spouses can harm not only the marriage relationship but also relationships with families and friends.

2. Fairness/Reciprocity versus Cheating

Most Christians recognize the difficulty in a relationship when one partner cheats on the other in the form of an extramarital affair. Betrayal in a marriage can also be a nonsexual emotional attachment to another person. Emotional cheating occurs in romantic relationships when one partner develops an emotional attachment to another person, which competes with love for one's spouse. This deep love for another is a betrayal that is deeply felt and can be worse than a nonromantic sexual cheating event.

Ultraconservative Christians focus on the sacredness of marriage and preserving the marriage at all costs—even when one partner has cheated. Some churches will hold biblically based seminars that address many of these topics. They may offer biblical counseling to help members get their relationships back on track.

Conservative Christians with more moderate views are open to accepting psychological counseling from a professional they trust to hold biblical values about the importance of marriage and the sinfulness of divorce. Cheating in the form of adultery is clearly condemned.

Progressive Christians will focus on the effects of fairness or cheating on the wellbeing of either marriage partner. They are more likely to support the wishes of the person who feels victimized by unfair treatment, which can include the extremes of cheating.

The other aspect of fairness was discussed earlier in the chapter at some length. In traditional views of marriage, the notion of fairness as equality is not evident—men were in the position of authority, and wives were to submit. Conservatives appear to have been influenced by equality movements within culture such that equality can now mean equally valued contributions to a marriage even though men and women have different roles. Progressive Christians view marriage as an egalitarian relationship. In this view, fairness means treating each other with respect as equals.

3. Ingroup Loyalty versus Betrayal

Conservative views rely heavily on biblical rules and guidance, which offer evidence for God's perspective on moral issues even if a particular text does not speak to a contemporary issue, such as spouse abuse. Conservatives are mindful of God's constant warnings about Israel's betrayal. Christian conservatives' close following of biblical teaching can be seen as being loyal to God. Conservative Christians are also loyal to the teachings of their tradition. To support other than traditional teachings about marriage and divorce would feel like betraying God and one's faith family.

Progressive Christians are more likely to focus on God's love and compassion for people who are victims of inflexible rules and oppressive laws. When progressive Christians focus on the commandment to love others as oneself, they interpret loyalty to mean being loyal to the principles taught by Jesus rather than following a rigid set of rules that fail to consider contemporary life situations.

4. Authority/Respect versus Disrespect

The conservative position is clear: in a biblical marriage, the husband is the head of the relationship in the same way Jesus is the head of the church.

Although there is a basis for respect and care between husband and wife, the wife is to obey, serve, and be under the authority of her husband. Many contemporary conservatives are quick to point out that men are to love their wives as Jesus loves the church and sacrificed himself for the church. Nevertheless, the hierarchy of authority remains a biblical principle to follow.

Progressive Christians view marriage as a partnership between equals. Moral relationships are about respect, which can only truly occur when each person views the other as an equal partner in the relationship. Serving the other partner may be a moral response when the other is in need. But serving the other should occur in either direction and not be a one-sided relationship for a lifetime.

5. Purity or Sanctity versus Degradation

Conservatives view marriage as a sacred institution ordained by God. People are joined together in *holy* matrimony. Anything that can degrade the marriage relationship can be sinful. Degradation can take many forms but at least includes such common forms as addiction to alcohol or other drugs, extramarital sexual relationships, and pornography. Conservative Christians are more likely to view many degrading activities as part of a sinful lifestyle that can be addressed through biblical counseling.

Progressive Christians focus on the integrity of the members in the relationship and recognize the degradation caused by various addictions. Progressive Christians are more likely to seek help from professionals who may use psychological or psychiatric interventions to treat substance dependence or harmful sexual practices.

6. Liberty versus Oppression

Conservatives value their right to follow God's plan for marriage as that between one man and one woman. They value their freedom to limit divorce and remarriage. They value their freedom from laws and rules that permit alternative lifestyles, such as same sex-marriage or plural marriage. They also value the freedom to act in society in accordance with their beliefs about marriage and divorce. Therefore, they feel oppressed when laws are enacted that would require them to hire divorced persons, support people who are living together or who are in a same-sex relationship.

Progressive Christians value freedom for all persons regardless of marital status. They are more likely to welcome unmarried couples and same-sex couples into their businesses and churches. Progressive Christians prefer to allow individuals the time they need to make moral decisions as they interact with God throughout a lifespan. Progressive Christians are concerned about oppression within a marriage.

Consent and Choice

Ultraconservative Christians continue the biblical custom of a man seeking consent in the form of approval from a woman's father before they marry. In conservative Christian weddings, the pastor traditionally asks the bride's parents, "Who gives this woman away?" The expected response comes from the father who is to declare to all present, "Her mother and I." This practice continues to fade, and those who keep it up view it as a tradition and sign of respect, though undoubtedly some continue to view the woman as unable to consent to marriage. Of course, conservative Christians would not consider the question of consensual sex a legitimate question.

In general, progressive Christians emphasize the dignity of the persons in the relationship and the importance of mutual respect. Mutual respect is in part evident when both persons consent to their relationship without coercion from other persons. All Christians would agree that the marriage partners should be strongly committed to respect each other.

Social context is important to understand the legal boundaries that govern consent. For example, laws may specify when a person is old enough to consent to sexual relations. Laws also define how old people must be to marry without a parent's consent.

Summary

In this chapter, I presented a selection of the major biblical texts Christians traditionally use as their basis for Christian marriage and teaching about divorce. The traditional Christian understanding of marriage begins with the first two chapters of the Bible. As further evidence of the importance of this text, Christians note that Jesus cited the Genesis verses when making the point that divorce was not part of God's original plan for marriage. Finally, many Christians observe that God's blessing on reproduction indicates that the proper place for sex is within the context of a marriage relationship.

I then looked at biblical texts in the New Testament. The texts present a man as the head of the marriage relationship. Men and women are instructed to respect each other and meet each other's sexual needs. The New Testament writers do not offer much in the way of options to obtain a divorce. And there is no support for sex outside of marriage.

In reviewing the biblical texts, I also presented progressive views, which do not necessarily contradict the traditional perspectives on marriage, divorce, and sexuality but rather allow for the use of reason when considering information about culture during biblical times and during contemporary times. For example, there are good reasons for divorce that are not covered in Scripture, such as when a woman is physically abused by her husband.

In keeping with the plan of this part of the book, I reviewed the six moral dimensions to illustrate how conservative and progressive Christians could reach different conclusions with respect to marriage and divorce.

Additional Resources

1. **Evans on *Real Marriage*.** In the text I referred to a bestselling book by Mark and Grace Driscoll. Popular writer and speaker Rachel Held Evans offers her comments on the book as well as marriage and sex. More than five hundred people commented. Her article may also lead to a rich discussion. http://rachelheldevans.com/blog/mark-driscoll-real-marriage

2. **Divorce is the end of a relationship.** Some suggest it could be time to view divorce as the start of a new life. Here's an article about throwing a divorce party. http://www.oprah.com/spirit/Throw-a-Divorce-Party

Discussion Questions

1. A number of American Christians deny evolution and insist that God had a personally active role in creating people. How might views about being created in God's image be different for creationists compared to those who accept the scientific account of human origins? Is there a way for Christians who accept evolution to maintain a conservative view of marriage?

2. Cohabitation is a popular form of relationships in many cultures, but people continue to want to marry. What do you think of Pastor Rob Bell's idea that a biblical marriage was pretty much about a sex act and a financial arrangement?

3. The story of Henry VIII illustrates the lengths to which powerful people would go to get what they wanted. Nowadays divorce is fairly easy

to obtain in cultures once dominated by official Christian doctrines. If you had the power to influence a change in divorce laws, what would you like to see happen?

9

SEXUAL ORIENTATION AND SAME-SEX RELATIONSHIPS

In recent years, various political entities ruled that people of the same sex have the right to marry or live together in a legal relationship identified as a "union." Examples of countries where same-sex marriage is legal include Canada, France, Mexico, New Zealand, South Africa, United Kingdom, and the United States. For many Christians, the problem with same-sex relationships is the existence of Old and New Testament texts prohibiting same-sex sexual activity and other texts identifying marriage as between one man and one woman. Christians have come to different views on the interpretation of these texts, which results in considerable conflict within families, churches, Christian schools, and public arenas.

In 2013, when many groups were advocating for or against changes in laws restricting marriage to only one man and one woman, I received an email that referred to the sins of the Sodomites. Sodom is where the problem of same-sex orientation begins for some Christians. And in fact, the term *sodomy* stems from the type of sexual sin traditionally associated with the biblical narrative. In this chapter I will review the primary texts Christians reference when expressing their views about same-sex orientation and same-sex relationships. Second, I will suggest how moral psychology may be applied to understand the range of Christian perspectives on biblical morality.

Same-Sex Relationships and the Bible: Christian Perspectives

Most Christians learn that sexuality and sexual relationships begin with the two creation narratives in Genesis 1 and 2. Because I included those verses in the chapter on marriage, I will not repeat them here. Conservative perspectives refer to these verses to make the following points relevant to same-sex relationships:

1. God only created two sexes—male and female. They were created with a desire to join together in physical union. Other forms of sexual interaction were not part of God's plan.
2. The union was a marriage blessed by God, which implies no other type of union or marriage can be blessed.
3. The original couple was commanded to reproduce, which implies that married couples need to be of the opposite sex.
4. Jesus referred to the union of Adam and Eve when answering a question about divorce. His answer indicates the verses are about God's design for marriage as a permanent relationship between a male and a female (Matt 19:4–6).

Progressive perspectives offer the following points:

1. The Genesis verses are stories about the origins of things and blessings. The Genesis stories are not commandments or laws to govern humanity.[1]
2. Since God is the continuous creator of all life, he made some people with two sets of sex organs. He made some with sexual desire for people of the same sex and others with a sexual desire for both men and women. And God created some people with no desire for sex.
3. The absence of comments in Genesis chapters 1 and 2 about sexual minorities and their relationships is not a logical basis for a prohibition of unmentioned relationships.
4. The Genesis verses refer to a helping relationship and affirm sexual activity. There is no command to have children.[2] The text indicates having children is a blessing rather than a commandment.[3]
5. Marriage is not just about having children. Many couples are unable to have children. And there is no biblical basis to limit marriage to women of childbearing age.
6. The earth is full. Overpopulation is a problem. Adding more children to the world is not necessarily a moral act.

---

1. Friedman and Dolansky, *The Bible*, 39–40.
2. Hornsby, *Sex Texts*, 16.
3. van Leeuwen, "Be Fruitful," 58–61.

Sodom and Gibeah

The reference to sin within the ancient city of Sodom is in Genesis 13 and 18 followed by Abraham's conversation with God and the story in which two angels come to visit Lot, Abraham's nephew, who resides in Sodom with his family. Here's the text in Genesis 19:4–8:

> But before they lay down, the men of the city, the men of Sodom, both young and old, all the people to the last man, surrounded the house; and they called to Lot, "Where are the men who came to you tonight? Bring them out to us, so that we may know them." Lot went out of the door to the men, shut the door after him, and said, "I beg you, my brothers, do not act so wickedly. Look, I have two daughters who have not known a man; let me bring them out to you, and do to them as you please; only do nothing to these men, for they have come under the shelter of my roof."

The people of the city press Lot to bring his guests out to them so they can *know* them. In the Bible, the verb *know* is usually taken to mean to have sexual relationships. A similar story can be found in Judges 19 at a place near Gibeah where the local men demanded that a host offer his male guest for sexual relations. The host protested and offered his daughter; however, the guest offered his concubine, who was taken and raped during the night. The stories evoke powerful responses of disgust, fear, and anger.

Conservative perspectives on these verses make the following points:

1. The sin of the men of Sodom was the aggressive demand for sex with Lot's male guests.
2. Lot's protest to offer his daughters was further evidence of the moral depravity of the Sodomites.
3. God does not tolerate sexual sinfulness. He will destroy the wicked.

Alternative perspectives note the following:

1. The people in Sodom were not necessarily all men because the Hebrew word *anasim*, sometimes translated "men," can also mean "women."[4]
2. Lot's offer of his virgin daughters as a substitute for his guests (Gen 19:8) indicates the story was not simply about same-sex sexual

---

4. Friedman and Dolansky, *The Bible*, 1–8.

activity. The story is about rape and illustrates the egregious violation of hospitality expected from hosts in this part of the ancient world.[5]

4. In the Gibeah story, the guest offers his concubine; the offer is accepted, and she is raped. Given the different sexes involved in this brutish report, the story does not establish a basis for comments on loving same-sex relationships.

5. Jesus' reference to the Sodom story also implied the sin was a failure of expected hospitality.[6]

6. The prophet Ezekiel and the book of Judges (chapter 19) refer to the sins of Sodom without mentioning sexual sin.[7]

7. Coogan comments on the use of the word *sodomy* or *sodomites* in some translations: "no such exact term derived from the name of the city of Sodom exists in either biblical Hebrew or biblical Greek."[8]

Was King David a Gay Man?

Another potential reference to biblical same-sex relationships is the poem known as "David's Lament," which memorializes the death of his good friend Jonathan. David wrote about his love for Jonathan as greater than the love for women (2 Sam 1:26).

It seems doubtful that David was gay. David appears to have practiced polygyny—having several wives as well as concubines. The biblical evidence—a verse in a poem and other verses indicating Jonathan's love—is far too limited to establish whether he was gay or bisexual. Men and women have lifelong same-sex friends that do not include sexual interaction. Also note that those who knew David brought a beautiful virgin named Abishag to him in his old age to see if he had sufficient libido to be king (1 Kgs 1:1–4). David was unable to have sex with her, so he lost his kingship to his son. Presumably, the courtiers would have brought a man if he were gay.

Coogan offers a few points about the culture.[9] The point of the early stories about David and Jonathan is to explain why David, and not one of Saul's sons, became king. The love relationship between the two men can be a celebration of the friendships between men in patriarchal societies.

5. Coogan, *God and Sex*, 119–32.
6. Ibid., 127.
7. Ibid., 128.
8. Ibid., 130.
9. Ibid., 117–19.

Coogan also notes that men who signed treaties were considered brothers, if they were political equals, or father and son if not equals. Love could be used to refer to either covenant relationship.

What about the Biblical Laws?

The laws from the two legal texts in Leviticus are often quoted in any Christian discussion about same-sex activity. "You shall not lie with a male as with a woman; it is an abomination" (Lev 18:22). "If a man lies with a male as with a woman, both of them have committed an abomination; they shall be put to death; their blood is upon them" (Lev 20:13).

Both verses prohibit same-sex relationships for men. What is interesting is the lack of a prohibition against same-sex relationships for women even though proximal verses specifically identify prohibitions against sex with animals for both men (Lev 20:15) and women (Lev 20:16). Why did the law prohibit same-sex activity for men but not women? Some have spoken about the important role of a man's semen in ancient Israel. Thus in sex without a woman, a man wasted his semen ("seed" in some biblical translations) and concomitantly failed to engage in sexual relationships that would create children. However, the presence of semen appeared to be a moral purity issue taken care of by washing. Another possible explanation for the exclusive focus on men is the rules against mixing of sexes, as in the law that prohibited cross-dressing (Deut 22:5); but again, why was there no prohibition for same-sex relations for women since they were mentioned in the cross-dressing verse? Coogan suggests the laws do not prohibit lesbian relationships because the relationships "did not relate to patriarchy—or, for that matter, to paternity."[10]

Cultural factors have been considered by some scholars who observe that laws in other ancient cultures (e.g., Babylon, Greece) prohibited sex between people of unequal social classes. However, Friedman and Dolansky point out that the Hebrew Bible does not distinguish between people of different classes but rather treats men as equals before the law.[11] Finally, despite the class-based objection of Friedman and Dolansky, others have observed that the physical position of male-on-male sex was degrading because of the comparison with male-on-female sex and the widespread lower social position of women in ancient cultures. As written, the law appears to define the same-sex act between men as an abomination. How important were the purity laws? Tony Campolo recalls a comment offered to him by a

10. Ibid., 134.
11. Friedman and Dolansky, *The Bible*, 1–8.

Rabbi. That is, that the penalty helps determine importance, and the penalty is death.[12]

Those who offer other opinions note there is no evidence of same-sex activity in the context of a loving relationship. It is only in recent history that we have evidence of same-sex couples living in loving monogamous relationships. Also, most Christians do not consider themselves bound by the old laws and cite the words of Jesus about a new way to view old rules (e.g., Luke 5:37–39) and the experience of Peter revealing a change in what God calls "clean" or "unclean" (Acts 10). As with many other rules, people are left to decide which of the old laws they should follow today; however, Christians have another set of texts to consider, and these seem to be more precise when it comes to prohibitions against same-sex relations.

What do the Gospels Say?

There are no verses in the Gospels that directly deal with same-sex activity or relationships. As noted above, conservatives make the point that Jesus affirmed God's plan for marriage when he referenced the creation narrative about marriage between a male and a female. Alternative views make the point that Jesus was surely aware of same-sex activity and did not consider it important enough to condemn.[13] Conservatives remind people that the lack of a comment cannot be taken as an endorsement and one must take all of Scripture into consideration.

What Did the Apostle Paul Write?

The apostle Paul is traditionally considered to be the author of three letters to early churches that offer guidance on conduct, including sexual behavior. Those specific texts are Romans 1:24–31, 1 Corinthians 6:9–10, and 1 Timothy 1:8–11. Paul condemns same-sex activity for men and women as well as a plethora of other sins. I will review the common points made about each of the texts.

Romans 1:24–31

> Therefore God gave them up in the lusts of their hearts to impurity, to the degrading of their bodies among themselves, because

---

12. Campolo, "Missing," 198–213.
13. Ibid.

they exchanged the truth about God for a lie and worshiped and served the creature rather than the Creator, who is blessed forever! Amen. For this reason God gave them up to degrading passions. Their women exchanged natural intercourse for unnatural, and in the same way also the men, giving up natural intercourse with women, were consumed with passion for one another. Men committed shameless acts with men and received in their own persons the due penalty for their error. And since they did not see fit to acknowledge God, God gave them up to a debased mind and to things that should not be done. They were filled with every kind of wickedness, evil, covetousness, malice. Full of envy, murder, strife, deceit, craftiness, they are gossips, slanderers, God-haters, insolent, haughty, boastful, inventors of evil, rebellious toward parents, foolish, faithless, heartless, ruthless.

1 Corinthians 6:9–11

Do you not know that wrongdoers will not inherit the kingdom of God? Do not be deceived! Fornicators, idolaters, adulterers, male prostitutes, sodomites, thieves, the greedy, drunkards, revilers, robbers—none of these will inherit the kingdom of God. And this is what some of you used to be. But you were washed, you were sanctified, you were justified in the name of the Lord Jesus Christ and in the Spirit of our God.

1 Timothy 1:8–10

Now we know that the law is good, if one uses it legitimately. This means understanding that the law is laid down not for the innocent but for the lawless and disobedient, for the godless and sinful, for the unholy and profane, for those who kill their father or mother, for murderers, fornicators, sodomites, slave traders, liars, perjurers, and whatever else is contrary to the sound teaching that conforms to the glorious gospel of the blessed God, which he entrusted to me.

Conservative Comments on Paul's Writings

1. Same-sex activity is condemned in the context of other sinful activities.
2. Same-sex activity is condemned for both men and women.

3. Same-sex activity is condemned for people living in different cultures.
4. Regardless of translations of specific words, the descriptions of sexual activity by Paul in Romans make it clear that same-sex activity is condemned.
5. Paul's writings indicate the seriousness of the sins. The punishment is death and an inability to enter the kingdom of heaven.
6. Paul's writings are consistent with the rest of Scripture regarding the appropriate place for sex within marriage and the sinfulness of sex outside of marriage, including same-sex sexual activity.
7. Church leaders have consistently interpreted the teachings of Paul and the rest of Scripture to mean that same-sex relationships are sinful. To claim a new revelation or a better interpretation after thousands of years is not credible and lacks humility.

Alternative Comments on Paul's Writings

1. Paul's letter to the Romans focused on the sexual activity that is unnatural.[14] This does not apply to people who are naturally attracted to people of their same sex and who have relations in the context of a loving, monogamous relationship. Such situations were not a part of Paul's culture.
2. Paul's letter to the Corinthians focused on the sexual activity involved in the worship of Aphrodite, the hermaphrodite goddess. Heterosexuals worshipping her would engage in what for them was an unnatural act of sex with same-sex persons.[15]
3. The type of same-sex practice Paul condemned in the letter to Timothy was the common practice of teachers having sex with their same-sex students (i.e., pederasty).[16] All Christians agree with Paul that the sexual exploitation of vulnerable persons, especially children, is sinful.
4. Greater tolerance and humility is needed when it comes to various interpretations of biblical texts, including those regarding same-sex sexual activity.

14. Coogan, *God and Sex*, 136.
15. Furnish, *The Moral*, 55–92
16. Ibid.

5. Traditional interpretations of Scripture are indeed retained by some conservative groups, but most Christians find the example of the ill-treatment of women a compelling reason to change traditional interpretations. For example, a literal interpretation of Scripture requires women to remain in abusive relationships because the only listed acceptable reason for a biblical divorce is adultery.

6. When conservatives insist on the timelessness of biblical laws, they must logically insist on the death penalty as well, but most are selective in the parts of the texts they accept as commandments for contemporary living.[17]

Summarizing Conservative and Progressive Perspectives

Conservative Perspectives

When it comes to the prohibitions against same-sex sexual activity, many Christians share a conservative perspective: that sexual activity is restricted to married persons of the opposite sex. All other sexual activity, which includes same-sex activity, violates God's plan. Based on the biblical texts, same-sex acts are sinful; there is no provision for same-sex unions or same-sex marriage in traditions that interpret Scripture in a conservative manner, even if those traditions do not reflect Fundamentalist interpretive perspectives on other aspects of behavior.

When conservatives interact with the biblical texts, they offer the context of God-ordained marriage as discussed in the marriage chapter. Again, the quoted verses refer to the creation narratives in which God unites one man and one woman, which were referred to by Jesus in Matthew (19:4–5, 10–12). The conservative sources note the Leviticus laws and cite the New Testament teaching against same-sex relationships presented by the apostle Paul. Evangelical leaders generally support the conservative perspective. Evangelical preacher Billy Graham illustrates the marriage context and concomitant prohibitions against same-sex relationships in an online article titled "Does the Bible Approve of Some Homosexual Relationships?":

> The Bible provides God's blueprint for marriage and for His good gift of sex in Genesis 2:24. The gift is only to be enjoyed within a marriage between a man and a woman. There are no exceptions suggested, such as homosexual partnerships. From Genesis on, the Bible praises the marriage of a man and a

---

17. Coogan, *God and Sex*, 119–32.

woman, but it speaks only negatively of homosexual behavior whenever it is mentioned.[18]

Sociologist Tony Campolo affirmed the traditional Evangelical understanding that same-sex behavior is sinful. In his essay, he focused on the importance of building a loving community where people experiencing same-sex attraction feel welcomed and supported. He reviewed the Scriptures aforementioned, and, while not disagreeing with traditional interpretations of the texts, he suggested Christians consider alternative interpretations, including an awareness of the cultural context within which Paul wrote. Finally, he advised Christians not to hope or expect that people with a same sex-orientation can change their orientation. And he suggested alternative lifestyles to combat the loneliness experienced by Christians who love same-sex persons. One idea is to live in a covenant relationship without sexual activity, and a second is to live in a Christian community.[19] People change their minds. I used the past tense in this paragraph because in 2015 Tony Campolo created quite a stir by changing his mind and supporting same-sex marriage.[20]

Progressive Perspectives

Several mainline churches have made statements affirming the value of sexual minorities as children of God. Some groups have changed their rules to perform same-sex marriages and to welcome openly gay and lesbian persons into clerical positions. In 2003, Gene Robinson became the first openly gay bishop in the Episcopal Church and the larger Anglican Church. He told part of his story to Terry Gross on NPR.[21] Born Vicky Gene Robinson and not expected to live, he grew up with a sense of purpose. He prayed to be heterosexual and was married to a woman for fourteen years. His understanding of what it means to be gay has changed over the years, and when his state of New Hampshire changed their laws in 2010, he married his husband, Mark. One aspect of his perspective on Scripture is that God's communication to people did not end in the first century. He places the LGBT issues in the context of Bible-based attitudes toward slavery and women.

---

18. Billy Graham Evangelistic Association Staff, "Answers: Does the Bible," para. 1–2.
19. Campolo, "Missing," 198–213.
20. Gledhill, "Tony Campolo Calls."
21. Gross, "Retired Bishop," transcript.

> So the Holy Spirit will lead you into all truth. And I think, you know, look how many centuries we spent using Scripture to justify slavery. Look how some religions still use their holy texts to denigrate and subjugate women. But I believe it's the Holy Spirit who has been continuing to reveal God to us in those movements, and what we're trying to figure out right now is whether or not God is leading us to a different understanding of gay and lesbian, bisexual and transgender people that really does represent God's will, and before this we have just not been able to understand it.[22]

In congregations where there are traditional and alternative subgroups, the potential for conflict can be challenging, not only in dealing with those who are aggressive about their positions, but within families and the minds of those who wrestle with their conscience. A *New York Times* story illustrates this conflict in a report of a Methodist pastor, Dr. Thomas Ogletree, who officiated at his son's wedding in New York. Although same-sex marriage was legal at the time, the Methodist Church voted against changing their position on sexual orientation in 2012. Of interest is his argument defending his stance; Ogletree said, "Jesus of Nazareth broke the law; he drove the money changers out of the temple. So you mean you should never break any law, no matter how unjust it is?"[23]

I mentioned Tony Campolo's view under "conservative perspectives." Months after I wrote that section, Campolo garnered considerable attention because he changed his mind in support of gay marriage. He had long identified with the progressive movement but he did not support gay marriage. His stature in the U.S. Evangelical community is considerable as a sought-after speaker, a Baptist minister, a popular author, and spiritual adviser to former president Bill Clinton.[24]

Additional Perspectives

The Metropolitan Community Church (MCC) identifies itself as a movement founded by gay pastor Troy D. Perry, who was defrocked by a Pentecostal denomination because of his sexual orientation. The MCC was specifically focused on ministering to LGBT communities. As of 10 June 2013, their website (i.e., MCCChurch.org) reported a presence in twenty-two countries.

22. Gross, "Retired Bishop," para. 51.
23. Otterman, "Caught in Methodism's," para 11.
24. Gledhill, "Tony Campolo calls."

The MCC offers a paper by Mona West titled "The Bible and Homosexuality." As noted above, West interpreted the Sodom story from Genesis 19 as a condemnation of rape and inhospitality. She opined that the Leviticus rules were important to the structure of male Jewish society. The Leviticus writers did not address sexuality between people in loving relationships.

Turning to the New Testament texts, West quotes the aforementioned passages attributed to the apostle Paul and points out the difficulty with two Greek words, which different translators have rendered using different English words. One word, *arsenokoitai*, has been translated as "homosexuals," "sodomites," "child molesters," and "perverts." The other word, *malakoi*, has appeared as "catamites," "the effeminate," and "boy prostitutes." She adds a discussion of Greek culture and the exploitation of youth by older male mentors. Finally, she comments on the Romans text (1:26–27) by referencing the social context of unequal sexual relationships as the point of Paul's concern but also noting the larger context of a theology of grace. A closing section discusses biblical interpretation. She advises readers against making an idol out of Scripture. Instead of looking to Scripture alone, she suggests biblical interpretation should rely on the John Wesley tradition known as the "Wesleyan quadrilateral," which consists of the Bible, tradition, experience, and reason.

Nick Street reported a story about LGBT inclusive Pentecostal churches in Brazil. Street describes the context of widespread Pentecostalism in Brazil and identifies Pentecostal churches that have an LGBT-friendly approach,[25] which expands options for Christians who identify as LGBT beyond those offered by the MCC and mainline Protestant churches.

Social Trends

On 23 May 2013, the Boy Scouts of America (BSA) voted to include gay scouts but not gay leaders. The policy was effective on the first of January 2014.[26] America's largest religious groups, some of which sponsor scouting programs, responded in different ways. The Church of Jesus Christ of Latter-Day Saints supported the inclusion of gay youth as scouts, but the Southern Baptist Convention and the Assemblies of God did not.[27] U.S. Catholic leaders supported the Boy Scouts' decision.[28] On July 27 2015 The

---

25. Street, "LGBT-Inclusive," para. 7.
26. Boy Scouts of America, "Boy Scouts."
27. Dias, "Brave," 14.
28. Gibson, "Catholic Leaders," para. 1.

BSA officially ended the ban on "openly gay leaders." They did announce that churches could choose leaders consistent with church teaching.[29]

On 19 June 2013, Alan Chambers, former leader of Exodus International, made public apologies on his website and OWN (Oprah Winfrey Network) to members of the gay and lesbian community for the harm done as a result of Exodus Ministries.[30] The program offered gays and lesbians activities to change their orientation to heterosexual. The program offered an "exodus" from same-sex orientation, and some participants reported becoming "ex-gay." Because of its religious focus, it and similar approaches have been known as attempts to "pray the gay away." The apology suggests that although Mr. Chambers has retained his theological position about sexual orientation, he no longer believes in the effectiveness of the program and admits the program harmed people. Chambers stated that "99.9% have not experienced a change in their orientation."[31]

On 26 June, 2013, the U.S. Supreme Court found problems with the Defense of Marriage Act (DOMA). The case, *The United States v. Windsor*, involved a tax burden on Edith Windsor that would not have been present if the United States recognized her same-sex marriage to Thea Spyer. They were married in Ontario, Canada and lived in the state of New York, which recognized the marriage. However, DOMA excluded same-sex partners. The Supreme Court decision recognized the rights of same-sex couples who were legally married under state laws. The federal law (i.e., DOMA), interfered with the rights granted by certain states.[32] Some viewed the decision as a victory for states' rights. Others celebrated the decision as an advance for LGBT rights. Outspoken conservative Christians saw the decision as another example of a disturbing social trend and an infringement on their religious rights.

Finally, on June 26, 2015, the U.S. Supreme Court ruled that same-sex couples had the right to marry.[33] Christians are clearly divided over the opinion. Numerous stories appeared on the internet revealing both support and opposition to the ruling.

---

29. Richinick, "Boy Scouts."
30. Chambers, "Exodus Int'l President," para. 1.
31. Throckmorton, "Alan Chambers," para. 2.
32. For a summary and commentary see Entin, "The Supreme Court's," 823–28. A copy of the "Slip Opinion" is available from the U.S. Supreme Court at http://www.supremecourt.gov/opinions/12pdf/12-307_6j37.pdf.
33. Howe, "In Historic Decision."

Other Sexual Minorities

Bisexual, transsexual, and transgender issues are not on the radar screen of most Christians who seem only recently aware that there are so many people whose sexual identity is gay or lesbian. I have consulted with Christians and Christian organizations for most of my professional career. Most are sincere about maintaining biblical standards of acceptable moral conduct. To reduce temptation, they keep the sexes apart in colleges and treatment programs. It never seems to occur to them that sexual identification on an admissions document is not a reliable indicator of whom the applicant might find attractive. And they seem unaware of the struggle a person might have to remain loyal to the rules of an organization, such as a college or seminary, while feeling a strong desire to have an unapproved relationship.

Moral Psychology and Same-Sex Relationships

Christians are clearly divided on the morality of same-sex relationships. The moral judgments of the community in which LGBT persons live will have an effect on multiple dimensions of functioning represented in the SCOPES model. The judgments of some Christian are so strong that they would question the possibility that a same-sex couple could also be Christian. The spirituality of LGBT persons is usually challenged by referring to the authority of Scripture. The messages of condemnation and disapproval are widespread and likely part of the memories of most LGBT persons. But attitudes of condemnation go further that just spirituality and cognition to affect behavior patterns, physical health and access to health care, emotional functioning, and of course social relationships.

Regardless of their position on the conservative-to-liberal spectrum, Christians feel obligated to include references to the biblical texts to explain at least a part of the justification for their beliefs about same-sex relationships. The way in which they address the biblical verses supports the theory of intratextuality. The lengthy arguments and the quantity of articles dealing with same-sex relationships indicate the extensive commitment of religious groups to their invested positions. The principle of sunk costs helps explain the sizable investment of time and finances required to support legal battles and political campaigns aimed at changing laws related to LGBT issues.[34]

Christian conservatives sometimes refer to physiology when arguing about the naturalness of heterosexual sex. Persons advocating for LGBT

---

34. See chapter 2 for a discussion of the theory of intratextuality and the principle of sunk costs.

rights sometimes argue that their state is natural—that they were born the way they are and did not choose their sexuality. Philosophically, any argument based on a biological status offers no help in deciding what is moral. In other words, because something naturally occurs does not mean that it should or ought to occur. In the case of sexual orientation and sexual attraction, there appears to be evidence favoring a biological component. But there is also evidence that sexuality is more fluid for some people than for others. Regardless of the several factors leading to the sexual orientation of LGBT persons, a culture needs a firm basis for making a moral decision. People are not encouraged or punished for simply acting on the basis of a biological impulse. They are held morally responsible for how they manage their behavior in accordance with the rules of their society.

In the next section, I will review the six domains of moral psychology and suggest how they might inform an understanding of Christian perspectives on reasoning about the morality of same-sex relationships. I will also comment on the ethics of consent and choice. Here's a general question to assess the impact of a moral judgment: how does acting on a moral judgment affect an LGBT person spiritually, cognitively, behaviorally, physically, emotionally, or socially?

1. Care versus Harm

Conservative Christians focus on many aspects of care and harm. They care about their marriages and their families and believe that same-sex marriage and displays of same-sex relationships will destroy their understanding of God's plan for marriage between one woman and one man. Marriage is the foundation of the Christian family, so any weakening of God's plan for marriage also weakens the family and, by extension, society. They also care about their children, and because they believe sexual orientation is a choice, they do not want their children exposed to this alternative lifestyle in the public arena.

Because of the strident voices of some conservatives, it would be a mistake to ignore the compassion other conservatives feel for people in the LGBT community. Conservatives believe God loves all people, and they believe they should reach out with love and compassion toward all people. Conservative psychologist Melody Palm affirms the traditional teaching of her tradition but focuses on responding to people who identify as having same-sex attraction. In her list of ten key points she includes two items particularly consistent with a caring response. She writes, "People have a deep need to be accepted unconditionally. Demonstrate unconditional, positive regard for the person. Convey warmth and compassion for the person in the struggle. Be genuine, empathetic, and respectful."[35]

Finally, conservatives believe that God loves all people but does not tolerate sin; hence, the common refrain, "love the sinner but hate the sin." In attempts to identify that they too sin and need redemption, some conservatives are quick to point out that sexual sins are no worse than other sins.

Christians who identify with alternative views focus on the harm done to people who experience same-sex attraction. They recognize the assaults and abusive language aimed at sexual minorities that have caused them to hide their sexuality from friends and family based on religious teaching. They identify with the emotional pain and hurt that can be caused by rules that prevent sexual minorities from publicly being with the people they love and from enjoying the role of parenting children, living where they choose, maintaining their employment, or just living life free of harassment because of who they are. Progressive Christians are also keenly aware of the pain of loneliness and loss that occurs when sexual minorities lose their church family and, in many cases, their Christian friends and family members when they disclose their sexual identity. Because they do not accept the Fundamentalist perspectives on the Scriptures, progressive Christians do not fear harm to their marriages or children by people living together in different relationships. Instead, they are more likely to view same-sex attraction as a common aspect of human sexuality that occurs in a small, albeit significant, percentage of people. Finally, because these Christians do not consider same-sex orientation to be sinful, they do not attempt to separate a person's sexuality from their personal identity. They recognize the insult in the phrase, "love the sinner but hate the sin." Sexuality is part of a person's identity.

The 2013 decision by the Boy Scouts of America (BSA) offers an interesting illustration of variations in care-harm morality. The organization voted to include gay youth and noted in their statement that sexual activity is not part of scouting. In contrast, gay men will not be admitted to leadership positions. Many conservative groups voiced their disapproval and will no longer participate in the BSA programs. Other groups, like Catholics and the LDS, expressed their support. Why wouldn't the conservatives show care and love in welcoming America's young men? I suspect it is because the threat of harm remains. The threat of harm would be accepting gay men as scout leaders thereby providing boys with unacceptable role models. As noted above, the 2015 decision to include gay leaders confirmed the

---

35. Palm, "Desires in Conflict," points 7 and 9.

suspicions of conservatives, albeit, there is a provision that churches may select leaders compatible with their views.

2. Fairness/Reciprocity versus Cheating

Fairness and reciprocity norms represent a basic sense of social justice. Conservative Christians view the rules of Scripture as providing the basis for a fair and just society. They acknowledge that the Old Testament laws do not necessarily apply to contemporary Christians, but in the case of same-sex relationships, they point to the New Testament directives. On the other hand, some conservative voices appear willing to support various degrees of fairness within society as long as they retain religious freedom to maintain traditional rules governing sexual relationships in their places of worship, work, and education.

In contrast, progressive Christians rely heavily on the commandment to love others as they love themselves and find therein the basis for affirming the same rights for sexual minorities as for the majority. Fairness also extends to the way society treats sexual minorities. It is wrong to treat people differently based upon their sexual orientation. It is unfair and unjust to deny them employment, housing, or any other benefit available to others. The close 5–4 votes by the justices on the U.S. Supreme Court in both cases (*The United States v. Windsor* and *Obergefell v. Hodges*) reflect the difficulty in deciding matters of justice and fairness when it comes to same-sex marriage.

3. Ingroup Loyalty versus Betrayal

The Christian tradition is two thousand years old. By claiming the Old Testament Scriptures as part of their canon, Christians trace their spiritual heritage back to creation. To violate God's plan for marriage and relationships is disloyal to God, who has ordered marriage and relationships for the good of humankind. In addition, conservative Christians are loyal to their traditions. To speak against the teaching of their church is to betray their church and their spiritual family. Loyal followers of Jesus support his view on marriage as between one man and one woman.

Progressive Christians point to the Scriptures that show how Jesus, who followed the Jewish law, still spoke out against his fellow Jews who created burdensome rules and interpreted old texts in ways that failed to treat the poor and sick lovingly. Christians are loyal to the spirit of Jesus when they challenge the traditional doctrines or position statements that impose unjust burdens on others. Progressives can also point to early church disagreements about which rules new converts should follow (Acts 15) as support for the idea that disagreements do not mean disloyalty. Every breakaway Christian denomination was disloyal to some other group of Christians.

4. Authority/Respect versus Disrespect

Conservatives in many cultures value the social order. For Christians, the social order reflects God's plan. Conservatives view God as the ultimate authority. Because Scripture represents the very words of God, they must be taken seriously. The Bible as God's Word is the ultimate authority. Given the plain language against same-sex activity in the texts, conservative Christians feel they must be obedient to God rather than to man. When a government attempts to create a law—like the approval of same-sex marriage—that violates God's law, conservative Christians feel they have no choice but to obey God and work to defeat such legislation. In addition, some Christians who belong to traditions with a strong sense of hierarchy, such as the Roman Catholic Church or the LDS, are expected to respect the authority of their leaders.

Progressive Christians also respect authority but tend to view Scripture as offering principles that need to be worked out in contemporary situations. They begin with the two great commandments that Jesus used to summarize God's law, and they ask, "What does it mean to love sexual minorities as Jesus would love them?" Progressives view the laws in Leviticus and Deuteronomy and elsewhere as laws for the ancient Israelites. They see Paul's writings as guidance for the specific churches he was addressing in his letters. Like Bishop Robinson, they are open to new interpretations guided by God's Spirit.

5. Purity or Sanctity versus Degradation

Concerns about purity and holy living are powerful concerns when it comes to same-sex issues. Although contemporary conservative Christians may not follow the letter of the Jewish laws, conservatives see in the laws the character of God, who desires his people to have a pure heart and to separate themselves from sin and the ways of the world. The Christian ritual of water baptism illustrates the cleansing from sin. Amish Christians separate themselves from the general culture and thereby conserve their traditions. For centuries, Christians wore special clothing or dressed up in their finest clothes for worship. When hauling and heating water was a significant challenge, the Saturday-night bath was a ritual preparation to be "cleaned up" for the Lord's Day. While those cleanliness rituals have declined in the past century, sexual purity remains an important value that requires abstinence from all sexual activity outside of marriage. As Jesus taught, adultery can occur in the mind, so mental discipline is a part of sexual purity. The Christian church has consistently promoted values of chastity and control over sexuality. Because same-sex activity is a sin, it remains a violation of the Christian's call to live a holy and pure life.

Progressive perspectives focus on respect for each person as the temple in which God dwells through his spirit. The natural desire to love another person intimately is a gift from God. Experiencing sexual attraction is normal, and in a loving and caring relationship, that love is pure, and each person's holiness and worth is respected regardless of sexual orientation. To sexually exploit another person—to use other person to satisfy one's sexual desire—is to disregard their holiness and the image of God in them. Rape and all forms of sexual assault violate the holiness of God revealed in his creation. It is the sexual exploitation that Scripture condemns—not the relationship of people who love each other.

In public statements, Christian organizations opposing same-sex marriage attempt to avoid language that could be construed as hateful. However, in conversation it's easy to hear people referring to same-sex kissing as "disgusting." And people refer to same-sex activity with words like "yuck" and "gross." Understanding Christian perspectives on same-sex relationships requires an understanding of the emotion of disgust and its connection to purity. It's worth re-emphasizing the pervasive impact on the functioning (SCOPES model) of LGBT persons if subjected to a constant barrage of disgust-motivated language and actions. In many cases, their spirituality is considered marred by persistent sin and their cognitive functioning will include memories of the negative ways they have been treated. If they are under threat then they must find behavioral ways to cope with the threat. Obviously, many have hidden their sexual orientation until recently. Many still run the risk of losing employment and relationships if they reveal their sexual orientation. Concerns for health and mental health (including emotional functioning) add to the potential negative impact of harsh, purity-disgust based moral judgments.

6. Liberty versus Oppression

Throughout history, people have yearned for freedom from oppression. Liberators are revered and seen as agents of God (e.g., Moses and Joshua). Perhaps the quintessential biblical liberation story is the exodus from Egypt still celebrated by Jews each year during Passover. In the twentieth century, Dr. Martin Luther King Jr. led protests to free African Americans from rules and regulations that kept them from enjoying the freedoms so dear to the majority of U.S. citizens. Christians value freedom of religion, and many, like the Amish and Huguenots, left tyrannical regimes in search of this important moral virtue.

Conservative Christians focus on their right to be free to worship and live according to God's will as revealed in Scripture. The freedom of religion implies a freedom from government rules and regulations that would force them to give up their right to change their policies and rules regarding the sinfulness of sexual activity outside of marriage between one man and one woman. Their sense of freedom is not just a political sense but includes a sense of being free in Christ and simultaneously free from sinful lifestyles, such as gay and lesbian lifestyles.

Progressive Christians take the view that, like African-Americans and women in years past, sexual minorities are not free to live life to the fullest. They recognize that Christians misinterpreted Scripture to justify laws supporting slavery, racial segregation, and discrimination against women. Therefore, they seek to liberate sexual minorities from legal tyranny imposed on societies by conservative Christians. As most Christians eventually learned to reject laws that limited the freedoms of women and people of color, they will learn to reject laws that limit the freedom of all people, regardless of color, sex, or sexual orientation.

Consent and Choice

Consent implies choice, but psychologists and other human service professionals do not consider all persons capable of giving consent to sexual activity. For example, laws and ethical principles do not consider minors to have the right to consent to a variety of societal activities, including marriage and sex. Progressives support the protection of vulnerable persons from sexual exploitation regardless of their sexual orientation. Instead, they believe that consenting adults have the right to engage in relationships that do no harm. In contrast, conservative Christians do not believe adults should be free to choose lifestyles that violate God's laws, and they warn about the slippery slope that can occur when a culture allows a deviation from traditional marriage.

Summary

In this chapter on sexual orientation and same-sex relationships, I began with the Genesis verses about Adam and Eve because they are the traditional starting point for Christians who argue that, from the beginning, God's plan for marriage was between one man and one woman. And it is only in that relationship where sexual activity is blessed because sex is designed for procreation. To understand the range of Christian perspectives, I presented both conservative and alternative views.

The story of Sodom usually comes up in any discussion about same-sex relationships, so I reviewed the story along with comments commonly presented by conservative and alternative voices. I also commented on the relationship between David and Jonathan, which also arises in some discussions. Finally, any discussion of same-sex relationships would not be complete without a review of the Old Testament laws.

The writings of the apostle Paul explicitly condemn same-sex sexual activity. As with the other texts, I included conservative and progressive perspectives. The issues included concerns about accurate translations, cultural contexts, and what principles may rightly apply to contemporary cultures.

Following the text-focused analysis, I presented some social trends and comments from some Christian leaders to offer a sense as to the diversity within contemporary Christianity. The U.S. Supreme Court decision that same-sex couples had the right to marry is a major factor dividing Christians.

As before, I concluded by showing how Christians can reach different conclusions about the morality of same-sex relationships drawing upon psychological factors that influence morality, applying the rubric of six moral dimensions, and considering the ethical issue of consent.

Additional Resources

1. **Pray the Gay Away**. Alan Chambers was a leader of Exodus International, a Christian program designed to help gays change their sexual orientation. Chambers changed his mind on this practice and offered an apology. Several episodes on "Our America with

Lisa Ling" deal with the subject of gay conversion therapy. People tell of their experiences. http://www.oprah.com/ouramericalisaling/Episode-Recap-Pray-the-Gay-Away-Breaking-News_1

3. **Southern Baptist Pastor Changes His Views.** John Shore posted a story about Danny Cortez, a California pastor who became gay-affirming and embraced his gay son. The post contains links to YouTube videos by both the pastor and his son. http://www.patheos.com/blogs/johnshore/2014/05/southern-baptist-pastor-accepts-his-gay-son-changes-his-church/

4. **U.S. Supreme Court Overturns Defense of Marriage Act.** In a famous 2013 ruling, the U.S. Supreme Court found the Defense of Marriage Act (DOMA) unconstitutional. A married woman suffered economic harm when she was deprived of rights normally granted to spouses. But DOMA deprived her of those rights because her marriage to a same-sex spouse, though recognized in New York, was not recognized under U.S. law. The decision of the court can be found on their web site. http://www.supremecourt.gov/opinions/12pdf/12-307_6j37.pdf

5. **World Vision Blasted and Forgiven.** World Vision provides for the needs of poor people around the world. In March 2014, they announced they would hire people in same-sex marriages. They were highly criticized by many Evangelical Christians. Two days later, they reversed their decision and issued an apology. Here's the story in *The New York Times*. http://www.nytimes.com/2014/03/28/us/christian-charity-backtracks-on-gays.html

    And here is how it was reported by a leading Evangelical Christian magazine, *Christianity Today*. http://www.christianitytoday.com/ct/2014/march-web-only/world-vision-reverses-decision-gay-same-sex-marriage.html

6. **U.S. Supreme Court Decision on Same-Sex Marriage.** Read about the decision at SCOTUS Blog and consider searching for other interpretations in major news sources. http://www.scotusblog.com/2015/06/in-historic-decision-court-strikes-down-state-bans-on-same-sex-marriage-in-plain-english/

Discussion Topics and Questions

1. Some young Christians tell me they believe the issue of equal rights for sexual minorities will not be a moral issue in the future, just like most people no longer support discriminating against people based on the color of their skin or whether they are a man or a woman. What future do you see for LGBT persons in the next twenty years?

2. Some people argue that after approving same-sex marriages, countries or states will approve polygamy. They view changes in laws that define marriage as other than between one man and one woman as a slippery slope. One conservative Christian told me he could see the slope the other way. Based on history, polygamy has been widespread for centuries, but same-sex marriage is new. What changes do you expect to see as a result of legalized same-sex marriages?

3. Given the long heritage of religious teaching against same-sex sexual activity, should conservative Christian colleges and organizations have religious freedom to practice their beliefs even if it means denying some rights to LGBT persons? You might consider related topics, such as the extent of religious freedom and the idea of rights.

4. Think about a story like that of California pastor Danny Cortez (see under Additional Resources), who was changing his views based on his experience with LGBT persons and then learned his son is gay. How influential are personal connections to LGBT persons in changing attitudes?

10

SEX AND GENDER ROLES

In 2014, Rose held up a placard that read, "WOMEN: beautifully & wonderfully made in the image of God!" Twenty years ago she held that same placard as she worked with others to become a priest. Rose was attending a twentieth anniversary celebration of the ordination of women in the Church of England. Today she is known as Reverend Rose Hudson-Wilkin. In attendance at the rally were Catholic women. One leader, Lala Winkley, expressed her distress: "I am a Catholic and I am not envious of anything but I grieve for our particular tradition because it is so bereft of women's input and significantly the poorer because of it- and it does not realise it . . . ."[1]

The words *sex* and *gender* are often used interchangeably in common language. Scientists prefer to use the term *sex* to refer to a person's biological status as male or female or to sexual activity. Of course, the word *sexy* has become an adjective for an attractive appearance. When certain jobs or other social activities are different for men and women, they are sometimes referred to as "sex roles" instead of "gender roles." In this book, I refer to biological differences as "sex differences," and I refer to those different sets of activities considered socially or culturally appropriate for men or women as "gender differences" or "gender roles." Christians view men and women as created in God's image, and many Christians believe men and women have different roles to play in the church, in society, and in the home. The purpose of this chapter is to discover how Christians come to different appraisals about what activities are either right or wrong for men or women.

From the Beginning

As with many topics, an understanding of Christian perspectives on gender role differences starts with the first three chapters of Genesis. Although

1. The BBC, "March through London."

initially men and women were not obviously differentiated in terms of their life roles, following the eating of forbidden fruit, Adam and Eve were ashamed and sought cover for their nakedness. And they were cursed in their life roles. The woman was to suffer pain in childbearing, and the man was to endure hardship in fieldwork. When the laws were created as reported in Leviticus, biological sexuality made a difference in how bodily fluids were handled, and those differences affected the time spent in religious, communal, and sexual activities.

People were not to touch a woman when she was menstruating. The period of uncleanness was seven days (Lev 15:19-24; 18:19). Knust points out that in the early years of Christianity, women attempted to follow the Leviticus 15 rules by not attending church when they were menstruating.[2] These early Christians literally waited seven days and then bathed on the eighth day. The example reveals several aspects of morality. The focus is clearly on the purity and sacredness dimension. But the example also reveals the concern of these women to obey God. Looking more closely we see two aspects of purity morality. One, contact with an unclean person resulted in uncleanness. And two, a literal washing was required before a woman would be ritually clean.

Christian women were also limited in what they could do following childbirth. Knust illustrated this point by referring to instructions from Pope Gregory the Great (597 CE) to Augustine of Canterbury in which the Pope quotes from Leviticus to offer guidance about waiting periods following childbirth and participation in various aspects of worship, such as attendance and participation in holy communion.[3]

The cultural limitations for men were much lower than for women. They could bathe following ejaculation and be clean by sundown. Although the bodily fluids were not necessarily sinful, the fluids were associated with uncleanness and impurity. And people needed to become ritually clean before going on with life in general and religious life in particular. In contrast, the temple was a place of inner and outer purity. Knust asks a question about the blood of animals in the temple—why was that blood not defiling?[4] She suggests the difference might be one of control. The bodily fluids of people that were regulated by law were those that people could not control. In contrast, the blood of animals was carefully controlled by the religious leaders.

From the beginning, biological differences between the sexes provided a basis for differentiation. Rules delineated the requirements to become

2. Knust, *Unprotected Texts*, location 4132.
3. Ibid., location 4275.
4. Ibid., location 4012.

clean, and women had more rules than men. There appears to be a link between sexual differences and the development of gender roles. As time progressed, only men would become religious leaders known as "priests." And only men would be heads of state, which, in the days of ancient Israel, were kings. Most of the prophets were men, but there are references to women as prophets. And there are references to women in leadership. But for the most part, ancient biblical religion was a man's world. Following Jesus' ministry, there are increasingly frequent glimpses of women having a role in the early church. But again, for the most part, men ruled. There have been no female popes. And many Christian traditions continue to restrict priestly or pastoral and leadership roles to men.

Sexual Differences and Christianity

Perhaps the best-known example of distinct gender roles within Christianity is the Catholic Church's position that only men can be priests. In the past few decades, many non-Catholic groups (e.g., Church of England, Episcopalians, Methodists) have changed their rules to welcome both women and men to pastoral leadership positions. An unusual case is the conservative U.S. Assemblies of God, which has ordained women for years although in practice women often had difficulty obtaining senior leadership positions. The Bible contains other rules indicating different roles for men and women. Here are a few examples:

1. Men and women are not to wear each other's clothing (Deut 22:5)
2. Women are to submit to the leadership of their husbands (1 Cor 11:3, 8–9; Eph 5:22–33)
3. Women are to be silent in churches (1 Cor 14:34).
4. Women should not have teaching roles (1 Tim 2:11–15).

Following the teachings and patterns of leaders in the Old and New Testaments, Fundamentalists view men as leaders within religious organizations as well as in the family. Some denominations are careful to point out that God values both men and women. Men are seen as protectors of women and their families, and as leaders they should assume a respectful servant role. Women are to submit to and help men.

Different Clothes

News stories often depict Muslim men and women in modest clothing that covers most of the body. Women's clothes vary with some cultures, sometimes requiring a covering from head to foot in public. Christian men and women in Western cultures used to wear modest clothes. But that has changed in the last few decades.

At different points in our marriage, my wife worked for Christian organizations. When she did, she was required to wear a dress or skirt. Christian culture identified slacks as men's clothing. As such, women were forbidden to wear them. Although conservative Christian cultures changed since her childhood in that they no longer viewed wearing jeans and slacks as sinful, the rule in her workplace did not change until after the year 2000. For thousands of years religious groups have maintained rules about right and wrong clothes for women.

During the 1960s, the Beatles, a British rock band, invaded the United States and brought with them a hairstyle that was longer than traditional for men. Teenage girls swooned over The Beatles, and adolescent boys copied their look. It wasn't long before men began to let their hair grow even longer. Conservative Christians became upset and linked long hair to drugs and the casual sex that swept through Western cultures beginning in the 1960s. Conservative Christians forbid their young men from wearing long hair. And they found support for their position in the Bible—a verse that identified long hair as right for women and not men: 1 Corinthians 11:14.

Most conservative Christians have moved beyond concerns about women in slacks and men wearing long hair. But ultraconservative groups continue to have rules about different clothing for women and men. Amish women continue to wear dresses, and the men continue to wear suits for Sunday dress. LDS women and men derive modesty guidelines from 1 Corinthians.[5] Overall, conservative Christians have shifted to a focus on modesty in appearance regardless of whether one is a woman or a man. On the beach, modesty seems to have a new definition as both men and women wear very little regardless of religious affiliation. The obvious difference between men and women among most contemporary Christians is the custom that women cover their breasts. Although rules about clothing may seem trivial to many in Western cultures, many religious persons, including Christians, take their sacred texts seriously. In the case of Christianity, conservative women and men are expected to dress modestly.

---

5. The Church of Jesus Christ of Latter Day Saints, "Modesty."

Different Roles at Home

James and Phyllis Alsdurf retell horrifying stories of abuse in their book, *Battered into Submission*. One woman recalls the advice she got from Christian books and her husband who was a preacher. "Wives be subject to your husbands as unto the Lord," she quoted from the Bible (Eph 5:22). The authors declare, "And her role was abundantly clear."[6] This battered woman remembers she was expected to stay home with her kids, meet her husband's needs, and obey what her husband said. She believed a Christian marriage was for life with no way out. After multiple beatings, she shot him. The murder trial was in 1984. And Lucille Tisland was acquitted. In their research, the Alsdurfs found many examples of Christian women who suffered in silence. Although I will address violence in another chapter, the story reflects a common belief among conservative Christians for centuries: "a woman's place is in the home."

A quote from the Southern Baptist Convention (SBC) offers a conservative example of a woman's role.

> A husband is to love his wife as Christ loved the church. He has the God-given responsibility to provide for, to protect, and to lead his family. A wife is to submit herself graciously to the servant leadership of her husband even as the church willingly submits to the headship of Christ. She, being in the image of God as is her husband and thus equal to him, has the God-given responsibility to respect her husband and to serve as his helper in managing the household and nurturing the next generation.[7]

In a strong reaction to the position of the SBC, former U.S. president Jimmy Carter ended his six-decade relationship with the SBC. His words in the quote below reflect a significant change by a Christian who is also a world leader.

> It was, however, an unavoidable decision when the convention's leaders, quoting a few carefully selected Bible verses and claiming that Eve was created second to Adam and was responsible for original sin, ordained that women must be "subservient" to their husbands and prohibited from serving as deacons, pastors, or chaplains in the military service.
>
> This view that women are somehow inferior to men is not restricted to one religion or belief. Women are prevented from playing a full and equal role in many faiths. Nor, tragically, does

---

6. Alsdurf and Alsdurf, *Battered*, 14.
7. SBC, "Family."

its influence stop at the walls of the church, mosque, synagogue, or temple. This discrimination, unjustifiably attributed to a higher authority, has provided a reason or excuse for the deprivation of women's equal rights across the world for centuries.[8]

The only reason to mention the U.S. Southern Baptists is that they are the largest single conservative Protestant group in the U.S. and that a world leader, U.S. President Carter, happens to have been a Southern Baptist. As former president Carter observed, other conservative Christian groups—and, indeed, other faith traditions—continue to limit the role of women within religion and society.

An alternative view reflecting equality for women and men can be found in a quote from the *United Methodist Women Handbook*: "We equip women and girls around the world to be leaders in communities, agencies, workplaces, governments and churches."[9]

Knowing the gender role norms of a particular Christian group can help identify the likely role expectations for women and men who share the same household. In conservative households, we can expect men to be the sole or ultimate decision-makers for the couple or family. Although the man is expected to be loving and respectful toward his wife and children, his authority is not to be questioned because it comes from God. A Christian woman is expected to love and respect her husband and submit to his authority. Increasingly, such traditional households are significantly different from the equality norms of Western cultures and many Christians. Obviously, people do not always follow the norms of their group behind closed doors. Thus, we can expect to find more egalitarian relationships among some conservative Christians. And, given the divorce rate, many Christian women head their family units.

Different Roles in Church

In Western cultures, many Evangelicals have moved toward equality for women in nonreligious settings. They have slowly come to accept the changes in industry and government. Accepting women in leadership roles within an official church ministry is another matter. Groups that refer to scriptural teaching as the basis for limiting women's roles are de facto Fundamentalists. That is, their behavior is based on a Fundamentalist way of viewing the biblical texts. In the previous section, it was obvious in some

---

8. Carter, "Losing My Religion," para. 1–2.
9. *United Methodist Women*, 4.

quotes that limited roles for women in the home and society were linked to limited roles in Christian churches and organizations.

Christians for Biblical Equality (CBE) published a study of which Christian denominations include women in leadership positions.[10] In their review, they focused on ordination but clarified other positions. Many groups affirm women by ordination and by placement in leadership roles. Examples include American Baptist Churches USA, Episcopal Church in the USA, Evangelical Lutheran Church in America, Mennonite Church USA, Presbyterian Church (USA), Religious Society of Friends (Quakers), United Church of Christ, United Methodist Church, and the Vineyard Movement. The CBE also listed Christian denominations that do not affirm women in leadership positions. The list includes Christian and Missionary Alliance, Evangelical Free Church of America (EFCA), Lutheran Church–Missouri Synod, and Mennonite Brethren Churches. Because organizations change their stance, it would be wise to check the latest information before considering this list as current.

Conservative Christian groups do not ban women from church work altogether. Rather, conservative Christians restrict women from entering into high leadership positions. Within the Catholic Church, only men serve as priests and bishops, and, of course, the pope is always a man, as he is chosen from among those who have served as priests and bishops. Catholic nuns have a long history of service in such professions as education and healthcare. From time to time movements arise to challenge the churches' traditions, but the possibility of a female priest does not appear on the horizon.

A progressive perspective assumes the equality of men and women in Christian communities. Progressives refer to a statement in Paul's letter to the Galatians (Gal 3:28): "There is no longer Jew or Greek, there is no longer slave or free, there is no longer male and female; for all of you are one in Christ Jesus." Two examples will illustrate how women have been accepted into higher ranks in churches considered progressive or liberal.

First, in the United Methodist Church, Mary Evans Thorne began teaching a class in about 1770.[11] In 1787, John Wesley authorized Sarah Mallet to preach. When the state of New York abolished slavery in 1787, Isabella Bomefree was freed from slavery and cofounded Kingston Methodist Church. She is better known by the name Sojourner Truth. She began preaching in 1843. The history of women in the Methodist church is

---

10 Christians for Biblical Equality Staff, "US Denominations."
11. United Methodist Church, "Timeline of Women."

remarkable for the evidence of women in traditional male roles for more than two hundred years.

Second, the Church of England (C of E) and other members of the worldwide Anglican Communion allowed women to become priests in the twentieth Century. The first woman ordained as a priest was Li Tim-Oi, who served as a priest in Macau in 1944. Her case was a special exception brought on by a need for leadership. It would be another thirty years before the ordination of women as priests became official.[12] In January 2015, the C of E consecrated their first female bishop.[13]

Because the social changes favoring women are only recent, the number of women in official ministerial positions varies even when equality is official church policy. Normally very conservative when it comes to social values, two Pentecostal groups include women in high leadership positions. The U.S. Assemblies of God (AG) presents many conservative views in position papers on its website.[14] But when it comes to women, the AG ordains women, and they serve as senior pastors in their churches. In 2013, the AG hired its first woman to be president of their flagship institution of higher education, Evangel University.[15] To hold that position, one must be an ordained member of the clergy. In this role she also oversees the denomination's seminary, which is a part of the university. The official position of the AG regarding women in ministry affirms the important role of Scripture in deciding matters of faith. In addition, the paper cites the experiences of women filled with the Holy Spirit, thus emphasizing an important role for spiritual experiences in the worldview of at least this group of Pentecostals.[16]

Another group often classified as charismatic is the Vineyard.[17] Charismatic groups believe the Holy Spirit is within Christians to empower them for service according to their spiritual gifts. In a 2009 post, Winn Griffin explained how the Vineyard came to affirm equality. Men and women were created as equals, and there was no sex-based hierarchy until after they disobeyed God in eating the forbidden fruit. Throughout the Bible there were signs of women in leadership roles. But when Jesus came and introduced a

---

12. Anglican Communion News Service Staff, "Anglicans Mark."

13. The BBC, "Libby Lane," para. 1.

14. For a list of AG position papers, see http://ag.org/top/Beliefs/position_papers/index.cfm.

15. Temple, "Evangel to Install," para. 2.

16. General Presbytery of the Assemblies of God, "The Role of Women."

17. See their home page at www.Vineyard.org.

new creation, both men and women became equal in the kingdom of God, thereby recovering the original sense of equality.[18]

Finally, I include a comment on changing roles within the Catholic Church. Cindy Wooden reported comments by Pope Francis that affirmed, "Only men can be priests."[19] However, the Pope pointed to examples of roles women do play in pastoral care and offered a comment suggesting he is aware of the key issue—power. In the Catholic tradition, the celebration of the Eucharist, or the Lord's Supper, is of high importance. Scripture links men in this role to Christ as the head of the church. Here's a key quote.

> "The reservation of the priesthood to males, as a sign of Christ the spouse who gives himself in the Eucharist, is not a question open to discussion," the Pope said, "but it can prove especially divisive if sacramental power is too closely identified with power in general."[20]

The pope appears to be saying that women can and should have more decision-making power within the Catholic Church.

The challenge for women and men to consider is how women and men can be considered equal if there are social or religious roles restricted to one person or the other based on their biological sex characteristics. The challenge for people working with Christians is to recognize the inequality of gender roles within most church groups. Even when changes have become official, many do not accept the change as valid. All things considered, how can you change what God said?

Moral Psychology and Gender Roles

In this section, I will use the six dimensions of moral psychology to illustrate how conservative and progressive Christians can affirm different views on appropriate gender roles. Recall that Christian moral judgments are usually formed on the basis of an understanding of Scripture and arguments based on one or more moral foundations. As with the other chapters, consider the personal impact on functioning from moral judgments by thinking about the SCOPES model. The general question about the effects of acting on a moral judgment can be framed this way: how does acting on a moral judgment affect a person spiritually, cognitively, behaviorally, physically, emotionally, or socially?

18. Griffin, "The Story."
19. Wooden, "Evangelii Gaudium."
20. Ibid., para. 5.

1. Care versus Harm

Conservatives believe that God established different roles for men and women for a purpose. When people violate God's design, bad things happen, as illustrated by many punishments throughout the Bible. On a positive note, conservatives point to the guidance from the apostle Paul, who reminds husbands and wives to love each other and to submit to each other. No harm is done when people love and respect each other.

Progressive Christians find that women are harmed when their vocational opportunities are limited or they are paid less than men. Given the high number of divorces and the fact that most children continue to reside with their single mothers, harm is extended to children. In Western secular societies, women have made great strides in terms of equality of opportunity and pay, but most Christians limit leadership roles for women. In addition to the obvious differential in income and benefits, women can also be harmed by a decrease in wellbeing when their desires are thwarted by religious or social policies.

Referring to the SCOPES model, we can see potential harm for women who do not share the spiritual beliefs of men who may be in a position to control one or more aspects of women's lives. A woman's spirituality, thinking, emotional responses, health and relationships can all be positively or negatively (care vs. harm) impacted by the way the people and organizations in her life apply their moral beliefs about a woman's role. In turn, she may have to adapt her observed behavior patterns to cope with the expectations leaders have about her role.

2. Fairness/Reciprocity versus Cheating

From a philosophical perspective, it is clearly unfair to grant better positions or pay to men instead of women based on differences in biological sex. Because the leaders of any organization are normally paid more than those in lower ranks, and because women cannot hold leadership positions in some Christian groups, a state of unfairness exists. Progressive Christians oppose inequity and the concomitant discrimination.

A conservative might argue for separate but equal roles and suggest that women and men offer different and complementary gifts to a Christian community. It is not known if fairness in pay is also considered by those who hold this complementary position.

3. Ingroup Loyalty versus Betrayal

People who challenge traditional interpretations of the Bible will appear to be troublemakers and disloyal to the leadership of their group. An example of alleged disloyalty can be found in the case of U.S. Catholic nuns, who have sometimes been at odds with the male leadership, as when they supported President Obama's healthcare policies. Bill Donohue said of the nuns' movement: "It is run by people who are disloyal daughters of the Catholic Church."[21]

Women who wish to hold leadership positions within Christian communities may be forced to leave their conservative Christian community to join a progressive tradition that affirms women in leadership. The choice highlights the tension that comes from divided loyalty. If a woman feels called to ministry, she must leave her church family and friends to be loyal to her calling. But leaving her church, friends, and family members also feels disloyal both to the woman leaving as well as to those left behind. Leaving a group that has been part of one's life for years often means exchanging one source of distress for another. The loss of opportunities must be weighed against the loss of relationships.

4. Authority/Respect versus Disrespect

In the traditional view of most Christian groups, a woman is to function under the authority of a man. Over the years, I have heard ways that conservative Christians tried to deal with this rigid interpretation of the Bible. One example is the case of male preachers sitting on the platform when a woman speaks so they can be a "spiritual covering" for the woman. In other words, the presence of a man meant the woman was speaking under male authority. In another case, I found the teaching ability of one woman was clearly evident in conversation. She understood the Bible better than most lay persons and had teaching experience. When asked why she did not teach at church, she explained it was against the rules. Clearly, for conservatives, to go against a church's teaching about a woman's role is to show disrespect for the authority of the leadership. And ultimately, to go against the leadership of the church is seen as challenging God's authority.

Respecting the authority of legitimate leaders is a challenge in any group or organization. Challenges to authority can be particularly disruptive in religious groups who view God as the source of their authority. The large group of capable women in churches and the need for clergy may help

---

21. Saloomey, "Nuns Driving," para. 15.

women reframe their pursuit of equality as helping the church rather than challenging authority.

Progressive Christians view the leadership distinctions between men and women as cultural and find the limitations on authority inconsistent with biblical evidence that women were prophets, included in conversations with Jesus, and active in the early church, and, as noted previously, there is no difference between women and men in spiritual matters.

5. Purity or Sanctity versus Degradation

As noted above, based on how a culture interpreted the Leviticus laws dealing with menstruation, women were limited in their interactions with others, including religious activities. It appears that those laws persisted into the Christian era and affected how women and men dealt with church attendance. Because blood and bodily fluids were associated with concepts of uncleanness, which in the case of menstruation lasted several days, there exists the possibility for biological differences affecting both social and religious activities. Concepts of being pure and clean are linked to being sanctified or holy before God. Being impure is to be unholy and requires a separation from God until one is made ritually clean. Rituals of washing and baptism symbolize restoring acceptability.

It is obvious that some people have an aversion to blood and respond with a sense of disgust to blood and other bodily fluids. I am not aware to what extent the aversion of people to bodily fluids affected the ancient laws and the concomitant limitations placed on women. However, given the commonness of the aversion and the accompanying disgust response, it seems at least plausible that disgust motivated the creation of some discriminatory rules.

Although it may be possible that some contemporary differences between men and women are based on old purity codes, the link is not so obvious today. One aspect of life where differences based on purity may persist is sexual purity. Sexual purity means no sexual activity until marriage. Anecdotally, the burden placed on young women to be virgins appears greater than the burden on young men. Because young people are not expected to have sex, there is no obvious need for birth control. In this context, teen pregnancy in conservative Christian communities offers visible evidence of impurity for months. In contrast, there is no visible evidence of impurity linked to her male partner. The failure of living up to sexual purity codes is a sizeable moral failure for some Christian groups that place a high emphasis on holiness.

Progressive Christians tend to expand the metaphor in the apostle Peter's vision of unclean animals, in which God challenged Peter's views about clean and unclean. In this view, God redeems and sanctifies people—sex or gender does not matter. The pregnant young woman shares the same moral status as do other human beings; her life is sacred. In Christ, she is pure, holy, and restored. Sexual purity distracts a community from focusing on holistic spiritual growth.

6. Liberty versus Oppression

The bottom line regarding liberty is that women have not been as free as men have been in most societies for most of recorded history. And the limitations on freedom are also found in Christian communities.

Conservative women do not necessarily feel themselves oppressed. Women who accept the traditional ordering of roles can feel comfortable and resent "outsiders" obsessed with changing the status quo. A longstanding saying among conservative women is that the man may be the head of the family but the woman is the neck that turns the head.

Women and men from progressive traditions support the liberation of women from oppression in all aspects of society, including church and parachurch organizations. Progressives object to the paternalistic mentality that continues to oppress women by limiting them in any way.

Summary

Gender roles have changed in Western cultures, but they have been slow to change within Christian churches and organizations. Christians have long justified male leadership based on biblical teaching and examples and, for the most part, ignored examples of female leaders within the biblical texts. Some non-Catholic churches have changed their polices in the last few decades to include women as clergy. However, many churches still do not have women in key leadership positions. An unusual finding is the fact that some conservative groups ordain women and hire them to serve in leadership roles, including positions where women have authority over men. I reviewed the six dimensions of moral psychology and suggested how conservatives and progressives emphasize different perspectives within these dimensions.

After some two thousand years, Christianity continues to be dominated by male leadership. Although some women are able to see openings in some hierarchies, conservative perspectives are the norm.

Additional Resources

1. **Catholic Women as Priests.** Roman Catholic women have broken with official church rules (Canon Law) to serve as priests. Their positions and activities can be viewed at the website, RomanCatholicWomenPriests.org/

2. **Church History.** Those who study Christian history find that most leaders were men and most writings were produced by men. But as women entered the profession of history, things began to change. The PBS organization produced *Women in Ancient Christianity: The New Discoveries* for their *Frontline* program. http://www.pbs.org/wgbh/pages/frontline/shows/religion/first/women.html

3. **Power in The Church.** In 2013, Pope Francis made several comments about power and decision-making within the church. His comments suggest a reframing of the roles of men and women. The story contains a number of quotes that might suggest a shift is on the way, at least in terms of power. http://www.catholicherald.co.uk/news/2013/11/26/evangelii-gaudium-pope-says-only-men-can-be-priests-but-women-must-have-voice-in-church/

Discussion Topics and Questions

1. Do you think it is possible for women and men to have different roles within a Christian organization and still be considered equal?

2. Do you think biological factors may have influenced religious roles for men and women? For example, until recently, a fertile woman may have had many pregnancies and several children during her childbearing years. There were no reliable means of birth control and no social programs offering childcare. Women had few choices when it came to nursing their own children. And men, obviously free from pregnancies and nursing, were available to provide for their families in other ways, which became traditional roles for men.

3. Some churches restrict women from teaching men. If a woman cannot teach a man, does that imply she is inferior to a man?

11

SEXUAL VIOLENCE AND CHRISTIANITY

Rachel felt depressed by her marriage, which had deteriorated in the past two years. Her husband had been working late, and she suspected he was having an affair. As a devout Christian, she sought pastoral counseling. Her pastor offered support and encouragement. Rachel found the counseling sessions helpful and continued to meet with her pastor on a weekly basis. A strong bond developed between the two. Eventually friendly hugs became longer and more intense. The counseling relationship became romantic. Emotional infidelity led to sexual infidelity.

The story of Rachel and her pastor is not uncommon. Those who have defended pastors sometimes assert that both the pastor and the congregant were equal partners in the immoral relationship. However, among professionals, counselors are held to a higher standard because they are expected to recognize and maintain professional boundaries in counseling relationships and because, by virtue of their position, they have more social power in the relationship. Clients like Rachel are in a vulnerable position when they seek counseling. Clients cannot be expected to understand how professional relationships can devolve into romantic relationships when they are seeking help for depression, anxiety, or other sources of personal distress.

The Bible contains stories and rules related to incest, stranger rape, and sex workers. This chapter is about sexual violence. And sexual violence is officially condemned by contemporary Christian groups. Nevertheless, attitudes toward rape and sexual abuse have only recently changed within Western Christian cultures. Reports of the extensive sexual abuse of girls and boys within churches and church-based institutions have shocked contemporary members of Western societies—not only because of the horror of the lifelong suffering of the victims, but also because of the appalling lack of safety and protection within the church. In many cases, matters were made even worse as victims and their families felt insulted and outraged when religious organizations covered up the abuse and placed known offenders in new positions where they could continue to re-offend. Finally, we should be aware that sexual violence is not just about the abuse of children but also about women and men as well. The driving question is "why have Christians failed to protect their most vulnerable members from sexual abuse?"

Sex Workers and Sexual Violence in the Bible

Before considering contemporary issues, I will review some of the key biblical texts to appreciate how sex workers and abuse victims were treated.

Tamar and Judah

An early story of a temporary "sex worker" can be found in Genesis 38:13–26. In the story, a widowed woman named Tamar expected to have her dead husband's brother as a mate, but her father-in-law, Judah, refused to honor the tribal custom. She changed her clothes to appear as a sex worker and tricked Judah into having sex with her. She asked for payment, but Judah offered to send a goat along later. Showing her business sense, Tamar asked for a security deposit. Later, Judah returned for his things. He asked a local person for the location of the "holy" woman, but she could not be found. Later, Tamar showed up as pregnant, and Judah, as the tribal leader, ordered her to be burnt. Tamar produced Judah's deposit, and he acknowledged that she is more righteous than he is. Several points are noteworthy about this story:[1]

1. Neither Judah nor Tamar is condemned by God for the sex act.
2. The descendants of the couple include King David and Jesus
3. The Hebrew meaning of *Tamar* is "whore."
4. Judah's question about the location of the *holy* woman is odd and may indicate a euphemism for prostitutes.

Rahab and the Spies

Joshua sends spies into Jericho before making plans for an attack (Josh 2:1–21). The spies visit a sex worker named Rahab. When the local king searches for the spies, Rahab hides them and lies to protect them. The spies

---

1. Hornsby, *Sex Texts*, 114–17.

are grateful and vow to protect her and her family if she marks her house with a red cord. Notice again that there is no condemnation of Rahab's lifestyle.

Paul's Warning

The apostle Paul condemns sexual relations with prostitutes in his first letter to the Corinthians (6:15–16). He refers to the Genesis creation story to graphically illustrate that just as the sexual union creates one flesh, so Christians who have sex with prostitutes are uniting Jesus with prostitutes. Hornsby observes that Paul is showing the effect of sexual immorality on the whole community.[2]

Christian groups do not support legalized commercial sex. The lack of condemnation of sex workers in the Old Testament is a puzzlement for some, but the prohibitions against adultery and the teaching of the apostle Paul make the condemnation of prostitution clear. Despite the choices of some sex workers to engage in commercial sex on a voluntary basis, the sexual abuse and exploitation of so many persons, including children, is horrific. Although conservative Christians have been known to preach against prostitution and preach to prostitutes about salvation in a spiritual sense, it is only in recent years that Christians have been active in social programs to meet the multiple needs of those forced into the sex trade.[3]

Incest in the Bible

I am separating stories or laws about incest from those about rape on the basis of how the texts present the story. The obvious first case of incest involved Cain, the first son of Adam and Eve (Gen 4:1–5:5). Because conservative Christians believe all humans are descendants of Adam and Eve, Cain must have had a relationship with a sister or his mother. Not surprisingly, many have challenged a literal biblical interpretation of the creation narratives with the question, "Who did Cain marry?" Such a question was posed at the famous U.S. Scopes trial in 1925 by Defense Attorney Clarence Darrow.[4]

---

2. Ibid., 124.

3. A notable exception to the way Christians historically treated prostitutes can be found in the work of Josephine Butler, who viewed her nineteenth-century work on behalf of English prostitutes as a "divine calling." Her efforts included a successful overturning of the Contagious Disease Acts, which victimized women, and advocacy for the rights of women to a university education. http://www.josephinebutler.org.uk/.

4. Linder, "Day 7."

William Jennings Bryan, the prosecuting attorney, failed to provide a response. Why bring up the question of Cain's wife? The importance of the question is that it serves to illustrate how conservative Christians think differently about an issue of sexual morality. The question about Cain's wife is not an issue for progressive Christians who could expect Cain to obtain a wife from another family. But as noted above, for conservative Christians, the only women would have been close relatives. When conservative Christians offer a defense of Cain having relations with his sister, they argue that laws against intermarriage did not appear until many years later. This of course raises a philosophical issue for such Christians: is incest or other sexual activity only wrong when a biblical law exists?

Father-Daughter Incest

Genesis 19:30-38 tells about the incest between Lot and his two daughters. They had escaped the destruction of Sodom and were on the run. Out of fear, Lot and his daughters lived in a cave. Here's the story.

> And the firstborn said to the younger, "Our father is old, and there is not a man on earth to come in to us after the manner of all the world. Come, let us make our father drink wine, and we will lie with him, so that we may preserve offspring through our father." So they made their father drink wine that night; and the firstborn went in, and lay with her father; he did not know when she lay down or when she rose. On the next day, the firstborn said to the younger, "Look, I lay last night with my father; let us make him drink wine tonight also; then you go in and lie with him, so that we may preserve offspring through our father." So they made their father drink wine that night also; and the younger rose, and lay with him; and he did not know when she lay down or when she rose. Thus both the daughters of Lot became pregnant by their father. The firstborn bore a son, and named him Moab; he is the ancestor of the Moabites to this day. The younger also bore a son and named him Ben-ammi; he is the ancestor of the Ammonites to this day. (Gen 19:31-38)

Contemporary scholars find the story disquieting for many obvious reasons. Lot is portrayed as having no responsibility in the story. And one wonders how the girls could force their father to drink alcohol. But there is another interesting angle to the story. The verses at the end may be the key to the tale. Two foreign tribes, the Moabites and Ammonites, would be known as the descendants of bastards. Ancestry was obviously important given the biblical record of generations. Being a descendant of royals and heroes was a prize then as it is now. Being the descendants of bastards was a shame and represented an inferior status. Perhaps the biblical writers did not need to offer any harsh comments because just telling the tale of Lot and his daughters would be enough of a social insult.[5]

Learning from Other Stories

The biblical stories of incest were not just about problems among tribal members. As Calum Carmichael points out, the men in the stories were leaders: Abraham, Jacob, Judah, Moses, and David. Abraham married his half-sister.[6] Jacob married two sisters that were his cousins. Ruben, Jacob's oldest son, had sex with one of his father's wives. Nahor married his brother's daughter. Moses' father married his father's sister. Tamar had sex with her father-in-law Judah whilst posing as a prostitute. And David's daughter, another Tamar, referred her brother Amnon to their father to obtain permission before having sexual relations. In his essay, Carmichael wonders why the Bible has rules against incest. He suggests the rules addressed the problems of incest reported in the stories communicated by the ancestors. So, for example, the rule against child-parent incest in verse 7 can refer to Ham's sin against his father in Genesis 9 and the acts of Lot's daughters.

Laws against Incest

Leviticus 18:7–18 contains Hebrew laws that limit the people available for legitimate sexual relationships. There are other rules in Leviticus and in Deuteronomy (e.g., Deut 27:20–13). I will just use Leviticus 18:7–18 as an example. Notice the focus. Consistent with other aspects of ancient culture, the laws tell men who is not available and why. The verses use the euphemism "uncover the nakedness" to represent sexual intercourse. And notice that there is no prohibition against father-daughter incest. Why is this? Hornsby suggests the absent prohibition could be that it was obvious or that because a daughter was the property of her father, he could do as he wished.[7] Of course, the father would have much to lose if his daughters were not virgins. Men paid fathers for their virgin daughters.

---

5. Hornsby, *Sex Texts*, 154.
6. Carmichael, "Incest in the Bible," 123–47.
7. Hornsby, *Sex Texts*, 158.

Finally, notice the first rule in verse 7. It prohibits a child from having sex with his father or mother. As Carmichael notes, the usual problem in society is a problem of a parent sexually abusing his or her child rather than a child sexually abusing his or her father or mother. As noted above, Carmichael suggests the order of the rules has to do with how the laws came into existence; rules were developed as needed to address significant problems in Israel's history.[8]

> You shall not uncover the nakedness of your father, which is the nakedness of your mother; she is your mother, you shall not uncover her nakedness. You shall not uncover the nakedness of your father's wife; it is the nakedness of your father. You shall not uncover the nakedness of your sister, your father's daughter or your mother's daughter, whether born at home or born abroad. You shall not uncover the nakedness of your son's daughter or of your daughter's daughter, for their nakedness is your own nakedness. You shall not uncover the nakedness of your father's wife's daughter, begotten by your father, since she is your sister. You shall not uncover the nakedness of your father's sister; she is your father's flesh. You shall not uncover the nakedness of your mother's sister, for she is your mother's flesh. You shall not uncover the nakedness of your father's brother, that is, you shall not approach his wife; she is your aunt. You shall not uncover the nakedness of your daughter-in-law: she is your son's wife, you shall not uncover her nakedness. You shall not uncover the nakedness of your brother's wife; it is your brother's nakedness. You shall not uncover the nakedness of a woman and her daughter, and you shall not take her son's daughter or her daughter's daughter to uncover her nakedness; they are your flesh; it is depravity. And you shall not take a woman as a rival to her sister, uncovering her nakedness while her sister is still alive. (Lev 18:7–18)

The Problem at Corinth

The apostle Paul wrote about the attitude of the Corinthians toward a man who was living with his father's wife (1 Cor 5:1–2): "It is actually reported that there is sexual immorality among you, and of a kind that is not found even among pagans; for a man is living with his father's wife. And you are arrogant! Should you not rather have mourned, so that he who has done this would have been removed from among you?" Paul is obviously outraged by

---

8. Carmichael, "Incest," 123–47.

what the Corinthian Christians have done—not only the act itself, but also how it contrasts with the morality of the pagans. Why were the Corinthians so proud of their acceptance of this couple? Carmichael suggests it has to do with the Jewish and Christian views about conversion.[9] Both groups believed that after conversion people were born again. Old relationships ended. The logical extension of this way of thinking was a freedom to marry anyone. According to Carmichael, the Jewish leaders did not want problems with the gentiles, so they did not permit relationships prohibited by the local culture, despite believing in the miracle of transformation when people converted. In contrast, it appears Paul had to instruct the Corinthians, who were obviously more focused on their freedom in Christ than how immoral they appeared.

There is another curious passage in 1 Corinthians 7:36–38. The meaning hinges on how people translate *autos parthenos* (his virgin). Some have attacked Paul and his teaching for justifying father-daughter incest. Others interpret the verses to mean that Paul was offering guidance in how a father could handle plans for the marriage of a daughter to her fiancé.

In closing this section on incest, it is clear that the Bible contains several stories about incest. The Bible also contains rules prohibiting a variety of close kinship relationships. The laws against incest appear following early stories. And the laws condemn a number of relationships. But other kinship relationships were encouraged. On a practical level, the old Hebrew rules of inheritance meant that male children would inherit the land and wealth of their fathers. The growing nation would lose their possessions if the Israelites were bound by marriage to those in other cultures. In the New Testament, people became eligible marriage partners when they converted. In a sense, it seems Paul had to separate spiritual rebirth and the idea of a family of God for those who took their newly found freedoms too literally. Prohibitions against incest are close to universal and are probably driven by feelings of disgust. Despite some unusual stories in the Old Testament and the notion that women were the property of fathers and husbands, readers can expect Christians to condemn incest and sexual abuse.

Rape

To state the obvious, Christians are opposed to rape. The reason for looking at a few biblical accounts of rape is to gain an understanding of how Christians might think about sexual violence and the primary target of such violence, women. Sometimes biblical stories appear to be about rape, but

9. Ibid.

we do not always have the details to appraise the situation. In the chapter about same-sex relationships, I examined the story of Sodom and found that, in addition to demands for sex, the biblical authors condemned the townspeople for their profound lack of hospitality.

Dinah's Story

In Genesis 34:2–3, Dinah, the daughter of Leah and Jacob, was visiting local women. Prince Shechem, the son of Hamor, "saw her, he seized her and lay with her by force. And his soul was drawn to Dinah daughter of Jacob; he loved the girl, and spoke tenderly to her." The story is often portrayed as a rape, but the biblical writer does not tell us how Dinah felt.[10] Although the Hebrew phrasing indicates sex, not all translators indicate that force was involved. However, the rest of the story is about sex and violence. Dinah's brothers were angry and considered their sister defiled. The prince asked his father's help in recruiting Dinah. The father spoke with Jacob, but Jacob's sons contrived a plan of revenge. They claimed that Hamor and his people could not enter into marriage with Jacob and his clan unless they became circumcised. Hamor agreed. On the third day after the mass circumcision, the sons of Jacob and Dinah's brothers attacked the city, killed the men, and took their wealth, children, and wives. Knust views the story as a rape, and the actions of Dinah's family are portrayed as saving Dinah's honor.[11] Also at stake was the separate identity of the Israelites as a different group of people.

Although the details of the Dinah story are not entirely clear, there is a law in Deuteronomy 22:25–29 stating what should happen in cases when a man takes a virgin and has sex with her:

> But if the man meets the engaged woman in the open country, and the man seizes her and lies with her, then only the man who lay with her shall die. You shall do nothing to the young woman; the young woman has not committed an offense punishable by death, because this case is like that of someone who attacks and murders a neighbor. Since he found her in the open country, the engaged woman may have cried for help, but there was no one to rescue her. If a man meets a virgin who is not engaged, and seizes her and lies with her, and they are caught in the act, the man who lay with her shall give fifty shekels of silver to the young woman's father, and she shall become his wife. Because

---

10. Hornsby, *Sex Texts*, 140.
11. Knust, *Unprotected Texts*, locations 3158–214.

he violated her he shall not be permitted to divorce her as long as he lives.

As Hornsby points out, the crime is against a girl's father, who is to be paid for the damage done to his daughter.[12] The woman is then bound to the man as a wife for life. There is no evidence of modern notions of justice for the woman. As noted previously, the story also suggests that the sex act sealed the husband-wife relationship.

A Concubine's Rape

When discussing the texts related to same-sex relationships, I also considered the story of the Levite who spent the night with an old man, as recorded in Judges 19:20–29. Similar to the Sodom story, men of the village came to the house and demanded sex. In this case, the Levite offered his concubine. The men had sex with her and abused her all night. The Levite appears to care very little about his concubine. He asks her to get up, then he takes his knife, cuts her to pieces, and sends her parts throughout Israel, which incites a violent revenge attack. What is striking to contemporary readers is the lack of concern for this woman. The story focuses on the profound dishonor shown to the man, but the story does not focus on the horrific destruction of the woman.[13]

The Tamar and Amnon Story

The story of Amnon's desire for his sister, Tamar, would seem to be about incest and rape, but Tamar appears to think it would be okay to have sex with her stepbrother if he obtained their father's permission (2 Sam 13). Tamar is a virgin and under the authority of her father. Amnon faked an illness, refused to eat, then asked his father, King David, to send Tamar to bring him a special cake. She did. Here's what happened (2 Sam 13:10–19):

> Then Amnon said to Tamar, "Bring the food into the chamber, so that I may eat from your hand." So Tamar took the cakes she had made, and brought them into the chamber to Amnon her brother. But when she brought them near him to eat, he took hold of her, and said to her, "Come, lie with me, my sister." She answered him, "No, my brother, do not force me; for such a thing is not done in Israel; do not do anything so vile! As for me,

12. Hornsby, *Sex Texts*, 140–42.
13. Ibid., 144.

> where could I carry my shame? And as for you, you would be as one of the scoundrels in Israel. Now therefore, I beg you, speak to the king; for he will not withhold me from you." But he would not listen to her; and being stronger than she was, he forced her and lay with her.
>
> Then Amnon was seized with a very great loathing for her; indeed, his loathing was even greater than the lust he had felt for her. Amnon said to her, "Get out!" But she said to him, "No, my brother; for this wrong in sending me away is greater than the other that you did to me." But he would not listen to her. He called the young man who served him and said, "Put this woman out of my presence, and bolt the door after her." (Now she was wearing a long robe with sleeves; for this is how the virgin daughters of the king were clothed in earlier times.) So his servant put her out, and bolted the door after her. But Tamar put ashes on her head, and tore the long robe that she was wearing; she put her hand on her head, and went away, crying aloud as she went.

The story reveals much about the ugliness of rape: the overpowering of another person, the lust-inspired deception, and the suffering of the victims, who are usually women. Finally, we see the hatred and loathing that follows the sexual violence. Women have been victims of rape for thousands of years.[14] Who would care about Tamar? In Israel, the responsibility for daughters resided with their fathers until they married. King David did not act.[15]

Incest and Rape

The graphic accounts of incest and rape reveal an ugly violence in the lives of ancient Israel. Scholars like Knust have suggested that the stories, along with the laws, are presented by the religious leaders to show the wickedness of the kings—especially King David. For example, the prophet Ezekiel condemns various sexual acts (22:6, 10–12) and warns against becoming like the Canaanites. But other cultures did have strict laws as well. For example, Knust notes that the ancient laws of Hammurabi outlawed sexual relations among close relatives, including an explicit prohibition against father-daughter incest.[16] The punishments for violating the laws about incest and rape were

---

14. Ibid., 146.
15. Coogan, *God and Sex*, 148.
16. Knust, *Unprotected Texts*, location 2581.

harsh, but not all violators were punished. And some were punished outside the structure of the law (e.g., Absalom killing Amnon).[17]

By the time the New Testament was written, things had changed. The Israelites, now referred to as Jews, were under the governance of the Romans. Examples from the Gospels reveal a concern for people in general (e.g., "love thy neighbor"), especially women. Although many quotes that support an inferior role for women can be taken from the apostle Paul, Hornsby reminds us that Paul spoke out against domestic violence in Colossians 3:19: "Husbands, love your wives and never treat them harshly."[18]

Sex Workers, Sexual Violence, and Contemporary Christianity

In this section I look at sexual violence and the response of the Christian community. First, I take a look at contemporary sex workers. Different times and different cultures make it difficult to compare the circumstances of modern workers with those in ancient times. Although some workers report a high standard of living, many are trapped by traffickers and forced to work as slaves. Next I look at the problem of sexual violence that happens within Christian families and how churches have responded to those seeking help. Finally, I look at the disturbing reports of children and adults actually abused by clergy and other church leaders.

Sex Workers and the Church

Commercial sex is a term currently used for the sale of sexual services. Although some have used the term *willing prostitution* for this activity, those who sell sex services prefer the term *sex worker* rather than *prostitute*. Such activities may be casual or organized as a business.[19] In addition to interpersonal sexual activity, the sex industry encompasses a wide range of products and services related to sex. The world's largest sex industry trade show, Adult Entertainment Expo, is held annually in Las Vegas, Nevada, and represents a multibillion-dollar industry within the U.S. although a report in *Forbes* suggests it is difficult to accurately identify the size of the industry.[20]

Although many Christians object to various sex-related services, the focus of current concern has been for people trafficked for the specific

---

17. Coogan, *God and Sex*, 148.
18. Hornsby, *Sex Texts*, 150.
19. Oprea, "Female Sex Workers," 237–47.
20. Ackman, "How Big is Porn," para. 2.

purpose of providing sex services. Human trafficking is a contemporary form of slavery. Vulnerable persons are forced to work for little or no wages. Many people, mostly women and girls, are bought and sold to work as prostitutes. According to the U.S. Federal Bureau of Investigation (FBI), the average age range of child prostitutes was between eleven and fourteen.[21]

A number of Christian organizations exist to rescue people from the sex trade and help them find healing.[22] Despite these noteworthy efforts, many victims do not get help. The barriers are significant because the victims are controlled by fear of violence from their traffickers and fear of repercussions from police where their work is illegal.

Kathleen Deering and her colleagues reviewed research on violence against sex workers. In general, violence is linked to health problems, injury, and mental health problems such as depression, anxiety, and post-traumatic stress disorder. Sex workers also suffer from sexually transmitted infections and struggle with unwanted pregnancies.[23]

One solution to widespread sexually transmitted infections (STIs) has been efforts to encourage condom use. According to the World Health Organization (WHO), sex workers are at higher risk than others for STIs and HIV.[24] For example, the rate of HIV-positive sex workers was recently at 36.9 percent in sub-Saharan Africa and 10.9 percent in Eastern Europe. Significant reductions have been seen when safe sex guidelines were used.

A substantial barrier to the use of condoms has been the teaching of the Roman Catholic Church. The church provides a significant level of HIV/AIDS care but has been officially opposed to the use of condoms.[25]

Another solution found objectionable to many Christians is for governments to regulate commercial sex so that providers have access to health care and some level of protection. Sex workers are subject to many forms of sexual (e.g., rape and harassment) and nonsexual (e.g., beating, choking, and burning) physical violence and various forms of emotional violence, including threats of intimidation, withholding food, and denial of medical services.[26] Recent research indicates decriminalization of sex work can significantly reduce violence against sex workers and the incidence of HIV.[27]

---

21. "FBI: Combatting Human," para. 1–7.
22. Yancey, "Back from the Brothel," 80.
23. Deering, "A Systematic Review," 42–54.
24. World Health Organization, "New WHO guidelines," para. 3–6.
25. Suarez, "Vatican Maintains," para. 5.
26. World Health Organization Department of Gender et al., "Addressing Violence," 23.
27. Forbes and Patterson, "Decriminalizing Sex Work," para. 1–9.

Reductions in violence and improvements in health have been reported from Germany and New Zealand, where sex work has been legalized.[28] People are divided over the issue of legalization of sex work, which is also known as decriminalization. Radical feminists and Christians can find themselves opposing legalization. Some feminists support a woman's choice of work while others view sex workers as additional victims of male exploitation. Christians object to supporting prostitution because it is a violation of biblical teaching. Additional arguments against legalization come from reports of emotional and mental harm to sex workers as a result of selling sex and dealing with troubling memories for years.[29]

Sexual Abuse and the Church

When tragedy strikes, Christians pray. For centuries, Christians have turned to the church for help. Pastoral counseling and support is highly valued by people with spiritual, personal, and relationship struggles. In recent decades, people have become more aware of the significant problem of intimate partner violence (IPV). Precise estimates of IPV are hard to come by but may range from as low as 15 percent to as much as 71 percent depending on the country. Over one-third of U.S. women said they experienced rape and physical violence, with or without stalking.[30]

One of the most devastating effects of IPV is post-traumatic stress disorder (PTSD). PTSD represents a cluster of symptoms that persistently interfere with functioning. Recurrent thoughts of the traumatic event along with images of the trauma frequently appear in the mind like video clips on a screen. People relive highly anxious feelings, have trouble sleeping, and seek to avoid any reminders of their painful past. Sexual assault can be one source of severe PTSD symptoms. To make things worse, many people with PTSD often develop severe depression.

The results of a large-scale survey of Christian women in the U.S. South indicated that most drew strength from their Christian beliefs. A little more than half of the women reported IPV. Sexual assault was included with other forms of abuse.[31] Another study looked at violence in people attending U.S. Seventh-Day Adventist Churches and found that 46 percent experienced violence and 29 percent specifically reported sexual victimization.[32]

28. Reisenwitz, "Why It's Time," para. 6.
29. Borkett-Jones, "Why the Church."
30. Levitt et al., "Addressing Intimate," 213.
31. Wang et al., "Christian Women," 224–35.
32. Drumm, "Intimate Partner," 233–51.

Many Christian women hold beliefs about the importance of marriage and submission that do not support leaving an abusive relationship.[33] At this point, research findings are mixed. Some find involvement in churches to be a protective factor limiting abuse. But other studies find that certain beliefs keep people in abusive relationships.

Sexual Assault within the Church

Reports of sexual abuse within religious communities have recently come to light. Perhaps the most horrifying accounts in recent years come from the sexual abuse of children by Catholic priests. Karen Terry and others investigated the problem for the years 1950 through 2002 and found that about 4 percent of Catholic priests sexually abused children.[34]

Diarmaid MacCulloch reviewed the history of cover-up within the Catholic Church. He noted that clergy were certainly not unique in terms of adults who sexually abuse children, but he focuses on the damning effects of the long history of concealment: "The clergy seemed to regard the good name of the Church as more important than the damage done to the young victims."[35] Although old records are sparse, an interesting study found evidence of covering up sexual abuse perpetrated by Stefano Cherubini on students at a school in Naples.[36] In 1629, the matter was brought to the attention of Joseph Calasanz, who was head of the order responsible for the school. His expressed thinking suggests he weighed the cover-up as the better course of action. The idea of cover-up suggests hiding dirt a fairly obvious connection to disgust-purity based morality. But the reasoning associated with covering-up also suggests the power of loyalty to the church hierarchy as more powerful than loyalty to the church membership.

My colleagues and I have examined clerical sexual abuse within Christian churches in a series of studies. We noticed the devastating impact on both the victims of sexual abuse as well as the Christian community. Congregations often split following the revelation of abuse. And church members are divided when it comes to restoring fallen leaders.[37] The contemporary accounts of sexual abuse serve as important reminders that, regardless of biblical examples and laws, Christians continue to struggle as victims of

33. Levitt et al., "Addressing Intimate," 214–15.
34. Terry, "Understanding the Sexual," 31–44.
35. MacCulloch, *Silence*, 204.
36. Luxmoore, "British Historian," para. 3–8.
37. For example, Sutton et al., "Does Gender," 645–63; Sutton and Thomas, "Can Derailed," 583–99; Thomas et al., "Religious Leadership," 16–29.

sexual violence and as people responsible for protecting others from sexual violence. In biblical times and the present, sexual violence hurts. Not only is there physical pain from the use of force, but there is emotional pain as well. People—mostly women—are shamed, humiliated, and troubled by years of painful memories.

Moral Perspectives

Although there are no voices of support for sexual abuse among Christian leaders, there are differences in emphasis, which sometimes become apparent when speakers comment on specific sexual acts. Before looking at the six dimensions, I want to introduce you to a story used by Jonathan Haidt when he was studying moral decisions.[38]

> Julie and Mark, who are brother and sister, are traveling together in France. They are both on summer vacation from college. One night, they are staying alone in a cabin near the beach. They decide that it would be interesting and fun if they tried making love. At the very least it would be a new experience for each of them. Julie was already taking birth control pills, but Mark uses a condom too, just to be safe. They both enjoy it, but they decide not to do it again. They keep that night as a special secret between them, which makes them feel even closer to each other. So what do you think about this? Was it wrong for them to have sex?

When I present this to students, I see reactions of disgust. People know incest is wrong even when the situation is presented as consensual. People objected to incest in Haidt's research as well but had a hard time coming up with reasons why. Haidt refers to the problem as "moral dumbfoundness"— a condition in which people intuitively know something is wrong but have a hard time explaining their feelings. That idea of feeling something is horribly wrong—a moral intuition—may help explain the presence of the assault stories in the biblical texts. That is, it is possible that telling the story would evoke feelings of moral outrage and condemnation. The lack of recorded laws need not imply an act was condoned.

As a final reminder, it is important to consider the effects of sexual violence and the impact of moral judgments on a survivor's overall functioning represented in the SCOPES model. We should also remember that although most victims are women, men can be victims too. The impact question can

---

38. Haidt, *The Righteous*, 38.

be phrased: how do sexual violence and actions based on moral judgments affect a victim spiritually, cognitively, behaviorally, physically, emotionally, and socially?

1. Care versus Harm

Both conservative and progressive Christians express concern about the victims of sexual assault. In the biblical stories, we saw cases where the concern appeared to be more about the damage done to the father's reputation, or perhaps the nascent nation of Israel, than to the woman. Ironically, despite the fact that the apostle Paul has been accused of misogyny, we find he admonished husbands to love their wives.

Conservative Christians can seem less caring than progressive Christians when they focus on keeping a marriage intact despite the harmful effects of sexual violence. Additionally, regardless of conservative or progressive stance, when churches cover up sexual violence, they appear to care more about the reputation of the church than the victims. And when offending clergy are moved to other positions or receive only minor penalties, the church appears to care more about the offending clergy than their victims.

Christians ought to care for the victims of sexual violence. Some do and some do not. Clearly, sexual violence has the potential to disrupt and seriously harm a victim's spirituality to the point of turning them off to Christianity altogether. Their cognitions can be dominated by negative thoughts and images for a lifetime and these are accompanied by distressing emotions. Behavior patterns of avoidance are common as are health issues, and impaired social functioning in the form of broken relationships. All aspects of personal function covered in the SCOPES model reveal changes in functioning linked to sexual violence. Only caring aimed at all aspects of functioning offers a chance of undoing the harm.

2. Fairness/Reciprocity versus Cheating

In the biblical narratives, there was a price to be paid when a woman lost her virginity. Presumably, there was an agreement on what was a fair price. The stories of Dinah and Tamar (of David) indicated the revenge of her kin who were morally outraged by the news. Sexual violence, especially against loved ones, destroys many lives and illustrates the near impossibility of a "fair" response. Sexual assault is so life-destroying, regardless of the fact that a woman survives, that it is no wonder biblical protectors believed the only fair and just response is to kill the offender.

In recent years, Christians have increasingly acted to encourage abuse victims to separate—if not divorce—their abusive partners. And administrative bodies remove accused clergy from their posts and investigate sexual abuse allegations. Committees have been established to review allegations, respond to victims' needs, revise policies, and address systemic problems.

3. Ingroup Loyalty versus Betrayal

The account of Dinah particularly shows intense family loyalty at work. The protections of family are also reflected in the biblical laws. The problem of sexual violence is reported by Christians regardless of their affiliation with conservative or progressive churches.

When sexual violence occurs within family relationships, the issues of loyalty and betrayal can create significant tension for victims who wish to be loyal to their faith, and perhaps even the abusive spouse, yet feel betrayed. Anecdotally, many young women report that they cannot believe a Christian man could commit sexual violence.

When Christian leaders sexually violate their members, they offend the entire church family. But ingroup loyalty works two ways: some support the offender, and others rally to support the victims. At a minimum, people on the opposing side of the loyalty issue are viewed as disloyal, so it is not surprising to see church families divide following clergy sexual abuse. Nor is it surprising to see large numbers of people leave churches when sexual abuse is discovered—not just because of the abuse, but also because the church failed to be loyal to those they were supposed to serve and protect.

4. Authority/Respect versus Disrespect

There is a lot of support in the Bible and in contemporary Christian cultures for showing respect toward leadership. As noted previously, some scholars think the ancient priests and prophets avoided directly accusing King David by proclaiming a general warning to people not to live like Canaanites. However, by telling stories about David and his family likely to elicit moral outrage the writers were able to make their point about immorality.

As noted in the chapter, some women from conservative traditions hold beliefs about living in submission to their husbands. Such a stance can make it difficult to escape persistent sexual violence, especially if their clergy, family, and community focus more on the relationship than the victim.

In recent years, moral outrage has taken the form of lawsuits in an effort to bring about change and focus attention on the victims of those harmed by people in religious authority. By turning to the civil courts, people turned to a higher authority than the church, which revealed a greater respect for the courts than the church. The church and its leaders lost credibility. The irony for the church is that Christians sometimes appeal to God as a higher authority than people or governments. They might refuse to go along with same-sex marriage or abortion because of their Christian beliefs. But when leaders sexually abuse their followers, people have had to invoke the authority of earthly governments to remove the evil from the church.

5. Purity or Sanctity versus Degradation

The biblical accounts refer to women being defiled when they were raped. Traditionally, sexual purity was often symbolized by a woman's virginity or the absence of sexual relations until she was in a relationship approved by her father. The range of concerns raised by different people throughout the Scriptures shows an awareness of the many ways sexual violence destroys victims and their families—and even their cultures.

You may have noticed the absence of male sex workers in the biblical stories. And there were no stories of boys or young men as victims of sexual assault. Although some conservative groups continue to focus on being pure by abstaining from sex before marriage, other Christians have become more concerned about the need to protect all persons from sexual violence, especially those who are vulnerable.

It is a commonly observed phenomenon that many people blame the victims of sexual violence as if in some way a victim encouraged the harmful act. Women especially have been the target of purity-disgust-linked abusive language when they report a rape. If they wore certain clothes, engaged in unapproved behavior, or were in a particular location, they may be considered an immoral, impure, and unclean woman. Although honor killings directed at women are not common among Christian groups, a sexual assault victim may be identified as "immoral" and pay the consequences of social isolation from former family and friends as if she had a disgusting condition that might contaminate those purported to live a holy life.

6. Liberty versus Oppression

In the Bible, women were at the mercy of their fathers or husbands. The Israelite laws indicated intent to protect women, but it is not possible to know how much women suffered because laws were not enforced or women were unable to give voice to their plight. In recent years we have seen evidence of sexual abuse of children and women by religious leaders. And we find that the vulnerable are easily oppressed. When laws are enforced, we learn that the laws actually offer liberty to the oppressed by removing oppressors from the workplace and in some cases, leading to incarceration of perpetrators.

Summary

In this chapter I offered an overview of sexual violence. Even though Christians agree that sexual violence is morally wrong, the church has not always worked to protect its members from IPV, offending clergy, or other predators within the church. The challenge for Christians continues: do current teachings directly or indirectly support sexual violence? And how are churches responding to help victims heal after they have experienced sexual violence?

Christians have been quick to condemn prostitution. In recent years, many have been concerned about the extent of sex trafficking. The sordid business condemns many young persons to physical and psychological pain and suffering at the hands of those who enslave them. A challenge for the church will be to examine teaching and policies that may directly or indirectly interfere with the safety and health of the victims of the trade.

Some sex workers appear to choose their work. In such cases, Christians may be challenged to evaluate how their beliefs influence political activities that limit the ability of sex workers to obtain healthcare.

The Bible includes stories of incest and rules that prohibit incest. Most cultures have rules against incest. Although the decision about how close relatives can be so as not to violate incest rules may seem arbitrary, a sense of disgust may motivate the widespread feeling that incest is morally wrong.

Rape, or forcing another person to participate in sexual activity, is an obvious concern. Christians condemn rape and all forms of sexual violence. It is also clear that many men, women, and children have been sexually assaulted by church leaders and other predators within a congregation. The church has failed to protect vulnerable persons from sexual violence. All churches, regardless of their conservative or progressive beliefs, ought to actively protect their congregants from sexual violence and find ways to promote holistic healing for those who have been abused.

Although it may seem unusual to examine the six dimensions of morality when it comes to a matter of sexual violence that seems so wrong, it can be instructive to think of the many ways that sexual violence violates our moral sense. A consideration of the moral dimensions can help us be alert to misplaced concern for harm to the church, loyalty to one's tradition, and respect for the authority of church leadership as factors fostering a cover-up of sexual violence.

Additional Resources

1. **Catholic Clergy Sex Abuse**. Psychologist Tom Plante has studied the problem of clergy abuse in the Catholic Church. He offers readers six points to keep in mind about the abuse in the article within the "Do the Right Thing" section of *Psychology Today*. http://www.psychologytoday.com/blog/do-the-right-thing/201003/six-important-points-you-dont-hear-about-regarding-clergy-sexual-abus

2. **Clergical Sexual Misconduct**. Diana Garland of Baylor University looks at the prevalence of clergical sexual misconduct with adults. The article includes some statistics that illustrate the scope of the problem. http://www.baylor.edu/clergysexualmisconduct/index.php?id=67406

3. **Sex Trafficking**. The problem of sex trafficking has been a major concern in recent years. This 2011 article by Amelia Blanton offers a summary of a Christian response. http://www.stltoday.com/lifestyles/faith-and-values/civil-religion/deleted-bloggers/a-christian-response-to-human-trafficking/article_3a15d8ea-54cf-11e0-8c3c-0017a4a78c22.html

Discussion Topics and Questions

1. Some scholars have noted the lack of a woman's voice in the stories about incest and rape in the Bible. Would the stories have been worded differently if written by women?

2. Discuss any of Tom Plante's six points that appear surprising to you.

3. The discussion of the six moral dimensions examined possible bases for why Christians failed to protect people from sexual abuse. Can you think of other reasons sexual abuse was allowed to continue for so long?

PART III

Redemption and Reflections

12

SEXUALITY, MORALITY, AND REDEMPTION

After Kayla finished her presentation, a woman in front of me shook her head. "I can't believe it," she said. Kayla Jordan had reported the results of a study she designed to assess the effects of an apology by a Christian for the way Christians have treated people who identify as gay or lesbian. The woman who voiced her disbelief was a judge at the research conference and worked with LGBT students at a large university. The judge found it incredible that a student from a conservative school would even consider the notion of apologizing for the way Christians have treated sexual minorities.[1]

Canadian sociologist Michael Wilkinson observed that a number of public apologies have taken place since World War II. Germany apologized to Jews for the Holocaust. The Catholic pope apologized for the church's treatment of Jews and Muslims as well as slavery. The LDS church apologized to African Americans for refusing to include them in leadership positions. Southern Baptists apologized for slavery. Methodists apologized for a leader who murdered Native Americans. South African whites apologized for using the Bible to support apartheid. And Canadian churches apologized to First Nations people for many acts, including the destruction of cultural practices as well as physical and sexual abuse of those in residential schools.[2]

In this brief chapter, I will look at ways that Christians can focus on redemption rather than condemnation. The processes of confessing, apologizing, forgiving, reconciling, and restoring can promote healing within individuals and churches as well as between groups of Christians that often seem to be on different sides of cultural wars. If Christians wish to have a

---

1. Kayla later published her results. See Jordan et al., "Effects on Forgiveness," 99–114.

2. Wilkinson, "Public Acts," 177–96.

credible voice when it comes to morality, they must find ways to heal the growing rift between Christians from different traditions.

A Call to Corporate Repentance

Forgiveness is a method of relationship repair that is motivated by love. Apologies are not always effective. But it is a moral duty for Christians to repair damaged relationships and restore those who have been hurt by their actions. Recognizing the harm that Christians have done requires humility. Recognizing the harm Christians have allowed to happen requires an honest investigation. Public confessions and apologies by representatives of groups of Christians are helpful first steps in seeking forgiveness and attempting to repair the harm caused by the policies and proclamations that have victimized or failed to protect vulnerable persons.

The good that some groups of Christians do can be erased by the harm done by other groups. Some have physically abused, sexually abused, insulted, ridiculed, and discriminated against women and sexual minorities. Christians have supported laws that interfere with the ability of women and sexual minorities to obtain education, employment, and housing. Christians who have not perpetrated acts of harm have often failed to protect minorities from the harmful actions of others. Before Christians can offer moral guidance, they must come to terms with their own sin. Self-examination, confession, and apologizing are first steps.

A Message of Truth and Reconciliation

"Truth and Reconciliation" has been a popular phrase since the efforts of Nelson Mandela and his government to bring healing following the end of apartheid in South Africa. Not surprisingly, some praised the Truth and Reconciliation Commission, and others found reasons to be critical. Many who have been hurt will respond to confessions and apologies with forgiveness and be open to reconciliation. Others who have been deeply hurt will remain skeptical and hostile.

The lead title of this book, *A House Divided*, represents the diverse voices of Christians who often seem poles apart on matters of sexuality and the sex-linked behavior discussed in the foregoing chapters. A focus on the Christian virtues of love, forgiveness, humility, compassion, and gratitude can promote an openness to consider alternative interpretations of Scripture and a concomitant genuine concern for people marginalized, devalued, and excluded from supportive and loving faith communities. Efforts at reconciliation begin with actively listening to the stories of pain and suffering from those who have been hurt. Trust is the essential ingredient in reconciliation. Trust grows when people feel they can safely disclose their concerns without feeling condemned.

Forgiveness Can Promote Reconciliation

Forgiveness has been a popular topic for more than a decade. In the Gospels, Jesus reminds his followers to forgive others as they have been forgiven (Matt 6:14–15) and to forgive multiple times (Matt 18:22). Christians come to their awareness of the need for forgiveness as they fail to meet their understanding of what it means to live a godly life. As we have seen in this book, Christians have different ideas of what it means to live a moral life. I suggest that one way to reduce the rhetoric of condemnation is to trust that God relates to people on the basis of love and forgiveness. Sincere Christians come to different understandings during their spiritual journeys. And what is right for one person may be wrong for another. Seeing fellow Christians as people who have also been forgiven and reconciled with God can serve as a basis for mutual respect.

The offensive language and actions of Christians toward other Christians who believe and live in different ways leads to deeply felt hurts that can be difficult to overcome. It is here that churches and individuals can be part of the process of healing rather than hurting. Letting go of past hurts requires considerable effort. Although reconciliation may be an outcome of forgiveness, it is more important to focus on the needs of the victim for inner healing and release from the anger, hatred, and bitterness that destroy inner peace and keep victims chained in their troubled memories to their offenders. The process can be slow and painful, but there is ample evidence that the effort is worthwhile. There are a few scientifically supported interventions that churches, clinicians, and individuals may find useful. I will summarize one model.

Using the acronym *REACH*, Ev Worthington offers a five-step model.[3] The model has research support and has been applied in secular and Christian settings.[4] In step one, victims *Recall* the hurt that was done to them along with the emotional pain. Step two asks victims to *Empathize* with the person who hurt them. Apologies help victims develop empathy. Researchers find that even imagining an offender apologizing helps develop empathy. Christians are encouraged to embrace Jesus' teaching about loving

---

3. Worthington, *Forgiveness and Reconciliation*, 169–86.
4. Worthington et al., "Religion, Spirituality, and Forgiveness," 476–97.

their enemies. The third step asks victims to offer an *Altruistic* gift to the offender. Victims are encouraged to remember how they felt when they were forgiven and how they can in turn do something good for others, including the one who hurt them. At step four, victims take various actions to *Commit* to forgiveness. Commitment can be evidenced by writing a letter expressing forgiveness, but the letter is not sent. Finally, aware that doubts arise, Worthington offers suggestions to help people *Hold* on to forgiveness.

Restoration

I use the term *restoration* to refer to the state of being reinstated in a community following a moral failure. One of the major problems in past centuries was permitting sexual predators to continue in their positions as if forgiveness implied they should be allowed to keep their jobs. Sexually abusing clergy were sometimes transferred to another location only to reoffend. Clergy who apologized for their adultery were often forgiven and allowed to stay in their positions without dealing with their pattern of sexual infidelity.[5]

Forgiveness figures into the restoration process in several ways. Repentant leaders can expect forgiveness from God. If married and in couple counseling, the leaders and their spouses may express and receive forgiveness as part of the process of reconciliation. A church may offer opportunities to offended congregants to work through their feelings of hurt and betrayal and eventually forgive the errant pastor. And as part of a restoration plan, some congregants may meet with the derailed pastor where expressions of forgiveness are given and received. Ideally, these efforts promote healing for the pastor, the spouse, and the congregants. Nevertheless, a successful restoration plan may not result in restoration to church ministry.

Restoring people following a sexual offense is a good idea. But wisdom is needed to assess what form of restoration is wise for the offender and those who may suffer if the person has a relapse. The small percentages of persons who commit sexual offenses gain a lot of attention because they can do so much damage. A sexual offense by one member of the clergy destroys the lives of the immediate contact victims as well as those of family members. And those in the church or religious organization also experience strong feelings of anger and betrayal. Churches that fail to protect their congregants from sexual violence have no credible voice when it comes to proclamations about sexual morality. The idea of restoring fallen leaders must be viewed from the perspective of traumatic damage done to the victims.

5. Sutton and Thomas, "Restoring Christian Leaders," 27–42.

Summary

In previous chapters I reviewed a number of ways Christians are divided over interpreting the Scriptures pertaining to sexual morality. At times the disagreements are heated, and the church appears to offer a message of hate and contempt for their fellow Christians who hold different opinions as well as for Christians considered to be living in sin. The rhetoric is far from redemptive.

In recent decades, church leaders have apologized to groups harmed by the actions of various church leaders and church policies. Public acts of repentance and apology can promote reconciliation between groups and provide a basis for individuals to engage in processes of forgiveness and reconciliation. Christians can replace condemnation with redemption. I suggest that Christians lack a credible voice when it comes to morality to the extent they focus on attacking fellow Christians and failing to offer a message of redemption for all persons.

Churches, Christian organizations, and individuals can also be involved in helping victims of sexual offenses or sex-linked discrimination to heal by offering forgiveness-education programs and counseling. Although many people learn to overlook slights or even forgive more serious offenses by God's grace, many need assistance to find peace and inner healing. Christians can also be involved in programs that promote forgiveness and reconciliation in couples.

Finally, Christian organizations can promote healing and redemption when sex-linked behavior has resulted in the destruction of many lives, as in the case of moral failure in clergy. The moral failures of clergy have been exacerbated by the actions of superiors that worsened the damage done to victims.

13

REFLECTIONS: SEXUALITY, MORALITY, AND CHRISTIAN CULTURES

I hope that after reading this book you gained a new perspective on the diverse ways Christians assess the morality of various activities related to human sexuality. For the most part, contemporary Christians have learned to celebrate sexuality, in contrast to the restrictions of centuries past. I find this is a good and healthy appreciation of the joy possible in intimate relationships, which many continue to enjoy for a lifetime. Of course, the added bonus for so many is the joy of nurturing children and grandchildren. Sex is a good thing.

    I live in a country where obesity is a significant problem. Large calorie-filled chunks of food accompanied by colorful, caloric, oversized drinks dangle before my eyes in all the ways advertisers discover to reach my daily activities. People gorge on sex, too. Marketers skillfully place subtle and not-so-subtle sex-saturated references and images of sex, which are linked to fun and excitement, in songs, stories, games, videos, and just about anywhere people live, learn, and work. Like an unhealthy diet, unrestricted sex damages health. Relationships suffer—and people miss out on savoring the joy of sex within a committed and loving relationship.

    As we have seen, the Bible is rich with stories and teachings about sex. Many of the stories illustrate what can happen when sex is uncontrolled or forced upon a vulnerable person. People get hurt. And relationships suffer—sometimes for generations. Throughout biblical history, laws and teachings appear in the text to help people understand that not all sexuality is right, good, or healthy. Christians and non-Christians alike can see the joy that comes with sex in a loving relationship and the horrible effects when sex is forced on vulnerable persons. We have a moral sense of right and wrong.

    It's the sense of right and wrong expressed in six moral foundations that captured my thinking. As I taught a course on the psychology of religion, one of my students, Kayla Jordan, brought Haidt's book, *The Righteous Mind*, to my attention. I read it. We both discussed it and created a unit on moral psychology for the course. Since then, I have examined the arguments of Christian leaders as they passionately advocated for one position or another in response to the sex-linked social issues that divide Christians. This book is the result of those studies. I learned that progressive, or liberal, thinkers emphasize concerns about harm, fairness in the form of equality, and freedom from oppressive rules and policies. I also found that conservatives care about harm, fairness, and freedom from oppression but focus on different aspects of an issue. And consistent with Haidt's six dimensions, conservatives also spoke about respect for authority, the importance of loyalty to one's tradition, and a deep concern about that which is sacred, holy, and pure.

I expect Christians to turn to the Bible and see how those inspired writers addressed the problems of their day. After all, people haven't changed that much in the few thousand years of the biblical era. People still want to have sex. People still want to marry. Then as now, many want to have children and feel saddened or even depressed when their efforts fail. Of course, people still betray their partners and hurt others in sex-linked violence. So the Bible has much to offer, but not every nuance of sexuality is covered. As I reviewed the biblical texts, I found not only were Christian leaders forming statements derived from different assortments of teachings and stories, but they were doing so in ways that emphasized one or more of the six moral foundations.

As a psychologist with experience in both clinical psychology and psychological science, I wish to point out that information derived from research in moral psychology can change as new data become available. New studies often result in revising existing ideas and suggesting better ways to understand human nature. The way that psychologists view moral foundations may change in the future. Even now it is possible to see that the reasoning associated with some of the six dimensions overlaps with others. For example, considerations of respect for authority and loyalty share ideas in common. Liberty may not be clearly pitted against oppression unless one defines liberty in a specific way akin to liberation. These nuances need not distract us from a broad appreciation of people's viewing moral issues from multiple perspectives. And those lenses suggested by recent research can help us broaden our understanding so that we thoughtfully consider the perspectives of others when appraising an action as consistent with Christian morality.

Moral Philosophy

I should also like to point out to readers unfamiliar with philosophy that much can be learned from the theologians and philosophers who have wrestled with matters of ethics. I am not making a distinction between that which is moral and that which is ethical. Like many, I consider the terms moral and ethical to be interchangeable. There are several ways philosophers analyze different approaches to morality. One approach I find particularly relevant to understanding Christian morality and forming my own opinions is thinking in terms of a morality based on principles rather than a morality based on a consideration of consequences. Moral views based on a consideration of general principles are commonly linked to the writings of Immanuel Kant and represented in the Christian ethical principle of loving one's neighbor as oneself. The focus on considering the consequences of an act is usually associated with the writings of John Stuart Mill. A Christian application of such thinking can be found in Jesus's teaching about the Jewish Sabbath. He challenged the belief that the rule of honoring the Sabbath by doing no work meant you could not heal (Luke 13:10–17). Both approaches to morality have a long history, and contemporary philosophers have identified the problems inherent in trying to apply either approach.

I would like to share a few thoughts about my approach to morality in general and to Christian morality in particular. I take a mixed approach. I think we need principles to live by but we also need wisdom to consider harmful consequences that can occur when a rigid application of principles can do more harm than good. Based on my understanding of human nature, we need principles to live by because it is far too inefficient to constantly analyze our actions to determine consequences. And we can never be sure that our analysis is ever complete because we may discover unintended consequences of a present action in the distant future. What seems right now may turn out to be a bad thing in fifty years. Therefore, my approach to Christian morality is to focus on principles and to learn from the examples in Scripture and life to understand how principles can have both positive and negative consequences. Loving one's neighbor is a moral principle, but understanding how to love someone can require careful consideration when we learn that some actions may hurt those we love. A lifetime commitment in marriage is a biblical principle. It is a good thing for the church to help couples resolve their differences, enhance their relationships, and enjoy life together. Adultery is a hard thing to overcome, so it is understandable that we find adultery as a biblical basis for divorce. Adultery seriously damages the relationship and often causes psychological harm. Physical abuse was not included as a biblical basis for divorce, but the damage done by abusers can lead to permanent damage, if not death. Therefore, divorce for reasons of physical abuse is consistent with Christian morality.

Another consideration I have learned from philosophers is the important distinction between understanding what *is* true is different from deciding what *ought to be* true. It is far too easy for human beings to fall into the trap of thinking that what is the case ought to be the case. As my philosophy professors often said, "you cannot get an *ought* from an *is*." The fact that women are biologically different from men is true, but it does not mean women and men ought to be treated differently in matters of law, education, employment, or many other aspects of life. It does mean that women ought to be treated differently than men when it comes to some medical actions linked to medically relevant biological differences. When it comes to Christian service, I find no basis for sex-linked discrimination.

Common Ground

Before closing, I think it important to keep in mind that, although Christian cultures do take different perspectives on key issues of morality dealing with human sexuality, the majority of Christians do have many things in common when it comes to morality. Despite the public debate about some "hot-button" sex-linked topics that can make Christians seem so divided, Christians do agree on some principles. Christians may also agree that some actions are always wrong but disagree on why an action is wrong. For example, Christians agree that adultery is wrong. A conservative may emphasize God's commandment prohibiting adultery as the basis for judging adultery as wrong. But a progressive may emphasize the incredible harm, disrespect, and betrayal when explaining why adultery is wrong and violates the core Christian principle of love. Thus, one last time, I turn to the six moral dimensions and consent to consider where the majority of Christians might find common ground.

1. Care versus Harm

Christians can find common cause in showing compassion toward those victimized by sexual practices that do not affirm life, fail to respect human dignity, and result in spiritual, emotional, physical, and social harm. Although methods vary, Christians need to find ways to reduce teen pregnancy and protect our most vulnerable people from sexual exploitation. Birth control saves lives. And pregnancy care is important to women and their unborn children. Any Christian morality ought to find ways to help those women who do not have access to adequate care and support. Regardless of beliefs about sexual minorities, it is incumbent on all Christians to show love and respect to all persons, which at a minimum includes the removal of social and legal barriers that interfere with access to the basic rights afforded others within a given culture. As noted above, adultery harms relationships and causes measurable pain to one or more persons. Christians ought to be involved in strengthening marriages and promoting self-control.

2. Fairness/Reciprocity versus Cheating

Christians ought to review their policies and political efforts to ensure they are not treating others in unfair ways. Favoring one group above another is surely contrary to righteous living. Making decisions about how to treat others based on a person's biological sex characteristics surely deserves a challenge.

Christians must be fair in the sense of equal treatment for people when hiring, promoting, transacting business, and educating. Access to housing and healthcare ought to be available to all persons regardless of sexual orientation or gender. Christians ought to support laws and policies that promote the equal treatment of all persons. Christian leaders must ensure they are fair when they investigate allegations of sexual abuse and harassment. Favoring those in power and leadership positions fails to recognize the importance that all people deserve to be treated fairly.

3. Ingroup Loyalty versus Betrayal

The natural tendency to be loyal to one's family and friends interferes with the core of Christian teaching about God as the creator of all persons. Time after time, churches, Christian organizations, and families have covered up sexual offenses out of misguided loyalty to an organization or group. In fact, when wrongdoing is eventually discovered, the loyalty-based cover-up only reduces the credibility of Christians to have a moral voice. Loyalty can be a virtue. But misplaced loyalty is a vice. Christian morality seeks to encourage Christians to be loyal to the broad principles of Christian morality derived from an understanding of God's love for all humanity.

4. Authority/Respect versus Disrespect

I admit that respect for authority can be difficult for Christians who only recognize the authority of the leaders in their faith tradition when it comes to understanding how the Bible should be interpreted on moral matters. Here I wonder if a reminder of humility can be of value. Jesus was not shy about challenging the interpretation of Scripture by the religious leaders of his day. The apostle Paul referred to Scripture and reason when responding to moral matters in the early days of Christianity. Today Christians face new challenges not specifically covered in biblical texts. Godly people will disagree. May we learn to disagree in a charitable and respectful way as we prayerfully consider a right course of action.

Christians must actively hold their leaders accountable for their statements and behavior. The sins of Christian leaders often make headlines because they are expected to live up to high standards of morality. Repentant leaders need support and assistance to get back on track. But those leaders bent on destroying the lives of others must be stopped. Most churches and organizations have procedures for dealing with an errant leader. Christians in churches and organizations that do not have ways to respectfully call attention to wrongdoing ought to prepare policies.

5. Purity or Sanctity versus Degradation

As we have seen, many of the concerns Christians have about immorality are framed in language indicating strong feelings of disgust. Christians express disgust when exposed to explicit images of sex. We feel disgusted when graphic details of an abortion are shown in a video. We feel disgust when a young woman recounts a horrific story of rape. Close on the heels of disgust is our natural reaction to distance ourselves from that which is disgusting and dirty. And many of us feel a strong sense of righteous anger. One danger is a quick and ill-considered strike against an available target rather than the true source of the offense. Another danger is failing to consider all relevant facts before reaching a moral judgment and acting accordingly.

Though a natural response pattern, objects of disgust are learned within our culture. Anyone who has traveled extensively has likely encountered foods that seem disgusting. The point is, Christian morality ought to transcend culture. It is too easy to develop a "distaste" for people and customs that seem strange or different.

Another point worth noting is the tendency of people to demonize people who appear so different from us. Richard Beck writes about the tendency of people to turn unsavory characters into "monsters" when motivated by strong feelings of disgust.[1] It's easy to think of rapists and sex traffickers as monsters, especially when the victims tell us of the brutal and callous way they were treated.

Beck also notes the problem of creating false monsters in order to have a target for feelings of outrage. He cites the example of Nazi propaganda art that depicted Jews as rodents. When ordinary people think of another group as disgusting, dirty, depraved, perverted, or in other ways less than human, the stage is set for unmitigated destruction. It is important that Christians be aware of this human propensity to dehumanize and degrade others with whom we disagree. It is not long ago that some American Christians treated slaves as less than human and undeserving of basic human rights. The language some Christians use about sexual minorities reveals a similar aversion to their fellow humans.

6. Liberty versus Oppression

Some will find any restrictions on personal liberty to be oppressive. Others may be too quick to impose the limitations of their conscience on others. Living the Christian life involves living with others, which necessitates some loss of personal liberty with respect to the liberties of another. Relational sexuality is perhaps the most intimate of experiences. Limitations are necessary to ensure that all persons are free from the oppression of others. Laws and regulations serve liberty best when they restrict individuals and groups from oppressing others—especially those most vulnerable. Christian morality ought to negotiate the boundaries between the irresponsible downside of unbounded liberty and the unmitigated burden of oppression. In this context, Christians ought to speak out against sexual violence within relationships, on campuses, and in the work place. Christians have a responsibility to take action against human trafficking of all kinds, especially sex trafficking.

Consent

Without choice there is no morality. When it comes to sexuality, consent to participate is a critical component to ensure that people are not harmed, treated unfairly, betrayed, degraded, or oppressed. Consent alone does not justify an act as moral or immoral but consent must be a consideration in

---

1. Beck, *Unclean*, 91–106.

judging sexual activity as right or wrong. An appreciation of consent and the importance of choice ought to be a key component of Christian sex education and sexual harassment prevention programs.

Summary and Conclusion

As a final summary, I will list a few key points along with questions I hope you find useful in analyzing the arguments Christians use when making a moral judgment about sex-related moral issues.

1. Most Christians form moral judgments by combining their understanding of Scripture, human nature, one or more reasons derived from six moral foundations, and an understanding of human sexuality.
2. Christians interpret Scripture based on several theological and psychological factors.
3. Christians reveal the moral foundations important to their moral judgment in the language they use. There are six moral foundations. Conservative Christians may draw upon all six foundations of care, equality, loyalty, authority, purity, and liberty. Progressive Christians tend to emphasize two or three foundations: care, equality, and liberty.
4. People understand sexuality and sex-linked issues differently. Some biological aspects of sexuality are relevant to questions about what is natural and the degree of choice a person has over sex-related functioning. I also considered factors relevant to understand sex-related harm.
5. It is possible that Christians will employ arguments derived from the same moral foundation but emphasize different aspects.
6. When Christians act on moral judgments, there may be an impact on one or more areas of a person's wellbeing. We can think about wellbeing in terms of six dimensions of functioning represented in the SCOPES model: spiritual, cognitive, behavioral, physical, emotional, and social.
7. We can analyze moral reasons by using two questions derived from the positive and negative dimensions of the six moral foundations. How does their language reveal concerns about care, equality, loyalty, authority, purity, or liberty? How does their language reveal concerns about harm, inequality, betrayal, disrespect, degradation, or oppression?

8. The impact of a moral judgment on wellbeing can be framed by using a question like the following: how does the judgment impact a person's spirituality, thinking, behavior patterns, health, feelings, and relationships?

A Final Note

In closing, I hope I have helped you think broadly about the sex-related issues that divide so many Christians. I hope I have stimulated your thinking about how to consider the role of Scripture in creating a moral foundation or examining the foundation of others. I hope you find some value in thinking about human nature in multiple ways such as in the SCOPES model. I also hope that using the six lenses derived from the discussion of moral foundations along with consent allows for more productive thinking when it comes to establishing a Christian moral compass. Moreover, I hope you learned something new about sexuality that may help your thinking about sex-related issues. And for those readers who are parents, I hope you too formulate robust Christian principles to guide your children in ways that help them select a moral course of action for their sexuality that honors God, themselves, and those they love.

BIBLIOGRAPHY

Ackman, Dan. "How Big is Porn." *Forbes,* May 25, 2001. Online: http://www.forbes.com/2001/05/25/ 0524porn.html.

Ainsworth, Mary D. S. "Object Relations, Dependency, and Attachment: A Theoretical Review of the Infant-Mother Relationship." *Child Development* 40 (1969) 969–1025.

Alsdurf, James, and Phyllis Alsdurf. *Battered into Submission: The Tragedy of Wife Abuse in the Christian Home.* Downers Grove, IL: InterVarsity, 1989.

Altemeyer, Bob, and Bruce Hunsberger. "Authoritarianism, Religious Fundamentalism, Quest, and Prejudice." *International Journal for the Psychology of Religion* 2 (1992) 113–33.

American Psychiatric Association. *Diagnostic and Statistical Manual of Mental Disorders.* 5th ed. Washington, DC: American Psychiatric, 2013.

American Psychological Association. *Answers to Your Questions: For a Better Understanding of Sexual Orientation and Homosexuality.* Washington, DC: American Psychological Association, 2008. Online: http://www.apa.org/topics/lgbt/orientation.pdf.

American Society for Reproductive Medicine. *Third-Party Reproduction: Sperm, Egg, and Embryo Donation and Surrogacy.* American Society for Reproductive Medicine, 2012. Online: https://www.asrm.org/uploadedFiles/ASRM_Content/Resources/Patient_Resources/Fact_Sheets_and_Info_Booklets/thirdparty.pdf.

Anglican Communion News Service Staff. "Anglicans Mark 70 Years Since Ordination of First Woman Priest." *Anglican Communion News Service,* January 8, 2014. Online: http://www.anglicannews.org/news/2014/01/anglicans-mark-70-years-since-ordination-of-first-woman-priest.aspx.

Bancroft, John. "Sexual Desire and the Brain Revisited." *Sexual and Relationship Therapy,* 25 (2010) 166–71.

Barna Group. "Christian Women Today, Part 2 of 4: What Women Want." Last updated August 17, 2012. Online: https://www.barna.org/culture-articles/585-christian-women-today-part-2-of-4-a-look-at-womens-lifestyles-priorities-and-time-commitments://.

Barrett, Duncan. "British War Brides Faced Own Battles During 1940s." *L.A. Times,* October 20, 2014. Online: http://www.latimes.com/opinion/op-ed/la-oe-barrett-war-brides-immigration-20141021-story.html

The BBC. "Divorce in Christianity." *The BBC,* June 23, 2009. Online: http://www.bbc.co.uk/religion/religions/christianity/ritesrituals/divorce_1.shtml.

———. "Libby Lane: First Female Church of England Bishop Consecrated." *The BBC,* January 26, 2015. Online: http://www.bbc.com/news/uk-politics-30974547.

———. "March through London to Mark 20 Years of Women Priests." *The BBC*, May 3, 2014. Online: http://www.bbc.co.uk/news/uk-27265039.

Bateson, Melissa, et al. "Cues of Being Watched Enhance Cooperation in a Real-World Setting." *Biology Letters* 2 (2006) 412–14.

Bell, Rob. *Love Wins*. New York: Harper One, 2011.

———. *Sex God: Exploring the Endless Connections between Sexuality and Spirituality*. New York: Harper One, 2007.

Beck, Richard. *Unclean: Meditations on Purity, Hospitality, and Mortality*. Eugene, OR: Cascade, 2011.

Bering, Jesse M., and Dominic D. P. Johnson. "'O Lord . . . You Perceive my Thoughts from Afar': Recursiveness and the Evolution of Supernatural Agency." *Journal of Cognition and Culture* 5 (2005) 118–42.

Billy Graham Evangelistic Association Staff. "Answers: Does the Bible Approve of Some Homosexual Relationships?" Billy Graham Evangelistic Association, 2004. Online: http://billygraham.org/answer/does-the-bible-approve-of-some-homosexual-relationships/.

Black, David A. *Linguistics for Students of New Testament Greek*. Grand Rapids: Baker, 1995.

Blanton, Amelia. "A Christian Response to Human Trafficking." *St. Louis Post-Dispatch*, March 22, 2011. Online: http://www.stltoday.com/lifestyles/faith-and-values/civil-religion/deleted-bloggers/a-christian-response-to-human-trafficking/article_3a15d8ea-54cf-11e0-8c3c-0017a4a78c22.html.

Borg, Marcus. J. *Reading the Bible Again for the First Time: Taking the Bible Seriously but not Literally*. New York: HarperCollins, 2001.

Borkett-Jones, Lucinda. "Why the Church Needs to Stop Being Prudish about Prostitution." *Christian Today*, March 26, 2015. Online: http://www.christiantoday.com/article/why.the.church.needs.to.stop.being.prudish.about.prostitution/48855.htm.

Bornstein, Brian H., and Monica K. Miller. "Does a Judge's Religion Influence Decision Making?" *Court Review* 45 (2008–2009) 112–15.

Boy Scouts of America. "Boy Scouts of America Statement." Last updated May 23, 2013. Online: http://www.scouting.org/sitecore/content/MembershipStandards/Resolution/results.aspx.

Brakke, David. "Canon Formation and Social Conflict in Fourth-Century Egypt: Athanasius of Alexandria's Thirty-Ninth Festal Letter." *Harvard Theological Review* 87 (1994) 395–419.

Bretherton, Inge. "Attachment Theory: Retrospect and Prospect." *Monographs of the Society for Research in Child Development* 50 (1985) 3–35.

Brook, Tom Vanden. "Pentagon Opening Front-Line Combat Roles to Women." *USA Today*, June 18, 2013. Online: http://www.usatoday.com/story/news/politics/2013/06/18/women-expected-on-front-lines-by-2016/2434911/.

Cain, Virginia S., et al. "Sexual Functioning and Practices in a Multi-Ethnic Study of Midlife Women: Baselines Results from SWAN." *Journal of Sex Research* 40 (2003) 266–76.

Campolo, Tony. "Missing the Point: Homosexuality." In *Adventures in Missing the Point*, edited by Brian D. McLaren and Tony Campolo, 198–213. Grand Rapids: Zondervan, 2003.

Carbery, Baevin, et al. "Need For Physician Education on the Benefits and Risks of Male Circumcision in the United States." *AIDS Education and Prevention* 24 (2012) 377–87.

Carmichael, Calum. "Incest in the Bible." *Chicago-Kent Law Review* 71 (1995) 123–47. Online: http://scholarship.kentlaw.iit.edu/cklawreview/vol71/iss1/6.

Carter, Jimmy. "Losing My Religion for Equality." July 15, 2009. *The Age*. Online: http://www.theage.com.au/federal-politics/losing-my-religion-for-equality-20090714-dkov.html

Chambers, Alan M. "Exodus Int'l President to the Gay Community: 'We're Sorry'" Last updated June 19, 2013. Online: http://alanchambers.org/exodus-intl-president-to-the-gay-community-were-sorry/.

Chivers, Meredith L. "A Brief Update on the Specificity of Sexual Arousal." *Sexual and Relationship Therapy* 25 (2010) 407–14.

Christians for Biblical Equality Staff. "US Denominations and their Stances on Women in Leadership." *E-quality* 6 (2007). Online: http://www2.cbeinternational.org/new/E-Journal/2007/07spring/denominations%20first%20installment--FINAL.pdf

The Church of Jesus Christ of Latter Day Saints. "Modesty." Online: https://www.lds.org/topics/modesty?lang=eng.

Cohn, D'vera, et al. "Barely Half of U.S. Adults are Married—A Record Low." *Pew Research Center*, December 14, 2010. Online: http://www.pewsocialtrends.org/2011/12/14/barely-half-of-u-s-adults-are-married-a-record-low/.

Collins, Matthew A. "Examining the Reception and Impact of the Dead Sea Scrolls: Some Possibilities for Future Investigation." *Dead Sea Discoveries* 18 (2011) 226–46.

Coogan, Michael. *God & Sex: What the Bible Really Says*. New York: Hachette, 2010.

Coontz, Stephanie. *Marriage, a History: From Obedience to Intimacy or How Love Conquered Marriage*. New York: Penguin, 2005. Kindle edition.

Copen, Casey E., et al. "First Premarital Cohabitation in the United States: 2006–2010 National Survey of Family Growth." *National Health Statistics Reports*, no. 64 (April 4, 2013). Online: http://www.cdc.gov/nchs/data/nhsr/nhsr064.pdf.

Danziger, Shai, et al. "Extraneous Factors in Judicial Decisions." *Proceedings of the National Academy of Sciences of the United States of America* 108.17 (2011) 6889–92.

Deering, Kathleen N., et al. "A Systematic Review of the Correlates of Violence against Sex Workers." *American Journal of Public Health* 104 (May 2014) 42–54.

Dennett, Daniel C., and Linda LaScola. *Caught in the Pulpit: Leaving Belief Behind*. Durham, NC: Pitchstone, 2015. Kindle edition.

Dias, Elizabeth. "Brave, Clean, Reverent . . . and Split." *Time* 181.22 (2013) 14.

DiBlasio, Fred A. "Marital Couples and Forgiveness Intervention." In *Evidence-Based Practices for Christian Counseling and Psychotherapy*, edited by Everett. L. Worthington Jr. et al., 232–54. Downers Grove, IL: InterVarsity, 2013.

Duggar, Michelle, and Jim Bob Duggar. *A Love that Multiplies: An Up-Close View of How They Make It Work*. New York: Howard, 2011.

Duin, Julia. *Quitting Church: Why are the Faithful Fleeing and What to Do About It*. Grand Rapids: Baker, 2008.

"Drapes Removed from Justice Department Statue." *USA Today*, June 24, 2005. Online: http://usatoday30.usatoday.com/news/washington/2005-06-24-doj-statue_x.htm?csp=34.

Driscoll, Mark, and Grace Driscoll. *Real Marriage: The Truth about Sex, Friendship & Life Together.* Nashville: Thomas Nelson, 2012.

Drumm, René, et al. "Intimate Partner Violence in a Conservative Christian Denomination: Prevalence and Types." *Social Work & Christianity* 33 (2006) 233–51.

Edelman, Benjamin. "Red Light States: Who Buys Online Adult Entertainment?" *Journal of Economic Perspectives* 23 (2009) 209–20.

Elledge, Casey D. "'From the Beginning it was not so . . .': Jesus, Divorce, and Remarriage in Light of the Dead Sea Scrolls." *Perspectives in Religious Studies* 37 (2010) 371–89.

Elliott, James K. "Manuscripts, the Codex and the Canon." *Journal for the Study of the New Testament* 19 (1997) 105–23.

Enright, Robert D. *Forgiveness is a Choice: A Step-by-Step Process for Resolving Anger and Restoring Hope.* Washington, DC: American Psychological Association, 2001.

Entin, Jonathan L. "The Supreme Court's Treatment of Same-Sex Marriage in *United States v. Windsor* and *Hollingsworth v. Perry*: Analysis and Implications." *Case Western Reserve Law Review* 64 (2014) 823–28.

Exline, Julie J. "Godly Love from the Perspective of Psychology." In *The Science and Theology of Godly Love*, edited by Matthew T. Lee and Amos Yong, 141–56. DeKalb, IL: Northern Illinois University Press, 2012.

Fantz, Ashley. "Reality Show Snake-Handling Preacher Dies—of Snakebite." *CNN*, February 18, 2014. Online: http://www.cnn.com/2014/02/16/us/snake-salvation-pastor-bite/.

The Federal Bureau of Investigation. "Combatting Human Trafficking." September 23, 2013. Online: http://www.fbi.gov/news/testimony/combating-human-trafficking.

Feinberg, John S., and Paul D. Feinberg. *Ethics for a Brave New World.* Wheaton, IL: Crossway, 1993.

Finer, Lawrence B. "Trends in Premarital Sex in the United States, 1954–2003." *Public Health Reports* 122 (2007) 73–78.

Flint, P. W. "The Significance of the Biblical Dead Sea Scrolls." *Southwestern Journal of Theology* 53 (2010) 15–25.

Focus on the Family Issue Analysts. "Revisionist Gay Theology." Focus on the Family, 2008. Online: http://www.focusonthefamily.com/socialissues/social-issues/same-sex-revisionist-theology/revisionist-gay-theology-issue

"Food for Thought: Paul Rozin's Research and Teaching at Penn." *Penn Arts & Sciences*, Fall 1997. Online: http://www.sas.upenn.edu/sasalum/newsltr/fall97/rozin.html.

Forbes, Anna, and Sarah E. Patterson. "Decriminalizing Sex Work Could Reduce HIV Infections, So Why Isn't Everyone on Board?" *Our Bodies Ourselves*, August 29, 2014. Online: http://www.ourbodiesourselves.org/health-info/decriminalizing-sex-work-could-reduce-hiv/.

Foster, David K. "Covenant: The Heart of the Marriage Mystery." Online: http://www.focusonthefamily.com/marriage/gods-design-for-marriage/marriage-gods-idea/covenant-the-heart-of-the-marriage-mystery.

Francis. "Pope Francis General Audience St. Peter's Square." Wednesday 2 April 2014. Online: http://w2.vatican.va/content/francesco/en/audiences/2014/documents/papa-francesco_20140402_udienza-generale.html.

Franklin, Ruth M., and Sharon Dotger. "Sex Education Knowledge Differences between Freshmen and Senior College Undergraduates." *College Student Journal* 45 (2011) 199–213.

Friedman, Richard E., and Shawna Dolansky. *The Bible Now*. New York: Oxford University Press, 2012.

Furnish, Victor P. *The Moral Teaching of Paul: Selected Issues*. 3rd ed. Nashville: Abingdon, 2009.

Gabel, John B., and Charles B. Wheeler. *The Bible as Literature*. New York: Oxford University Press, 1986.

Gangel, Kenneth O. "Toward a Biblical Theology of Marriage and Family, Part 1: Pentateuch and Historical Books." *Journal of Psychology & Theology* 5 (1977) 55–69.

Garland, Diana R. "The Prevalence of Clergy Sexual Misconduct with Adults: A Research Study Executive Summary." Online: http://www.baylor.edu/clergysexualmisconduct/ index.php?id=67406.

General Presbytery of the Assemblies of God. "Can Born-Again Believers Be Demon Possessed?" *AG Position Papers*, May 1972. Online: http://ag.org/top/beliefs/Position_Papers/pp_downloads/pp_ 4176_possessed.pdf.

———. "Homosexuality, Marriage, and Sexual Identity." *AG Position Papers*, August 2014. Online:http://ag.org/top/Beliefs/Position_Papers/pp_downloads/pp_4181_homosexuality.pdf

———. "The Role of Women in Ministry as Described in Holy Scripture." *AG Position Papers*, August 2010. Online: http://ag.org/top/Beliefs/Position_Papers/pp_downloads/ PP_The_Role_of_Women_in_Ministry.pdf.

Gibson, David. "Catholic Leaders Urge Support for Boy Scouts after Shift on Gays." *Religious News Service*, May 31, 2013. Online: http://www.religionnews.com/2013/05/31/catholic-leaders-urge-support-for-boy-scouts-after-shift-on-gays/.

Gibson, Megan. "The Long, Strange History of Birth Control." *Time*, February 2, 2015. Online: http://time.com/3692001/birth-control-history-djerassi/.

Gilligan, Carol. *In a Different Voice: Psychological Theory and Women's Development*. Cambridge: Harvard University Press, 1982.

Gilmore, Alec. "Langton." In *A Concise Dictionary of Bible Origins and Interpretation*, 111. London: T. & T. Clark, 2006.

———. "Stephanous." In *A Concise Dictionary of Bible Origins and Interpretation*, 186. London: T. & T. Clark, 2006.

Gizitdinov, Nariman. "Polygamy Offers Young Women of Kazakhstan a Ticket Out of Poverty." *The Independent*, December 8, 2013. Online: http://www.independent.co.uk/news/world/europe/ polygamy-offers-young-women-of-kazakhstan-a-ticket-out-of-poverty-8991759.html.

Gledhill, Ruth. "Tony Campolo Calls for Full Acceptance of Gay Christian Couples in the Church. *Christian Today*, June 8, 2015. Online: http://www.christiantoday.com/article/tony.campolo.calls.for.full.acceptance.of.gay.christian.couples.in.the.church/55718.htm

Goldfeder, Mark. "Polygamy and DOMA." *The Salt Lake Tribune*, May 11, 2013. Online: http://www.sltrib.com/sltrib/opinion/56282277-82/marriage-plural-polygamy-court.html.csp.

Goldingay, John E., et al. "Same-Sex Marriage and Anglican Theology: A View from the Traditionalists." *Anglican Theological Review* 93 (2011) 1–50.
Gonzalez, Justo. *The Story of Christianity: The Early Church to the Present Day*. Peabody, MA: Prince, 1999.
Good, Deidre J., et al. "A Theology of Marriage Including Same-Sex Couples: A View from the Liberals." *Anglican Theological Review* 93 (2011) 51–87
Goodstein, Laurie. "Christian Charity Backtracks on Gays." *The New York Times*, March 27, 2014. Online: http://www.nytimes.com/2014/03/28/us/christian-charity-backtracks-on-gays.html.
Gorsuch, Richard L., and Susan E. McPherson. "Intrinsic/Extrinsic Measurement: I/I-Revised and Single-Item Scales." *Journal of the Scientific Study of Religion* 28 (1989) 348–54.
Gracey, Celeste, and Jeremy Weber. "World Vision Reverses Decision to Hire Christians in Same-Sex Marriages." *Christianity Today*, March 26, 2014. Online: http://www.christianitytoday.com/ct/2014/ march-web-only/world-vision-reverses-decision-gay-same-sex-marriage.html.
Graham, Billy. "A Sacred Institution." Online: http://billygraham.org/devotion/a-sacred-institution/.
———. "God's Best." Online: http://billygraham.org/devotion/gods-best/
Graves, Marlena. "Getting to the Root of Female Masturbation." *Christianity Today*, January 5, 2012. Online: http://www.christianitytoday.com/women/2012/january/getting-to-root-of-female-masturbation.html.
Greene, Joshua. *Moral tribes: Emotion, Reason, and the Gap between Us and Them*. New York: Penguin, 2013.
Grenz, Stanley. *Sexual Ethics: An Evangelical Perspective*. Louisville, KY: Westminster John Knox, 1997.
Griffin, Winn. "The Story of God and Women in Ministry." Vineyard USA, 2009. Online: http://www.vineyardusa.org/site/task-forces/women/article/story-god-and-women-ministry.
Gross, Terry. "Retired Bishop Gene Robinson on Being Gay and Loving God." *National Public Radio*, January 10, 2013. Online: http://www.npr.org/templates/transcript/transcript.php?storyId=169066917.
Gulley, Phillip. *If the Church Were Christian: Rediscovering the Values of Jesus*. New York: HarperCollins, 2010.
Gushee, David P. "A Crumbling Institution: How Social Revolutions Cracked the Pillars of Marriage." *Christianity Today* 48, September 2004, 42–45.
Haggard, Ted. "Suicide, Evangelicalism, and Sorrow." *The Pastor's Pen: Official Blog of Ted Haggard*. Online: http://tedhaggardblog.com/2013/12/12/suicide-evangelicalism-and-sorrow/.
Haidt, Jonathan. "The Emotional Dog and Its Rational Tail." *Psychological Review* 108 (2001) 814–34.
———. "Individual Differences in Sensitivity to Disgust: A Scale Sampling Seven Domains of Disgust Elicitors." *Personality and Individual Differences* 16 (1994) 701–13.
———. *The Righteous Mind: Why Good People are Divided by Politics and Religion*. New York: Pantheon, 2012.
Haidt, Jonathan, Fredrik Bjorkland, and Scott Murphy. "Moral Dumbfounding: When Intuition Finds No Reason." Unpublished manuscript, 2000. Online: http://

faculty.virginia.edu/haidtlab/articles/manuscripts/haidt.bjorklund.working-paper.when%20intuition%20finds%20no%20reason.pub603.doc

Haidt, Jonathan, and Selin Kesebir. "Morality." In *Handbook of Social Psychology*, 5th ed., edited by Susan Fiske et al., 797–832. Hoboken, NJ: Wiley, 2010.

Haidt, Jonathan, Paul Rozin, et al. "Body, Psyche, and Culture: The Relationship of Disgust to Morality." *Psychology and Developing Societies* 9 (1997) 107–31.

Hansen, Klaus. J. "Mormonism." In *Sex & Religion*, edited by Christel Manning and Phil Zuckerman, 142–59. Belmont, CA: Wadsworth, 2005.

Hagerty, Barbara B. "Some Muslims in U.S. Quietly Engage in Polygamy." *National Public Radio*, May 27, 2008. Online: http://www.npr.org/templates/story/story.php?storyId=90857818.

Harris Interactive. "Americans' Belief in God, Miracles and Heaven Declines: Belief in Darwin's Theory of Evolution Rises." Last updated December 16, 2013. Online: http://www.harrisinteractive.com/NewsRoom/HarrisPolls/tabid/447/ctl/ReadCustom%20Default/mid/1508/ArticleId/1353/Default.aspx.

Haselton, Martie G., and Timothy Ketelaar. "Irrational Emotions or Emotional Wisdom? The Evolutionary Psychology of Emotions and Behavior." In *Hearts and Minds: Affective Influences on Social Cognition and Behavior*, edited by Joseph P. Forgas, 21–40. New York: Psychology, 2006.

Hayes, Richard D. "Circular and Linear Modeling of Female Sexual Desire and Arousal." *Journal of Sex Research* 48 (2011) 130–41.

Hill, Craig A., and Leslie K. Preston. "Individual Differences in the Experience of Sexual Motivation: Theory and Measurement of Disposition Sexual Motives." *Journal of Sex Research* 33 (1996) 27–45.

Hill, Peter C. "Measurement Assessment and Issues in the Psychology of Religion and Spirituality." In *Handbook of the Psychology of Religion and Spirituality*, 2nd ed., edited by Raymond F. Paloutzian and Crystal L. Park, 48–74. New York: Guilford, 2013.

Historica Canada. "Departure of Black Loyalists." *Black History Canada*. Online: http://www.blackhistorycanada.ca/events.php?themeid=21&id=2.

Holst, Robert. "Polygamy and the Bible." *International Review of Mission* 56 (1967) 205–13.

Hood, Ralph W., Jr., Peter C. Hill, and Bernard Spilka. *The Psychology of Religion: An Empirical Approach*. 4th ed. New York: Guilford, 2009.

Hood, Ralph W., Jr., Peter C. Hill, and W. Paul Williamson. *The Psychology of Religious Fundamentalism*. New York: Guilford, 2005.

Hornsby, Teresa J. *Sex Texts from the Bible: Selections Annotated & Explained*. Woodstock, VT: Skylight Paths, 2007.

Howe, Amy. "In Historic Decision, Court Strikes Down State Bans on Same-sex Marriage: In Plain English." *Scotusblog*, June 26, 2015.

Humphrey, Edith M. "Recovering Christian Marriage: What God Hath Not Joined: Why Marriage was Designed for Male and Female." *Christianity Today* 48, September 2004, 36–41.

Hyatt, Eddie. "Why the 'Woman as the Weaker Vessel' Teaching is Wrong." *Charisma Magazine*, April 15, 2015. Online: http://www.charismamag.com/life/women/23086-why-the-woman-as-the-weaker-vessel-teaching-is-wrong.

Jayson, Sharon. "Remarriage Rate Declining as More Opt for Cohabitation." *USA Today*, September 12, 2013. Online: http://www.usatoday.com/story/news/nation/2013/09/12/remarriage-rates-divorce/2783187/.

Jones, Rachel K., and Joerg Dreweke. *Countering Conventional Wisdom: New Evidence on Religion and Contraceptive Use*. New York: Guttmacher Institute, 2011.

Jordan, Kayla, et al. "Effects on Forgiveness and Attitudes toward Christians of Self-Identified LGBTQ People to Hearing a Public Apology from a Christian and to Taking the Perspective of the Church." *Journal of Christianity and Psychology* 32 (2013) 99–114.

Just the Facts Coalition. "Just the Facts about Sexual Orientation and Youth: A Primer for Principals, Educators, and School Personnel." Washington, DC: American Psychological Association, 2008.

"Justice Department Covers Partially Nude Statues." *USA Today*, January 29, 2002. Online: http://usatoday30.usatoday.com/news/nation/2002/01/29/statues.htm.

Kahneman, Daniel. *Thinking, Fast and Slow*. New York: Farrar, Straus and Giroux, 2011.

King, Martin Luther, Jr. "I Have A Dream . . . ." 1963. Online: http://www.archives.gov/exhibits/featured_documents/mlk_speech/index.html.

Kirkpatrick, Lee A., and Phillip R. Shaver. "Attachment Theory and Religion: Childhood Attachments, Religious Beliefs, and Conversion." *Journal for the Scientific Study of Religion* 29 (1990) 315–34.

Kluger, Jeffrey, and Alice Park. "Frontiers of Fertility." *Time* 181, June 10, 2013, 50–54.

Knight, George W., III. "New Testament Teaching on the Role Relationship of Male and Female with Special Reference to the Teaching/Ruling Functions in the Church." *Journal of Psychology & Theology* 3 (1975) 216–29.

Knights of Columbus. "Abortion in America." *Marist Poll*, January 2014. Online: http://www.kofc.org/un/en/resources/communications/marist-poll-abortion-restrictions2014.pdf.

Knust, Jennifer W. *Unprotected Texts: The Bible's Surprising Contradictions about Sex and Desire*. New York: Harper Collins, 2011. Kindle edition.

Kohlberg, Lawrence, and Richard H. Hersh. "Moral Development: A Review of the Theory." *Theory into Practice* 16 (1977) 53–59.

Kolb, Bryan, and Ian Q. Whishaw. *Fundamentals of Human Neuropsychology*. 6th ed. New York: Worth, 2009.

Kumar, Anugrah. "John Piper Explains Why Women Shouldn't Lead Men." *The Christian Post*, October 30, 2011. Online: http://www.christianpost.com/news/john-piper-explains-why-women-shouldnt-lead-men-59818/.

Lang, Joshua. "What Happens to Women Who are Denied Abortions?" *The New York Times Magazine*, June 12, 2013. Online: http://www.nytimes.com/2013/06/16/magazine/study-women-denied-abortions.html?pagewanted=all&_r=2&.

Lazarus, Arnold A. *The Practice of Multimodal Therapy: Systematic, Comprehensive, and Effective Psychotherapy*. Baltimore: Johns Hopkins University Press, 1989.

Lee, Matthew T., and Amos Yong, eds. *Godly Love: Impediments and Possibilities*. New York: Lexington, 2012.

Levitt, Heidi M., et al. "Addressing Intimate Partner Violence within a Religious Context." In *Spiritually Oriented Psychotherapy for Trauma*, edited by Donald F. Walker et al., 211–31. Washington, DC: American Psychological Association, 2015.

Liebelson, Dana. "The 8 Best Lines from Ginsburg's Dissent on the Hobby Lobby Contraception Decision." *Mother Jones*, June 30, 2014. Online: http://www.motherjones.com/politics/2014/ 06/best-lines-hobby-lobby-decision.

Linder, Douglas O. "Day 7: Darrow Examines Bryan." *State v. Scopes: Trial Excerpts*. Online: http://law2.umkc.edu/faculty/projects/ftrials/scopes/day7.htm.

Ling, Lisa "Our America with Lisa Ling: Exodus Head Alan Chambers' Full Apology to the LGBT Community." Online: http://www.oprah.com/own-our-america-lisa-ling/Exodus-Head-Alan-Chambers-Full-Apology-Video.

Liptak, Adam. "Supreme Court Rejects Contraceptives Mandate for Some Corporations: Justices Rule in Favor of Hobby Lobby." *The New York Times*, June 30, 2014. Online: http://www.nytimes.com/2014/07/01/us/hobby-lobby-case-supreme-court-contraception.html.

LoPresti, Anthony F. "Christianity." In *Sex & Religion*, edited by Christel Manning and Phil Zuckerman, 117–41. Belmont, CA: Wadsworth, 2005.

Luhrmann, Tanya M. *When God Talks Back: Understanding the American Evangelical Relationship with God*. New York: Vintage, 2012.

Lunn, Pam "Anatomy and Theology of Marriage: Is Gay Marriage an Oxymoron?" *Theology & Sexuality* 4 (1997) 10–26.

Luscombe, Belinda. "The End of Alimony." *Time*, May 27, 2013, 44–49.

———. "I do, I do, I do, I do: Polygamy Raises its Profile in America." *Time*, July 26, 2012. Online: http://healthland.time.com/2012/07/26/i-do-i-do-i-do-i-do-polygamy-raises-its-profile-in-america/.

Luxmoore, Jonathan. "British Historian: Church Has Not Learned from Abuse in Past Centuries." *National Catholic Reporter*, June 14, 2012. Online: http://ncronline.org/news/british-historian-church-has-not-learned-abuse-past-centuries.

Macchia, Frank D. "Baptized in the Spirit: Towards a Global Pentecostal Theology." In *Defining Issues in Pentecostalism*, edited by Steven M. Studebaker, 12–28. Eugene, OR: Pickwick, 2008.

MacCulloch, Diarmaid. *Silence: A Christian History*. New York: Viking, 2013.

Mahoney, Kelli. "What the Bible Says About . . . Modesty." Online: http://christianteens.about.com/ od/whatthebiblesaysabout/f/Modesty.htm.

Major, Brenda, et al. "Abortion and Mental Health: Evaluating the Evidence." *American Psychologist* 64 (2009) 863–90.

Maner, John, et al. "Adaptive Relationship Cognition: The Sights and Smells of Sexual Attraction." In *New Directions in Close Relationships: Integrating across Disciplines and Theoretical Approaches*, edited by Omri Gillath et al., 153–68. Washington, DC: American Psychological Association, 2012.

McCombs, Brady. "Utah Appeals Ruling on Anti-Polygamy Laws in 'Sister Wives' Case." *The Salt Lake Tribune*, October 16, 2014. Online: http://www.sltrib.com/news/polygamy/1689789-155/utah-ruling-law-families-family-multiple.

McCullough, Michael E., and Brian Willoughby. "Religion, Self-Regulation, and Self-Control: Associations, Explanations, and Implications." *Psychological Bulletin* 135 (2009) 69–93.

McGrath, Alister E. *Christian Theology: An Introduction*. 4th ed. Malden, MA: Blackwell, 2007.

McGrath, James F. "Progressive Religion." *Patheos*, June 4, 2014. Online: http://www.patheos.com/blogs/exploringourmatrix/2014/06/progressive-religion.html

McIver, Robert K. *Memory, Jesus, and the Synoptic Gospels*. Atlanta: Society of Biblical Literature, 2011.

McLeland, Kelly. C., and Geoffrey W. Sutton. "Spirituality, Mental Health, Sexual Orientation, and Gender: An Experimental Study of Attitudes and Social Influence." *Journal of Psychology & Theology* 36 (2008) 104–13.

McMinn, Mark R., and Clark D. Campbell. *Integrative Psychotherapy: Toward a Comprehensive Christian Approach*. Downers Grove, IL: InterVarsity, 2007.

McNamara, Patrick, and P. Monroe Butler. "The Neuropsychology of Religious Experience." In *Handbook of the Psychology of Religion and Spirituality*, 2nd ed., edited by Raymond F. Paloutzian and Crystal L. Park, 215–33. New York: Guilford, 2013.

Menn, Esther M. "Sexuality in the Old Testament: Strong as Death, Unquenchable as Fire." *Currents in Theology and Mission* 30 (2003) 37–45.

Mezey, Nancy J. *LGBT Families*. Washington, DC: Sage, 2015.

Milar, Katherine S. "The Myth Buster: Evelyn Hooker's Groundbreaking Research Explored the Notion That Homosexuality Was a Mental Illness, Ultimately Removing It from the DSM." *Monitor on Psychology* 42 (2011) 24.

Mitchell, Melissa E., et al. "Need Fulfillment in Polyamorous Relationships." *Journal of Sex Research* 51 (2014) 329–39.

Mohler, Albert "Pointing to Disaster—The Flawed Moral Vision of World Vision [Updated]." Last updated March 26, 2014. Online: http://www.albertmohler.com/2014/03/25/pointing-to-disaster-the-flawed-moral-vision-of-world-vision/.

Moon, Ruth. "Does Plan B Cause Abortion?" *Christianity Today*, April 5, 2013. Online: http://www.christianitytoday.com/ct/2013/may/does-plan-b-cause-abortion.html.

Murray, David. "Blacks in Britain, 1942." *The New York Times*, March 6, 1988. Online: http://www.nytimes.com/1988/03/06/books/blacks-in-britain-1942.html.

Myers, David G. *Psychology*. 8th ed. New York: Worth, 2006.

National Association of Evangelicals. "Abortion." Last modified 2010. Online: http://nae.net/abortion-2/.

———. *Theology of Sex: Honoring God's Good Gift*. 2012. Online: http://nae.net/theology-of-sex/

National Geographic Channel. "Polygamy USA." Online: http://channel.nationalgeographic.com/channel/polygamy-usa/.

Obermeyer, Carla M. "The Consequences of Female Circumcision for Health and Sexuality: An Update on the Evidence." *Culture, Health & Sexuality* 7 (2005) 443–61.

Olatunji, Bunmi O. "The Disgust Scale: Item Analysis, Factor Structure, and Suggestions for Refinement." *Psychological Assessment* 19 (2007) 281–97.

Oman, Doug. "Defining Religion and Spirituality." In *Handbook of the Psychology of Religion and Spirituality*, 2nd ed., edited by Raymond F. Paloutzian and Crystal L. Park. 23–47. New York, Guilford, 2013.

Oprea, Cristina. "Female Sex Workers: A Vulnerable Social Group." *Social Work Review / Revista De Asistenta Sociala* 4 (2014) 237–47.

Otterman, Sharon. "Caught in Methodism's Split over Same-Sex Marriage." *The New York Times*, May 5, 2013. Online: http://www.nytimes.com/2013/05/06/nyregion/caught-in-methodisms-split-over-same-sex-marriage.html?pagewanted=all&_r=0.

Paik, Anthony. "Adolescent Sexuality and the Risk of Marital Dissolution." *Journal of Marriage and Family* 73 (2011) 472–85.

Palm, Melody D. "Desires in Conflict: Hope and Healing for Individuals Struggling with Same-Sex Attraction." *Enrichment Journal*. Online: http://enrichmentjournal.ag.org/201004/201004_090_desires_confl.cfm

Paloutzian, Raymond F., and Crystal L. Park, eds. *Handbook of the Psychology of Religion and Spirituality*. 2nd ed. New York: Guilford, 2013.

Paloutzian, Raymond F., and Crystal L. Park. "Recent Progress and Core Issues in the Science of the Psychology of Religion and Spirituality." In *Handbook of the Psychology of Religion and Spirituality*, 2nd ed., edited by Raymond F. Paloutzian and Crystal L. Park, 3–22. New York: Guilford, 2013.

Pargament, Kenneth I. *The Psychology of Religion and Coping: Theory, Research, Practice*. New York: Guilford, 1997.

Parry, Donald W. "The Dead Sea Scrolls Bible." *Studies in the Bible and Antiquity* 2 (2010) 1–27.

PBS Online. "The Pill: Timeline." Online: http://www.pbs.org/wgbh/amex/pill/timeline/timeline2.html.

Pedzek, Kathy. "Fallible Eyewitness Memory and Identification." In *Conviction of the Innocent: Lessons from Psychological Research*, edited by Brian L. Cutler, 105–24. Washington, DC: American Psychological Association, 2012.

Penner, Clifford, and Joyce Penner. *A Gift for all Ages: A Family Handbook on Sexuality*. Waco, TX: Word, 1986.

Pew Research Center. "Global Christianity: A Report on the Size and Distribution of the World's Christian Population." *The Pew Forum on Religion & Public Life*, December 2011. Online: http://www.pewforum.org/files/2011/12/Christianity-fullreport-web.pdf.

———. "Public Opinion on Abortion Slideshow." Last updated January 16, 2013. Online: http://www.pewforum.org/2013/01/16/public-opinion-on-abortion-slideshow/.

———. "Public's Views on Human Evolution." Last updated December 30, 2013. Online: http://www.pewforum.org/ 2013/12/30/publics-views-on-human-evolution/.

———. "Women, Work and Motherhood." Last updated April 13, 2012. Online: http://www.pewresearch.org/2012/04/13/women-work-and-motherhood/.

Phipps, William E. *The Apostles' Creed: The Ongoing Struggle of the Church to Define Its Basic Beliefs*. Lewiston, NY: Mellen, 2010.

Piaget, Jean. *The Moral Judgment of the Child*. New York: Free, 1997.

Pierceson, Jason. *The Road to the Supreme Court: Same-Sex Marriage in the United States*. Lanham, MD: Rowman & Littlefield, 2013.

Planned Parenthood. "A History of Birth Control Methods." Last updated January 2012. Online: http://www.plannedparenthood.org/files/2613/9611/6275/History_of_BC_Methods.pdf.

Plante, Thomas. "Six Important Points You Don't Hear about Regarding Clergy Sexual Abuse in the Catholic Church." *Psychology Today*, March 24, 2010. Online: https://www.psychologytoday.com/blog/do-the-right-thing/201003/six-important-points-you-dont-hear-about-regarding-clergy-sexual.

Poston, Larry. "Islam." In *Sex & Religion*, edited by Christel Manning and Phil Zuckerman, 181–97. Belmont, CA: Wadsworth, 2005.

Rapp, Jacqueline, and Pete Vere. "Catholic Marriage and Annulments." *Catholic News Agency*. Online: http://www.catholicnewsagency.com/resources/life-and-family/marriage/catholic-marriage-and-annulments/.

Raushenbush, Paul B. "The Role of Faith in Family Planning." *Huffington Post*, July 28, 2013. Online: http://www.huffingtonpost.com/paul-raushenbush/faith-family-planning_b_3350027.html.

Regan, Pamela C. *The Mating Game: A Primer on Love, Sex, and Marriage*. 2nd ed. Los Angeles: Sage, 2008.

Reisenwitz, Cathy. "Why It's Time to Legalize Prostitution." *Daily Beast*, August 15, 2014. Online: http://www.thedailybeast.com/articles/2014/08/15/why-it-s-time-to-legalize-prostitution.html.

Richinick, Michele. "Boy Scouts to Officially End Ban on Openly Gay Leaders." July 27, 2015. *Newsweek*. Online: http://www.newsweek.com/boy-scouts-end-ban-openly-gay-leaders-357385

Rosenbaum, Janet E., and Byron Weathersbee. "True Love Waits: Do Southern Baptists? Premarital Sexual Behavior among Newly Married Southern Baptists Sunday School Students." *Journal of Religion & Health* 52 (2013) 263–75.

Rozin, Paul, et al. "Disgust." In *Handbook of Emotions*, 3rd ed., edited by Michael Lewis et al., 757–76. New York: Guilford, 2008.

Saad, Lydia. "Three in Four in U.S. Still See the Bible as Word of God." *Gallup*, June 4, 2014. Online: http://www.gallup.com/poll/170834/three-four-bible-word-god.aspx.

Saloomey, Kristen. "Nuns Driving the Debate on US Immigration." Last updated May 31, 2013. Online: http://blogs.aljazeera.com/blog/americas/nuns-driving-debate-us-immigration.

Sanders, James A. "Canon: Hebrew Bible." In vol 1 *Anchor Bible Dictionary*, edited by David Noel Freedman, 837–52. New York: Doubleday, 1992.

Schirmer, Annett. *Emotion*. Los Angeles: Sage, 2015.

Schniedewind, William M. *How the Bible Became a Book: The Textualization of Ancient Israel*. Cambridge: Cambridge University Press, 2004.

Schuessler, Jennifer. "The Dark Side of Liberation." *The New York Times*, May 20, 2013. Online: http://www.nytimes.com/2013/05/21/books/rape-by-american-soldiers-in-world-war-ii-france.html?_r=0

Schwartz, John. "A Utah Law Prohibiting Polygamy Is Weakened." *The New York Times*, December 14, 2013. Online: http://www.nytimes.com/2013/12/15/us/a-utah-law-prohibiting-polygamy-is-weakened.html?_r=0.

Serovich, Julianne. "A Systematic Review of the Research Base on Sexual Reorientation Therapies." *Journal of Marital and Family Therapy* 34 (2008) 227–38.

Sheppard, Kate. "'The Loving Story': How an Interracial Couple Changed a Nation." *Mother Jones*, February 13, 2012. Online: http://www.motherjones.com/media/2012/02/the-loving-story-documentary-hbo.

Shiota, Michelle N., and James W. Kalat. *Emotion*. 2nd ed. Belmont, CA: Wadsworth, 2012.

Shore, John. "Southern Baptist Pastor Accepts His Gay Son, Changes His Church." *Patheos*, May 29, 2014. Online: http://www.patheos.com/blogs/johnshore/2014/05/southern-baptist-pastor-accepts-his-gay-son-changes-his-church/.

Sifferlin, Alexandra. "I Want My IUD. How Public-Health Experts are Rebranding the Much Derided Contraceptive." *Time* 182, November 2013, 19.

Smith, Timothy B., et al. "Religiousness and Depression: Evidence for a Main Effect and the Moderating Influence of Stressful Life Events." *Psychological Bulletin* 129.4 (2003) 614–36.
Smith, Tom W., and Jaesok Son. *Final Report: Trends in Public Attitudes about Sexual Morality*. Chicago: NORC University of Chicago Press, 2013.
Snyder, Graydon F., and Kenneth M. Shaffer. "On Male and Female." *Brethren Life and Thought* 54 (2009) 108–13.
Southern Baptist Convention "Resolution on Abortion: Kansas City, Missouri—1984." Date accessed July 17, 2015. Online: http://www.sbc.net/resolutions/21.
Speigelhalter, David. "Sex: What are the Chances?" Last updated March 15, 2012. Online: http://www.bbc.com/future/story/20120313-sex-in-the-city-or-elsewhere.
Street, Nick. "LGBT-Inclusive Pentecostal Churches Growing in Brazil," *GlobalPost*, April 10, 2013. Online: http://www.globalpost.com/dispatches/globalpost-blogs/belief/lgbt-inclusive-pentecostal-churches-growing-brazil.
Suarez, Ray. "Vatican Maintains Stance on Condoms at HIV/AIDS Summit." *PBS NEWSHOUR*, May 30, 2011. Online: http://www.pbs.org/newshour/bb/health-jan-june11-vatican_05-30/.
Sun, Eryn. "Mark Driscoll Affirms Men as Head of Wives in Latest 'Real Marriage' Sermon." *Christian Post*, January 31, 2012. Online: http://www.christianpost.com/news/mark-driscoll-affirms-men-as-head-of-wives-in-latest-real-marriage-sermon-68307/.
Sutton, Geoffrey W. "The Psychology of Forgiveness, Reconciliation, and Restoration: Integrating Traditional and Pentecostal Theological Perspectives with Psychology." In *Forgiveness, Reconciliation, and Restoration: Multidisciplinary Studies from a Pentecostal Perspective*, edited by Martin W. Mittelstadt and Geoffrey W. Sutton, 125–44. Eugene, OR: Pickwick, 2010.
Sutton, Geoffrey W., and Eloise K. Thomas. "Can Derailed Pastors be Restored? Effects of Offense and Age on Restoration." *Pastoral Psychology* 53 (2005) 583–99.
———. "Restoring Christian Leaders: How Conceptualizations of Forgiveness and Restoration used in Empirical Studies Can Influence Practice and Research." *American Journal of Pastoral Counseling* 8 (2005) 27–42.
Sutton, Geoffrey W., et al. "Does Gender Matter? An Exploration of Gender, Spirituality, Forgiveness and Restoration Following Pastor Transgressions." *Pastoral Psychology* 55 (2007) 645–63.
Sutton, Geoffrey W., and Martin W. Mittelstadt. "Loving God and Loving Others: Learning about Love from Psychological Science and Pentecostal Perspectives." *Journal of Christianity and Psychology* 31 (2012) 157–66.
Taggart, Peter. "Woman's Death Prompts Abortion Debate in Ireland." *CNN*, November 15, 2012. Online: http://www.cnn.com/2012/11/14/world/europe/ireland-abortion-controversy/.
Talbert, Charles H. "Are There Biblical Norms for Christian Marriage?" *Journal of Family Ministry* 15 (2001) 16–27.
Tatum, William O., IV, et al. "Sexuality." In *Epilepsy A to Z: A Concise Encyclopedia*. 2nd ed. New York: Demos Medical, 2009.
Temple, Christine. "Evangel to Install Taylor as President Today." *Springfield News Leader*, October 10, 2014. Online: http://www.news-leader.com/story/news/local/ozarks/2014/10/10/ evangel-install-taylor-president-today/17017873/.

Terry, Karen J. "Understanding the Sexual Abuse Crisis in the Catholic Church: Challenges with Prevention Policies." *Victims and Offenders* 3 (2008) 31–44.

Thobejane, Tsoaledi D., and Takayindisa Flora. "An Exploration of Polygamous Marriages: A Worldview." *Mediterranean Journal of Social Sciences* 5 (2014) 1058–66.

Thomas, Eloise K., et al. "Religious Leadership Failure: Apology, Responsibility-taking, Gender, Forgiveness, and Restoration." *Journal of Psychology & Christianity* 27 (2008) 16–29.

Thomas, Eloise K., and Geoffrey W. Sutton. "Religious Leadership Failure: Forgiveness, Apology, and Restitution." *Journal of Spirituality in Mental Health* 10 (2008) 308–27.

Thompson, Kirsten M. J. "A Brief History of Birth Control in the U.S." *Our Bodies Ourselves*, December 14, 2013. Online: http://www.ourbodiesourselves.org/health-info/a-brief-history-of-birth-control/.

Throckmorton, Warren. "Alan Chambers: 99.9% Have Not Experienced a Change in Their Orientation." *Patheos*, January 9, 2012 Online: http://www.patheos.com/blogs/warrenthrockmorton/2012/01/09/alan-chambers-99-9-have-not-experienced-a-change-in-their-orientation/.

Trembath, Kern R. *Evangelical Theories of Biblical Inspiration: A Review and Proposal*. New York: Oxford University Press, 1987.

Trimmer, Michael. "Teen Pregnancy Rate on the Decline." *Christianity Today*, February 26, 2014. Online: http://www.christiantoday.com/article/teen.pregnancy.rate.on.the.decline/ 36003.htm.

Tybur, Joshua, et al. "Microbes, Mating, and Morality: Individual Differences in Three Functional Domains of Disgust." *Journal of Personality and Social Psychology* 29 (2009) 103–22.

Uecker, Jeremy E. "Religion, Pledging, and the Premarital Sexual Behavior of Married Young Adults." *Journal of Marriage and Family* 70 (2008) 728–44.

United Methodist Church. "Abortion." Last modified 2004. Online: http://archives.umc.org/ interior.asp?mid=1732.

———. "Timeline of Women in Methodism." Online: http://www.umc.org/who-we-are/timeline-of-women-in-methodism.

United Methodist Women Handbook 2013–2016–English. Online: http://www.umwmissionresources.org/products/umw-handbook-2013-2016-1

United States Conference of Catholic Bishops. *Marriage: Love and Life in the Divine Plan: A Pastoral Letter of the United States Conference of Catholic Bishops*. United States Conference of Catholic Bishops, 2009.

Univision. "Voice of the People." Last updated February 6, 2014. Online: http://www.univision.com /interactivos/openpage/2014-02-06/la-voz-del-pueblo-portada-en.

U.S. Department of Health and Human Services. "Trends in Teen Pregnancy and Childbearing." Last updated May 29, 2015. Online: http://www.hhs.gov/ash/oah/adolescent-health-topics/reproductive-health/teen-pregnancy/trends.html.

van der Toorn, Karel. "Constructing the Canon." In *Scribal Culture and the Making of the Hebrew Bible*. Cambridge: Harvard University Press, 2009.

van Deusen, Stephanie, and Christine A. Courtois. "Spirituality, Religion, and Complex Developmental Trauma." In *Spiritually Oriented Psychotherapy for Trauma*, edited

by Donald F. Walker et al., 29–54. Washington, DC: American Psychological Association, 2015.
van Harn, Roger, ed. *Exploring and Proclaiming the Apostles' Creed*. Grand Rapids: Eerdmans, 2004.
van Leeuwen, Raymond C. "'Be fruitful and multiply': Is This a Command or a Blessing?" *Christianity Today* 45, November 12, 2001, 58–61.
van Seters, John. "The Origins of the Hebrew Bible: Some New Answers to Old Questions." *Journal of Ancient Near Eastern Religions* 7 (2007) 87–108.
Wallace, Daniel B. "The Number of Textual Variants: An Evangelical Miscalculation." Last updated April 13, 2009. Online: https://bible.org/article/number-textual-variants-evangelical-miscalculation.
Walsh, Michael J. *Roman Catholicism: The Basics*. London: Routledge, 2005.
Wang, Mei-Chuan, et al. "Christian Women in IPV Relationships: An Exploratory Study of Religious Factors." *Journal of Psychology & Christianity* 28 (2009) 224–35.
Wehner, Peter. "An Evangelical Christian Looks at Homosexuality." *Patheos*, June 11, 2013. Online: http://www.patheos.com/blogs/philosophicalfragments/2013/06/11/evangelical-christian-looks-homosexuality-peter-wehner/.
Wenger, Jay L. "The Implicit Nature of Intrinsic Religious Pursuit." *International Journal for the Psychology of Religion* 17 (2007) 47–60.
West, Mona. "The Bible and Homosexuality." Last updated May 20, 2010. Online: http://mccchurch.org/download/theology/homosexuality/BibleandHomosexuality.pdf
Wilke, Joy, and Lydia Saad. "Older Americans' Moral Attitudes Changing: Moral Acceptance of Teenage Sex among the Biggest Generational Divides." *Gallup*, June 3, 2013. Online: http://www.gallup.com/poll/162881/older-americans-moral-attitudes-changing.aspx.
Wilkinson, Michael. "Public Acts of Forgiveness." In *Forgiveness, Reconciliation, and Restoration: Multidisciplinary Studies from a Pentecostal Perspective*, edited by Martin W. Mittelstadt and Geoffrey W. Sutton, 177–198. Eugene, OR: Pickwick, 2010.
Wilkinson, Michael, and Peter Althouse. *Catch the Fire: Soaking Prayer and Charismatic Renewal*. Dekalb, IL: Northern Illinois University Press, 2014.
Williamson, W. Paul, et al. "The Intratextual Fundamentalism Scale: Cross-Cultural Application, Validity Evidence, and Relationship with Religious Orientation and the Big 5 Factor Markers." *Mental Health, Religion & Culture* 13 (2010) 721–47.
Wilton, Don. "You Shall Not Commit Adultery." *Decision Magazine*, January 20, 2013. Online: http://billygraham.org/decision-magazine/january-2013/you-shall-not-commit-adultery/.
Wise, Michael O., et al. *The Dead Sea Scrolls: A New Translation*. San Francisco: Harper, 1996.
Wooden, Cindy. "Evangelii Gaudium: Pope Says Only Men Can Be Priests, but Women Must Have Voice in Church." *Catholic Herald*, November 26, 2013. Online: http://www.catholicherald.co.uk/news/2013/11/26/evangelii-gaudium-pope-says-only-men-can-be-priests-but-women-must-have-voice-in-church/.
World Health Organization. "New WHO Guidelines to Better Prevent HIV in Sex Workers." Last updated December 12, 2012. Online: http://www.who.int/hiv/mediacentre/feature_story/ sti_guidelines/en/.

World Health Organization Department of Gender et al. "2 Addressing Violence against Sex Workers." Online: http://www.who.int/hiv/pub/sti/sex_worker_implementation/swit_chpt2.pdf.

Worthington, Everett L., Jr. *Forgiving and Reconciling: Bridges to Wholeness and Hope.* Downers Grove, IL: InterVarsity, 2003.

———. *Forgiveness and Reconciliation: Theory and Application.* New York: Brunner-Routledge, 2006.

Worthington, Everett L., Jr., et al. "Promising Evidence-Based Treatments." In *Evidence-Based Practices for Christian Counseling and Psychotherapy*, edited by Everett L. Worthington Jr. et al., 279–302. Downers Grove, IL: InterVarsity, 2013.

Worthington, Everett L., Jr., Don E. Davis, et al. "Religion, Spirituality, and Forgiveness." In *Handbook of the Psychology of Religion and Spirituality*, 2nd ed., edited by Raymond F. Paloutzian and Crystal L. Park, 476–97. New York: Guilford, 2013.

Wright, H. Norman. *The Premarital Counseling Handbook.* Chicago: Moody, 1992.

Wright, Paul J. "U.S. Males and Pornography, 1973–2010: Consumption, Predictors, Correlates." *Journal of Sex Research* 50 (2013) 60–71.

Yancey, Philip. "Back from the Brothel." *Christianity Today* 49, January 2005, 80.

Yarhouse, Mark A. "Narrative Sexual Identity Therapy." *The American Journal of Family Therapy* 36 (2008) 196–210.

Yarmey, A. Daniel. "Expert Testimony: Does Eyewitness Memory Research have Probative Value for the Courts?" *Canadian Psychology* 42 (2001) 92–100.

Young, Michael. "What's Wrong with Abstinence Education?" *American Journal of Health Studies* 19 (2004) 148–56.

www.ingramcontent.com/pod-product-compliance
Lightning Source LLC
Chambersburg PA
CBHW071245230426
43668CB00011B/1593